THE
SUCCESS
GURUS

THE
SUCCESS
GURUS

17 LESSONS IN GREATNESS FROM

THE BEST MINDS IN BUSINESS

ANDREW B. CLANCY

AND THE EDITORS OF SOUNDVIEW
EXECUTIVE BOOK SUMMARIES

PORTFOLIO / PENGUIN

PORTFOLIO / PENGUIN
Published by the Penguin Group
Penguin Group (USA) Inc., 375 Hudson Street,
New York, New York 10014, U.S.A.
Penguin Group (Canada), 90 Eglinton Avenue East, Suite 700,
Toronto, Ontario, Canada M4P 2Y3
(a division of Pearson Penguin Canada Inc.)
Penguin Books Ltd, 80 Strand, London WC2R 0RL, England
Penguin Ireland, 25 St. Stephen's Green, Dublin 2, Ireland
(a division of Penguin Books Ltd)
Penguin Books Australia Ltd, 250 Camberwell Road, Camberwell,
Victoria 3124, Australia
(a division of Pearson Australia Group Pty Ltd)
Penguin Books India Pvt Ltd, 11 Community Centre, Panchsheel Park,
New Delhi – 110 017, India
Penguin Group (NZ), 67 Apollo Drive, Rosedale, Auckland 0632,
New Zealand (a division of Pearson New Zealand Ltd)
Penguin Books (South Africa) (Pty) Ltd, 24 Sturdee Avenue,
Rosebank, Johannesburg 2196, South Africa

Penguin Books Ltd, Registered Offices:
80 Strand, London WC2R 0RL, England

First published in 2011 by Portfolio / Penguin,
a member of Penguin Group (USA) Inc.

1 3 5 7 9 10 8 6 4 2

The summaries of the following books are published for the first time in this volume: Drive: The Surprising Truth About What Motivates Us by Daniel Pink (Riverhead Books) and Getting Things Done: The Art of Stress-Free Productivity by David Allen (Penguin Books). The other summaries have been previously published by Soundview Executive Book Summaries.

Permission acknowledgments appear on the last page of the respective selection.

LIBRARY OF CONGRESS CATALOGING IN PUBLICATION DATA
Clancy, Andrew B.
The success gurus : 17 lessons in greatness from the best minds in business / Andrew B. Clancy and
Soundview Executive Book Summaries.
p. cm.
Includes bibliographical references and index.
ISBN 978-1-59184-404-4
1. Leadership.   2. Success in business.   3. Leadership—Abstracts.   I. Soundview Executive Book
Summaries.   II. Title.
HD57.7.C5316 2011
658.4'09—dc22   2011009126

Printed in the United States of America

Set in Joanna MT Std

For Michelle—YNWA

ACKNOWLEDGMENTS

As readers make their way through *The Success Gurus*, one lesson I hope they take away is that no person is a self-made success. The achievement of any goal does not belong to a single individual. It is the result of a collaborative effort by a network of dedicated professionals. I am fortunate to have worked with a fantastic group of people who helped make this book a powerful tool for any reader.

Josh Clement, president of Soundview Executive Book Summaries, has kept the company at the forefront as a business information resource. Under his leadership, Soundview has expanded and redefined its products to offer comprehensive coverage of today's most notable business books and thought leaders.

Publisher Rebecca S. Clement provided essential guidance in the selection of the seventeen summaries that fill this volume. We started with a sizable list, but Rebecca kept us on task and focused on collecting the summaries that create the most complete set of success-building skills.

Soundview's rights administrator, Sabrina Hickman, played a vital role in pulling together the works that appear in this book from the various publishers and rights holders around the world. Soundview's editor in chief, Sarah Dayton, deserves praise for her painstaking efforts to give my early drafts increased strength.

After her work on 2010's *The Sales Gurus*, I was delighted to find out that my editor on this book would be Jillian Gray. This project quickly came together under her guidance, and I envy the authors who have the pleasure of working with Jillian in the future. Additional thanks must be given to everyone at Portfolio for their support of Soundview and its book summary model.

A final thank-you goes to Soundview chairman George Y. Clement. Soundview's history of success is due in large part to his belief in each person's ability to demonstrate his or her strengths. This standard of excellence is the link between Soundview's employees and its thousands of subscribers.

CONTENTS

INTRODUCTION

Before a reader begins his or her journey through this book, he or she knows the desired destination: success. What's interesting is that the description of the destination is different for each individual. Asking someone to define success is the same as asking a person to name the ideal island paradise to visit. Some people would respond with Hawaii or Jamaica, while others might say Ireland or Japan. For most people the difficult part of the trip occurs while they're still standing on the mainland, staring across the vast ocean that divides them from success.

Philosophies on how best to achieve success are as numerous as the stars in the sky. They are also big business for hundreds of speakers and authors. With so many coaches, advisers, and consultants promising to lead a person to greatness, an individual can suffer from information overload. In addition, anyone actively pursuing his or her goals doesn't have the time or finances to evaluate which author provides a method that has been proven to get results.

The Success Gurus eliminates the waste and provides readers with a guide to success that balances the personal with the professional. This book features seventeen summaries of books on success by some of the top authors on the subject. While the systems and techniques featured in *The Success Gurus* cover a wide range of subjects, they all propel readers forward with insights focused on achieving results.

Any journey toward success begins with a goal. There is a correct method and an incorrect method of setting and achieving goals. In *Goals!*, Brian Tracy helps readers clearly identify what they want and how to unlock the potential necessary to achieve what they desire. The ability to achieve success is in part based on a person's level of motivation. Daniel Pink's *Drive* examines motivation and suggests that the traditional methods of motivation may be steering people away from their goals. Lest any reader believe that successful people are "born with it," Geoff Colvin argues in *Talent Is Overrated* that extreme levels of success are the result of a specific regimen he defines as "deliberate practice."

The pursuit of a successful career requires a combination of the right opportunities and high levels of performance. Seth Godin teaches readers how to get the best job with the most freedom in *Linchpin*. Jeffrey Pfeffer writes that the most successful individuals are those who combine political savvy with an ability to acquire and control power. His book, *Power*, guides readers through a responsible way to master this difficult skill. Powerful individuals also tend to possess an inner drive that keeps them going through any situation. Marshall Goldsmith defines this quality in his book *Mojo*. He helps readers find their internal source of positive energy and radiate it to the outside world.

Certain skills are required to achieve continued success. The ability to positively persuade others is near the top of this list of attributes. G. Richard Shell and Mario Moussa explore the strategic use of persuasion in *The Art of Woo*. In a world where twenty-four hours simply isn't enough time to accomplish anything, David Allen's *Getting Things Done* provides a more efficient system to make the most of each day. Success requires a constant refinement of one's objectives, strengths, and weaknesses. Jerry S. Wilson and Ira Blumenthal provide a much-needed tutorial in *Managing Brand YOU*.

For many people pursuing professional success, leadership is the skill that requires the most effort and has the greatest impact on their performance. *The Success Gurus* devotes a good portion of its pages to making readers better leaders. In an era of moral ambivalence Jon M. Huntsman offers a path to higher ground in *Winners Never Cheat*. Leaders must be equally adept at guiding themselves and others during difficult times and in better days. J. Barry Griswell and Bob Jennings provide insight into how best to handle tough times in *The Adversity Paradox*.

Few authors today have produced as much material on leadership as John C. Maxwell. *The 360-Degree Leader* is Maxwell's innovative teaching on leading from any level of an organization. Another renowned leadership expert, Brian Tracy, examines the finer points of what makes an elite leader in *How the Best Leaders Lead*. Leadership is a field where trends can cause as many problems as they solve. Fortunately, James M. Kouzes and Barry Z. Posner cultivate thirty years of research and share time-tested methods for successful leadership in *The Truth About Leadership*.

Success is a personal matter, and for many people the ultimate goal is to make a living pursuing their passions. In the realm of entrepreneurship, few people can match Guy Kawasaki in passion or knowledge. His book, *The Art of the Start*, is the go-to resource for, as he writes, "anyone starting anything." Jerry Porras, Stewart Emery, and Mark Thompson want readers to build a life of greatness. In *Success Built to Last*, they demonstrate why greatness comes in many forms and how readers can find the path that best fits them. Finally, since the bulk of one's life is spent working, why not enjoy it? Stephen R. Covey and Jennifer Colosimo show the way to a meaningful future in *Great Work, Great Career*.

The Success Gurus intends to serve as your compass on a voyage to greatness. It should inspire action and move you from dreaming to doing. No matter where the final destination, the advice in this book helps steer a steady course.

For more information on any of the authors or summaries featured in this book, visit www.summary.com.

GOALS!

by Brian Tracy

Training and development expert Brian Tracy believes that the key to success can be found in the mastery of one skill: goal setting. It's a philosophy as simple as the mission statement by which his company, Brian Tracy International, operates: Achieve your personal and business goals faster. Tracy perpetuates this message as both a best-selling author and an in-demand speaker and consultant. As the author of more than forty books, he provides readers with insights culled from decades of professional experience. Tracy considers himself a synthesizer of knowledge, and he is tireless in his dedication to deepening his own well of information. By his own admission, Tracy has devoted at least three hours per day every day for the past forty years to reading and scholarship.

One of the key titles written as a result of Tracy's study is his book *Goals! How to Get Everything You Want—Faster Than You Ever Thought Possible*. He helps readers understand the difference between goals and the ruminations of fantasy. Lack of focus in regard to goals is a problem that Tracy attacks from the outset. The average person mislabels his or her dreams as goals. Tracy demonstrates that goals deserve their own unique set of rules and regulations. A goal is a concrete destination about which a person can describe not only the route by which it's reached but also the specific mile markers that dot each leg of the journey.

The process of evolving from dreamer to pursuer requires intense work on a person's internal construct. Tracy devotes ample page space in *Goals!* to the training and strengthening of the mind. A successful person's mind has the dexterity to envision a goal, the clarity to recognize the necessary steps toward it, and the toughness to endure the failure that can often occur along the path. Readers will want to devote significant time to reading and understanding Tracy's analysis of the barriers that negative emotion places in the path to achieving a goal. These barriers, such as justification, rationalization, and hypersensitivity, are as seductive as any vice and as powerful as any narcotic. They have derailed many a person's potential for success, but Tracy provides the simple, powerful advice that enables anyone to conquer them.

Tracy's strength, as both writer and speaker, is his reliance on simple, honest messages that resonate with the recipient, regardless of the situation. His discussion of failure in *Goals!* may strike some readers as obvious, but anyone who dismisses Tracy's logic is likely unable to be honest about his or her own limitations. The path to a goal is one on which a person has never before set foot. As a result, a direct route to success, free from failure, is a rarity. The willingness to try different avenues, despite most ending in dead ends, is what separates the successful from the rest of the pack. Tracy pushes readers to embrace failure as a necessary part of achieving any goal. The attempt to rewire one's thinking is a goal that will intimidate many, but, as Tracy demonstrates throughout the text, those who persist and take measured steps will reach their destination.

GOALS!
How to Get Everything You Want—Faster Than You Ever Thought Possible
by Brian Tracy

CONTENTS

THE SUMMARY IN BRIEF

The most important quality you can develop for lifelong success is the habit of taking action on your plans, goals, ideas, and insights. In *Goals!*, renowned business strategist and motivation expert Brian Tracy provides you with the essential steps for setting and achieving goals and for living a successful professional and personal life as a result. By practicing these rules and principles, Tracy explains, you can accomplish more in a shorter period of time than you ever thought possible.

In *Goals!*, Tracy teaches you how to identify in clearest terms the things you want out of life, then how to make the plan to help you achieve those things. He covers the psychology and the physiology at work behind the goals you set and teaches you how to combat frustration and prolong the elation that accompanies the work you must do to reach your goals. Tracy also shows how goal achievement can be a process one can use again and again to reach ever-higher levels of success and happiness.

In addition, you will learn the following:

- How to unlock your potential, take charge, and create your own future by setting goals for the things you want out of life and creating a plan to achieve those goals.
- How to use vision, or "future orientation," to determine where you'll be in the future and how you will get there. By imagining the ideal future, you can set yourself on the path to making it happen.
- How to clarify your values and determine your major definite purpose—the quantifiable, measurable, achievable goal that is most important to you right now.
- How to eliminate the limiting beliefs about yourself that are holding you back from achieving all you can achieve.
- How to measure your progress, every step of the way, as you push forward toward your goals.
- How to maintain the fire and passion you feel for achieving your goals by building momentum and persisting every day until that which you desire is yours.

THE COMPLETE SUMMARY

Part One: Setting the Stage

Unlocking Your Potential

Success is goals; all else is commentary. All successful people are intensely goal oriented. They possess the master skill of success—the ability to identify what they want, make a plan to attain it, and use the full scope of their personal power to achieve their dreams.

What They Didn't Teach Them at Harvard Consider this: In his book *What They Don't Teach You at Harvard Business School*, Mark McCormack tells of a study conducted on students in the 1979 Harvard MBA program. In that year, the students were asked, "Have you set clear, written goals for your future and made plans to accomplish them?" Only 3 percent of the students had written goals and plans; 13 percent had goals, but they were not in writing; and a whopping 84 percent had no specific goals at all.

Ten years later, the members of the class were interviewed again, and the findings, while somewhat predictable, were nonetheless astonishing. The 13 percent of the class who had had unwritten goals were earning, on average, twice as much as the 84 percent who had had no goals at all. And what of the 3 percent who had had clear, written goals? They were earning, on average, *ten times as much as the other 97 percent put together.*

Why Don't People Set Goals? In spite of such proof of success, most people don't have clear, measurable, time-bound goals that they work toward. There are four reasons why people don't set goals:

They don't realize the importance of goals. If the people with whom you spend the most time—family, friends, colleagues, and so forth—are not clear and committed to goals, chances are you will not be either.

They don't know how to set goals. Some set goals that are too general ("Be happy" or "Make a lot of money"); these are, in actuality, fantasies common to everyone. Goals, on the other hand, are clear, written, specific, and measurable.

They fear failure. Failure hurts, but it is often necessary to experience failure in order to achieve the greatest success. Do not unconsciously sabotage yourself by not setting any goals in which you might fail.

They fear rejection. People are often afraid that if they are unsuccessful at achieving a goal, others will be critical of them. This is remedied by keeping your goals to yourself at the outset: Let others see your results and achievements once you've accomplished your goals.

A Little Every Day Make a habit of daily goal setting and achieving for the rest of your life. Focus on the things you want rather than the things you don't want. Resolve to be a goal-seeking organism, moving unerringly toward the things that are important to you.

Taking Charge and Creating Your Own Future

In a study done in New York several years ago, researchers discovered that the top 3 percent of people in every field had a special attitude that set them apart from the average performers in their industries. These people viewed themselves as self-employed throughout their careers, no matter who signed their paychecks. They saw themselves as responsible for their companies, exactly as if they owned the companies personally.

You should do the same—from this point forward, see yourself as the president of your own personal-services corporation. View yourself as self-employed, in charge of your life and career. Set goals, make plans, establish measures, and create strategies, just as the president of a company would. Market yourself well, enabling you to sell yourself for the very highest price in a competitive market. Know, also, how much of your services you want to sell, how much you want to earn, how rapidly you want to grow your income, and how much you want to be worth when you retire. This kind of financial strategy is up to you—you are responsible for that and all other aspects of your personal "corporation." You are, after all, the president.

The Barrier of Negative Emotions Most people don't take charge and set clear goals for their lives because they are dragged down by negative emotions. Negative emotions hold you back and take away all the joy in your life. You must free yourself from such negativity—fear, self-pity, jealousy, anger, and other pessimistic, ultimately harmful emotional reactions—if you are going to fulfill your full potential. Start by identifying in your life one or more of the sources of negative emotions. These sources include:

Justification. You can only be negative as long as you can justify that you are entitled to be angry or upset for some reason. As soon as you stop justifying and giving reasons why you're entitled to be angry, your anger and your negative emotions disappear.

Rationalization. When you rationalize your negativity, you attempt to give a socially acceptable reason for feeling bad or unhappy. You create ways of putting your negative emotions in a favorable light by explaining how they are acceptable. Stop rationalizing your negative emotions, as well as the events that cause you to feel negative.

Hypersensitivity. Some people base their entire self-image around the opinions of others, maintaining little sense of self-worth and leaving themselves prone to anger, shame, embarrassment, and even depression. Remember that what other people think of you has no effect on you at all, unless you allow it to have an effect. As Eleanor Roosevelt said, "No one can make you feel inferior without your consent."

The Blame Game. No one else is responsible for your lot in life or for the emotional reactions you have to various aspects of life. You are not a victim. Stop complaining, stop whining, stop making excuses, and start to take control of your life. Only when you accept full responsibility for your life can you start to set goals and move ahead rapidly.

FUTURE ORIENTATION

If there is one special quality that all great leaders have in common, it is vision. Leaders think about the future, where they're going, and what they'll do when they get there. They think about what they want, often many years in the future, and what can be done to achieve it. This leadership quality is called Future Orientation. Truly great leaders combine this orientation with an idealized long-term view of their lives—how their lives will look in x number of years, if they were perfect in every way—to create a personal strategic plan free of self-limiting beliefs.

For example, imagine if your work life was perfect five years from now. Answer these questions:

What would it look like?

What would you be doing?

Where would you be doing it?

With whom would you be working?

What skills and abilities would you have?

What level of responsibility would you have?

What kind of goals would you be accomplishing?

What level of status would you have in your field?

Imagine anything is possible. What would that future look like? What would it take between now and five years from now to achieve all those things? Answer similar questions for your financial life, your personal family life, and your health and fitness. Once you have this ideal in mind, switch from future orientation to action orientation, and do what it takes to make your ideal a reality!

Clarifying Your Values and Finding Your Purpose

The very core of your personality is your values; everything you do on the outside emanates from the values you have on the inside.

Think of your personality as a target with five concentric rings. The very center ring is your values—the core of your personality. Your values determine the next ring, your beliefs, about yourself and the world around you. If you have positive values, you will believe others are deserving of those values and you will treat them accordingly.

Your beliefs, in turn, determine the next ring out—your expectations. If you have positive values, you will believe yourself to be a good person; if this is the case, you will expect good things to happen to you, resulting in a positive, cheerful outlook.

Your expectations determine the next ring, your attitude—the outward manifestation or reflection of your values, beliefs, and expectations. If you have a positive attitude, others will be drawn to you, and you will be more likely to find success.

Your attitude determines the fifth ring: your actions. You are happiest when your outside actions are congruent with your values on the inside.

Integrity Perhaps the most important of all values is integrity. Someone once said that integrity is not so much a value in itself; it is, rather, the value that guarantees all other values. Once you have decided you are going to live consistently with a value, your level of integrity determines whether you follow through on your commitment. The higher your level of integrity, the happier and more powerful you will feel in everything you do.

Your Major Definite Purpose Since you become what you think about most of the time, a major definite purpose gives you a focus for every waking moment. Having a major definite purpose helps activate your subconscious mind on your behalf. Any thought, plan, or goal that you can clearly define in your conscious mind will be brought into reality by your subconscious mind.

Your major definite purpose can be defined as the one goal that is the most important to you at the moment. It is usually the one goal that will help you achieve more of your other goals than anything else you can accomplish. It must have the following characteristics:

It must be something that you personally really, really want.
It must be clear and specific.
It must be measurable and quantifiable.
It must be both believable and achievable.
It must have a reasonable probability of success when you begin.
It must be in harmony with your other goals.

Here is an exercise to help you find your major definite purpose. Take out a sheet of paper and write down (in the present tense, as if you had already achieved them) a list of ten goals you would like to accomplish in the foreseeable future. After you have written your list, ask yourself which goal on the list, if you were to accomplish it immediately, would have the greatest positive impact on your life. In almost every case, this one goal is your major definite purpose—the one goal that can have the greatest impact on both your life and the achievement of your other goals.

Write this goal on a separate sheet of paper, along with everything you can think of that you can do to achieve that goal. Take action on at least one item on your list. Think about your goal morning, noon, and night, continually looking for ways to achieve it.

Analyzing Your Beliefs

Perhaps the most important of all mental laws is the Law of Belief, which states that whatever you believe in, with conviction, becomes your reality. You do not believe what you see; you see what you already believe, viewing your world through a lens of beliefs, attitudes, prejudices, and preconceived notions. All improvement in your life comes from changing your beliefs about yourself and your possibilities. Personal growth comes from changing your beliefs about what you can do and about what is possible for you. Napoleon Hill once said, "Whatever the mind of man can conceive and believe, it can achieve."

Your Self-concept

Everything you do or achieve in life—every thought, feeling, or action—is controlled and determined by your self-concept. Your self-concept precedes and predicts your levels of performance and effectiveness in everything you do. It is the master program of your mental computer; everything you accomplish in your outer world is a result of your self-concept.

Even if your self-concept is made up of erroneous beliefs about yourself and your world, as far as you are concerned these are facts, and you will think, feel, and act accordingly. In truth, your beliefs about yourself are largely subjective, often not based on fact at all. Your beliefs have been shaped and formed by your childhood, your friends and associates, your positive and negative experiences, and innumerable other factors. You may believe yourself to be limited in some way, and regardless of whether that is true, it becomes true for you.

The good news about beliefs is that all beliefs are learned and can therefore be unlearned, particularly if they are limiting in any way. There are many things you think you know about yourself that are not true, and the starting point for unlocking your full potential is to identify self-limiting beliefs, then ask yourself, "What if they're not true at all?"

Imagine there is a "belief store," much like a computer software store, where you can purchase a belief to program into your subconscious mind. If you could choose any set of beliefs at all, which one would be most helpful to you?

Consider this one: "I am destined to be a big success in life." If you absolutely believe you are destined to be a big success, you will walk, talk, and act as if everything that happens to you is part of a great plan to make you successful. And if you act as if you are already the person you desire to be, your actions will generate the feelings that go with them.

IGNORE THE EXPERTS

*A*lbert Einstein was sent home from school as a young man with a learning disability. His parents were told he was incapable of being educated. They refused
to accept this diagnosis and eventually arranged for him to get an excellent
education.

Dr. Albert Schweitzer had the same problems at school as a boy. His parents
were encouraged to apprentice him to a shoemaker so that he would have a safe,
secure job when he grew up. Both men went on to earn doctorates before age
twenty and to leave their marks on the history of the twentieth century.

In fact, according to Fortune magazine, many presidents and senior executives
of today's Fortune 500 companies were diagnosed in school as being not particularly bright or capable. By virtue of hard work, however, they went on to achieve
great success in their industries. Imagine what would have happened—or, more
to the point, not happened—had Einstein or Schweitzer internalized the self-
limiting beliefs those in school tried to impose on them. Thank goodness they and
their parents recognized that limiting ideas about oneself are not based on fact at all!

Part Two: Getting Off the Ground

Starting at the Beginning

Once you have decided on your values, vision, mission, purpose, and goals, the
next step for you is to analyze your starting point. Exactly where are you today,
and how are you doing in each of the important areas of your life, especially as
they relate to your goals? If you want to lose weight, the first thing you do is
weigh yourself to determine how much you weigh today. If you decide to begin
an exercise program, the first thing you do is determine how much you are
exercising today. If you want to earn more money, the first thing you do is
determine how much you're making right now.

It is important to be as accurate with these calculations as possible; the more
accurate you are, the better and faster you can improve—and the better goals
you can set.

Zero-Based Thinking When you begin to plan your long-term future, one of the
most valuable exercises you can engage in is called zero-based thinking. In zero-
based thinking you ask this question: "Knowing what I now know, is there anything
that I am doing today that I wouldn't start up again today, if I had to do it over?"

It is difficult, if not impossible, to make progress in your life if you allow
yourself to be held back by decisions you have made in the past. No matter who

you are or what you are doing, there are certain things in your life that, knowing what you know now, you would not get into today if you had them to do over. The next question to ask yourself is "How do I get out of them?"

Apply this to every aspect of your life and career—to the people with whom you associate, the jobs you have taken, the activities in your business, and the investments you have made. Once you have identified these things, be prepared to make any necessary changes by doing the following:

Determine what is holding you back. What is the major reason you are not doing the things you truly want to do? Find others who are achieving success in these areas and determine what they are doing that you are not and what skills they have that you do not.

Determine your level of skills and ability. Identify the key result areas of your work—the critical tasks that you must accomplish in order to do your job well. You must be good at every one of these in order to achieve the highest levels of success in what you do.

Identify your weakest areas. Identify where you are below average or poor. How do these areas interfere with your ability to use your other skills? What key skills do you lack that are essential for your success? Identify them accurately and honestly, and make a plan to improve each one.

Imagine starting over. Never allow yourself to feel locked in or trapped by a particular decision from the past. At any time, you could start your career over again, if you feel there is a limited future in your current direction.

Be prepared to reinvent yourself. Stand back and think about starting your career over again today, knowing what you know now. If you had to start over again today, with your special combination of talents and skills, what would you choose to do differently from what you are doing now?

THE REALITY PRINCIPLE

*J*ack Welch, the former CEO of General Electric, once said that the most important quality of leadership is the "reality principle." He defined this as the ability to see the world as it really is, not as you wish it was. He would begin every meeting to discuss a goal or problem with a single question: "What's the reality?" Peter Drucker refers to this quality as "intellectual honesty"—dealing with the facts exactly as they are before attempting to solve a problem or make a decision.

If you want to be the best you can be and to achieve what is truly possible for you, you must be brutally honest with yourself. You must sit down and analyze yourself in detail to determine where you are today, as well as what you must do to get where you want to go.

Measuring Your Progress

You have incredible mental powers that you habitually fail to use to their full extent. By systematically setting goals for your life and making detailed plans to achieve them, you will save yourself years of hard work and use vastly more of your thinking powers than the average person.

While your conscious mind enables you to identify and analyze your environment, your subconscious mind contains the great powers that allow you to accomplish great things. It is essential that you learn to tap into these powers in order to achieve your goals.

Indeed, your subconscious mind functions best with clear goals, specific tasks, deliberate measures, and firm deadlines. The more of these you program into your subconscious mind, the more you will accomplish in a shorter period of time. Such things activate your mind's "forcing system," which helps eliminate procrastination and delay.

There are three keys to peak performance in achieving your goals—commitment, completion, and closure.

When you make a firm commitment to achieve a particular goal, you step on the accelerator of your subconscious mind, enabling you to be more creative, determined, and focused than ever before.

You must fight the temptations that keep you from completion of the tasks that lead to achievement. You must force yourself and discipline yourself to resist these temptations and push through to completion. Do what you must: Set benchmarks and create balanced scorecards, measures, metrics, and deadlines for every key task. These things activate your subconscious forcing system, enabling you to start earlier, work harder, stay later, and get the job done.

Bringing closure to an issue in your personal or professional life is absolutely essential for you to be in control of your situation. Lack of closure in the form of unfinished business or incomplete actions is a major source of stress, dissatisfaction, and even failure in business.

Eliminating the Roadblocks

Even with all the preparation, analysis, and effort that go into creating new goals, on average people give up on their goals after one attempt at achieving them. Some do not even get that far, giving up before they even try once. The reason they give up is because of all the obstacles, difficulties, problems, and roadblocks that appear as soon as one decides to do something one has never done before.

Consider this, though: Successful people fail far more often than unsuccessful people. Successful people try more things, fall down, pick themselves up, and try again, over and over again, before they achieve what they set out to achieve. Unsuccessful people try a few things, if they try at all, and soon quit to go back to their previous path.

There will always be obstacles that stand between you and anything you want to accomplish. The ability to solve problems is essential in any successful endeavor, and you possess that ability, if you desire the goal intensely enough; nothing can hold you back.

Dealing with Constraints Eliyahu Goldratt claimed a great breakthrough in thinking when he wrote about the "Theory of Constraints." This theory says that, between you and anything you want to accomplish, there is a constraint or limiting factor that determines how fast you get to where you want to go. This theory rings true in so many aspects of our personal and professional lives—there are always bottlenecks that we must identify accurately and then focus our energies on alleviating.

The 80/20 rule applies to the constraints between you and your goals— 80 percent of your constraints will be within yourself, 20 percent outside of yourself, in other people and situations. It is you personally who is usually the major roadblock setting the speed at which you achieve a goal. You may be afraid to make a change or doubtful that you can really reach a goal.

However, negative emotions, like limiting beliefs, can be unlearned. Have you ever seen a negative baby? Children come into the world with no doubts or fears or helpless feelings at all—they learn to feel those emotions over time. And whatever has been learned can be unlearned, through practice and repetition.

Unlearning Helplessness Indeed, the way to get over a tendency like helplessness is to set small goals, make plans, and work on them each day. Over time, your doubts and fears will weaken and your confidence will grow, becoming the dominant force in your thinking. Other related issues to keep in mind include the following:

Avoid the comfort zone. Many people become complacent with their current situations; they become so comfortable in their job or relationship that they avoid making any changes at all, even for the better. People who get stuck in a comfort zone, combined with learned helplessness, are almost impossible to help in any way.

Set big, challenging goals for yourself, then break each down into specific tasks, set deadlines, and work on them every day. Doing so will help break you out of your comfort zone.

Organize obstacles by priority. Make a list of all the obstacles standing between you and your goals, and organize those obstacles by priority. Look at each from different angles, until you find the best strategy to remove it.

For every obstacle that is standing between you and what you want to accomplish, there is a solution.

Part Three: Hitting Your Stride

Keeping Your Goals at the Front of Your Mind

Once your goals are in place, there are a number of things you can and should do to maintain the momentum of change and achievement, regardless of whether your goals are personal, professional, or both. Among these actions are managing your time, reviewing your goals daily, visualizing your goals continually, and persisting until you succeed. Consider the importance of each in the ongoing effort in which you must engage to make all your dreams a reality.

Manage Your Time Well To achieve all your goals and become everything you are capable of becoming, you must get your time under control—this is key to your feelings of happiness, confidence, power, and personal well-being. A sense of control is only possible when you practice excellent time-management skills.

The starting point of time management, once you have determined your goals, is the organization of your goals by priority and value. You must be clear, at any given moment, about exactly what is most important to you at that time. Start by dividing all of your activities into "A" activities (those that move you toward your goal) and "B" activities (those that do not move you toward your goal). Eliminate any activity that does not help you achieve something you want for yourself or which will not lead you to success. Focus all your time on the "A" activities.

Separate the urgent tasks (those that are determined by external pressures and requirements and must be done immediately) from the important ones (those that can contribute the very most to your long-term future). Apply the 80/20 rule to your task list, separating the 20 percent of your activities that will account for 80 percent of the total value of your activities. You can then practice "creative procrastination" on the less-valuable 80 percent, in order to focus your time and energies on the more valuable 20 percent. Keep yourself on track, focusing on the specific results you want and need to accomplish.

Review Your Goals Daily Get a spiral notebook that you can keep with you at all times. Each day, open up the notebook and write down a list of ten to fifteen of your most important goals, without referring to your previous list. Do this every day, day after day. As you do this, several remarkable things will happen.

The first day you write down your goals, you will have to give them some thought and reflection. The second day you rewrite your list (without referencing the first list), your ten to fifteen goals will change, in both description and order of priority. Some goals will drop off the list, only to reappear at a more appropriate time. Each day that you write down your list of ten to fifteen goals, your definitions will become clearer and sharper, until you are writing the same goals and descriptions every day.

About this time (which is after three to four weeks), something remarkable will happen in your life—it will take off! Your work and personal life will improve dramatically, your mind will brim with ideas and insights, you will attract people into your life to help you achieve your goals, and you will make progress at a rapid rate. Everything will begin to change in a positive way.

Put a deadline at the end of each goal to activate your subconscious mind's "forcing system." Even if you do not know how the goal is going to be achieved, deadlines will spur you to action, like an exclamation point after every goal.

This exercise is a test to determine how badly you really want to achieve these goals. The more you can discipline yourself to write and rewrite your goals each day, the clearer you will become about what you really want and the more convinced you will become that it is possible for you.

Visualize Your Goals Continually Your ability to visualize is perhaps the most powerful faculty that you possess. All improvement in your life begins with an improvement in your mental pictures. You are where you are and what you are today largely because of the mental pictures that you hold in your conscious mind. As you change your mental pictures on the inside, your world on the outside will begin to change to correspond to those pictures.

Indeed, the most successful people are those who visualize in advance the kind of success they want to enjoy. A successful salesperson, for example, will visualize and remember previous successful sales presentations. A successful trial lawyer will visualize and remember his or her performance in court during a successful trial. Successful doctors will visualize and remember their successful treatments of patients in the past. Always visualize the very best you've done, and you'll repeat it in your future.

Persist Until You Succeed Every great success in your life will represent a triumph of persistence. Your ability to decide what you want, to begin, and to persist through all obstacles and difficulties until you achieve your goals is the critical determinant of your success. Persistence is self-discipline in action; it is the true measure of individual human character. It is, in fact, the real measure of your belief in yourself and your ability to succeed.

Each time you move forward in the face of adversity and disappointment, you build up a habit of persistence. You become stronger, prouder, and more powerful; you deepen your levels of self-discipline and personal strength. You develop the iron quality of success, the one quality that will carry you forward and over any obstacle that life throws in your path.

In the later years of his life, Winston Churchill was asked to address a school class on what he believed to be the secret to his great success in life. His response was "I can summarize the lessons of my life in seven words—never give in; never, never give in."

THE FOUR PARTS OF VISUALIZATION

There are four parts of visualization you can learn and practice to ensure that you use this incredible power to its best advantage:

Frequency

How many times do you visualize a particular goal as achieved or yourself performing in an excellent way in a particular circumstance? The more frequently you repeat a clear mental picture of your very best performance or result, the more quickly it will be accepted by your subconscious and turned into reality.

Duration

How long can you hold the picture in your mind each time you replay it? The longer you can hold your mental picture, the more deeply it will be impressed into your subconscious mind and the more rapidly it will express itself in your subsequent performance.

Vividness

There is a direct relationship between how clearly you can see your desired goal and how quickly it comes into your reality.

Intensity

The intensity of a visualization refers to the amount of emotion you attach to your visual image. This is the most important part of the visualization process.

DRIVE

by Daniel H. Pink

The phrase "type-A personality" conjures images of Wall Street stockbrokers, cutthroat sales professionals, and executives who pound their fists on boardroom tables. This is the sort of person for whom the pursuit of success requires ample amounts of aggression, micromanagement, and, some would say, ruthlessness. Author Daniel Pink argues that when it comes to motivation, there are only two personality types: Type X and Type I. Which label fits the reader depends on whether he or she is motivated by extrinsic or intrinsic rewards. Type X and Type I each come with their own set of behaviors. Pink explores the difference between the two and the roles they play in performance on and off the job in his book *Drive: The Surprising Truth About What Motivates Us*.

In contributions to the *New York Times* and the *Harvard Business Review*, as well as his previous book, *A Whole New Mind*, Pink explored the nature of the brain and the shift in workplace culture toward more creative thinking. Pink's archetype of the creative worker would doubtless prefer the Type I work environment described in *Drive*. According to Pink, the creation of satisfaction relies on a combination of three elements: autonomy, mastery, and purpose. He explores the factors that contribute to the creation of the three elements and structures his argument against the traditional "carrot and stick" motivation method. The idea of reward and punishment is something he reserves for only a handful of specific, task-oriented jobs. Pink's claims are supported by fascinating examples from the past thirty years of psychological research into human behavior.

While *Drive* is best applied to organizations, it offers an important perspective for any individual. Pink reveals that once a person's basic needs are met, he or she will actively seek opportunities to grow and improve. This distinction is emphasized in Pink's discussion of mastery. No occupation is devoid of difficulties but how someone reacts to challenges can be a major determining factor in his or her success. A person who is intrinsically motivated never thinks twice about the hardest part of any job. He or she is engaged in an experience that challenges him or her without being unbearable or boring. *Drive* is a remedy for anyone who suffers from the frustration of being locked into a job, activity, or situation from which he or she takes no joy. There is a better way, and Pink helps readers find the path to their heart's delight.

Pink points out in *Drive* that Type X and Type I behaviors can equally lead to success. The difference is that extrinsic motivators are finite in their effectiveness. An individual who chases a financial or material reward will work every bit as hard to achieve his or her goal as someone who is intrinsically motivated. However, once that goal is achieved, the Type X person's journey is at its end. Pink maintains that for Type I individuals success comes from enjoying the endless ride.

DRIVE
The Surprising Truth About What Motivates Us
by Daniel Pink

CONTENTS

THE SUMMARY IN BRIEF

Most of us believe that the best way to motivate ourselves and others is with external rewards, like money—the carrot-and-stick approach. That's a mistake.

The secret to high performance and satisfaction—at work, at school, and at home—is the deep human need to direct our own lives, to learn and create new things, and to do better by ourselves and our world.

Drawing on four decades of scientific research on human motivation, Daniel H. Pink exposes the mismatch between what science knows and what business does—and how that affects every aspect of life. He demonstrates that while carrots and sticks worked successfully in the twentieth century, that's precisely the wrong way to motivate people for today's challenges.

In Drive, Pink examines the three elements of true motivation—autonomy, mastery, and purpose—and offers smart and surprising techniques for putting these into action. Along the way, he introduces us to the scientists, business leaders, and entrepreneurs who are pointing a bold way forward.

In addition, you will learn the following:

How "if-then" rewards not only are ineffective in many situations but can also crush the high-level, creative, conceptual abilities of your employees

A more accurate account of both human performance and the human condition

How to bridge the gap between what science knows and what business does

How to enlist new approaches to motivation

What truly motivates us and how we can use that knowledge to work smarter and live better

THE COMPLETE SUMMARY

Introduction: The Puzzling Puzzles of Harry Harlow and Edward Deci

In the middle of the last century, two young scientists conducted experiments that should have changed the world—but did not.

Harry F. Harlow was a professor of psychology at the University of Wisconsin. One day in 1949, Harlow and two colleagues gathered eight rhesus monkeys for a two-week experiment on learning. The researchers devised a simple mechanical puzzle. Solving it required three steps: Pull out the vertical pin, undo the hook, and lift the hinged cover. Pretty easy for humans, far more challenging for a thirteen-pound lab monkey.

The experimenters placed the puzzles in the monkeys' cages to observe how they reacted—and to prepare them for tests of their problem-solving prowess at the end of the two weeks. But almost immediately, something strange happened. Without any outside urging and unprompted by the experimenters, the monkeys began playing with the puzzles with focus, determination, and what looked like enjoyment. And in short order, they began figuring out how the contraptions worked. By the time Harlow tested the monkeys on days thirteen and fourteen of the experiment, the primates had become quite adept at solving the puzzles.

Now, this was a bit odd. Nobody had taught the monkeys how to remove the pin, slide the hook, and open the cover. Nobody had rewarded them with food, affection, or even quiet applause when they succeeded. And that ran counter to the accepted notions of how primates—including the bigger-brained, less hairy primates known as human beings—behaved.

The Third Drive

At the time, scientists knew that two main drives powered behavior. The first was the biological drive. Humans and other animals ate to sate their hunger, drank to quench their thirst, and copulated to satisfy their carnal urges. But that wasn't happening here. "Solutions did not lead to food, water or sex gratification," Harlow reported.

The only other known drive also failed to explain the monkeys' peculiar behavior. If biological motivations came from within, the second drive came from without—the rewards and punishments the environment delivered for behaving in certain ways. This was certainly true for humans, who responded exquisitely to such external forces. If you promised to raise our pay, we'd work harder. If you threatened to dock us for showing up late, we'd arrive on time. But that didn't account for the monkeys' actions either.

What else could it be?

To answer the question, Harlow offered a novel theory—what amounted to a third drive: "The performance of the task," he said, "provided intrinsic reward." The monkeys solved the puzzles simply because they found it gratifying to solve puzzles. They enjoyed it. The joy of the task was its own reward.

Edward Deci

In the summer of 1969, Edward Deci was a Carnegie Mellon University psychology graduate student who was intrigued by motivation but suspected that scholars and businesspeople had misunderstood it. So, tearing a page from the Harlow playbook, he set out to study the topic.

In an echo of what Harlow had discovered two decades earlier, Deci's experiment seemed to reveal that human motivation operated by laws that ran counter to what most scientists and citizens believed. From the office to the playing field, we knew what got people going. Rewards—especially cold, hard cash—intensified interest and enhanced performance. What Deci found, and then confirmed in two additional studies shortly thereafter, was almost the opposite.

"When money is used as an external reward for some activity, the subjects lose intrinsic interest for the activity," he wrote. Rewards can deliver a short-term boost—just as a jolt of caffeine can keep you cranking for a few more hours. But the effect wears off—and, worse, can reduce a person's longer-term motivation to continue the project.

Human beings, Deci said, have an "inherent tendency to seek out novelty and challenges, to extend and exercise their capacities, to explore and to learn." But this third drive was more fragile than the other two; it needed the right environment to survive. "One who is interested in developing and enhancing intrinsic motivation in children, employees, students, etc., should not concentrate on external-control systems such as monetary rewards," he wrote in a follow-up paper.

Part One: A New Operating System

The first human operating system—call it Motivation 1.0—was all about survival. Its successor, Motivation 2.0, was built around external rewards and punishments. That worked fine for routine twentieth-century tasks. But in the twenty-first century, Motivation 2.0 is proving incompatible with how we organize what we do, how we think about what we do, and how we do what we do.

Researchers such as Harvard Business School's Teresa Amabile have found that external rewards and punishments—both carrots and sticks—can work nicely for routine, algorithmic tasks. But they can be devastating for heuristic ones. Those sorts of challenges—solving novel problems or creating something the world didn't know was missing—depend heavily on Harlow's third drive. Amabile calls it the intrinsic motivation principle of creativity, which holds, in part: "Intrinsic motivation is conducive to creativity; controlling intrinsic motivation is detrimental to creativity." In other words, the central tenets of Motivation 2.0 may actually impair performance of the heuristic, right-brain work on which modern economies depend.

Enjoyment

Partly because work has become more creative and less routine, it has also become more enjoyable. That, too, scrambles Motivation 2.0's assumptions. This operating system rests on the belief that work is not inherently enjoyable—which is precisely why we must coax people with external rewards and threaten them with outside punishment.

Motivation 2.0 suffers from three compatibility problems. It doesn't mesh with the way many new business models are organizing what we do, because we're intrinsically motivated purpose maximizers, not only extrinsically motivated profit maximizers. It doesn't comport with twenty-first-century economic thought—because economists are finally realizing that we're full-fledged human beings, not single-minded economic robots. And perhaps most important, it's hard to reconcile with much of what we actually do at work—because for growing numbers of people, work is often creative, interesting, and self-directed rather than unrelentingly routine, boring, and other directed. Taken together, these compatibility problems warn us that something's gone awry in our motivational operating system.

Seven Reasons Carrots and Sticks (Often) Don't Work ...

When carrots and sticks encounter our third drive, strange things begin to happen. Traditional if-then rewards can give us less of what we want:

1. They can extinguish intrinsic motivation. "Careful consideration of reward effects reported in 128 experiments lead to the conclusion that tangible rewards tend to have a substantially negative effect on intrinsic motivation," Deci and his colleagues determined. "When institutions—families, schools, businesses and athletic teams, for example—focus on the short-term and opt for controlling people's behavior," they do considerable long-term damage.

2. They can diminish performance. In 2009, scholars at the London School of Economics analyzed fifty-one studies of corporate pay-for-performance plans. These economists' conclusion: "We find that financial incentives . . . can result in a negative impact on overall performance."

3. They can crush creativity. One study of artists shows that a concern for outside rewards might actually hinder eventual success. Among the starkest findings, especially for men: "The less evidence of extrinsic motivation during art school, the more success in professional art both several years after graduation and nearly 20 years later."

4. They can crowd out good behavior. In a study of 153 women who were interested in giving blood, two Swedish economists found that adding a monetary incentive didn't lead to more of the desired behavior. It led to less. The reason: It tainted an altruistic act and "crowded out" the intrinsic desire to do something good.

5. They can encourage cheating, shortcuts, and unethical behavior. When an Israeli day-care center announced a fine for parents who showed up late to pick up their children, the result was the opposite of what was intended. The economists who conducted the study wrote: "After the introduction of the fine we observed a steady increase in the number of parents coming late." The fine shifted the parents' decision from a partly moral obligation (be fair to my kids' teachers) to a pure transaction (I can buy extra time). There wasn't room for both. The punishment didn't promote good behavior; it crowded it out.

6. They can become addictive. Cash rewards and shiny trophies can provide a delicious jolt of pleasure at first, but the feeling soon dissipates—and to keep it alive, the recipient requires ever larger and more frequent doses.

7. They can foster short-term thinking. Extrinsic motivators—especially tangible, if-then ones—can reduce the depth of our thinking. They can focus our sights on only what's immediately before us rather than what's off in the distance.

...and the Special Circumstances When They Do

Carrots and sticks aren't all bad. The scholars exploring human motivation have revealed not only the many glitches in the traditional approach but also the narrow band of circumstances in which carrots and sticks do their jobs reasonably well.

The starting point, of course, is to ensure that the baseline rewards—wages, salaries, benefits, and so on—are adequate and fair. Without a healthy baseline, motivation of any sort is difficult and often impossible.

But once that's established, there are circumstances where it's okay to fall back on extrinsic motivators.

Routine Tasks For routine tasks, which aren't very interesting and don't demand much creative thinking, rewards can provide a small motivational booster shot without the harmful side effects. In some ways, that's just common sense.

As Deci, Richard Ryan, and Richard Koestner explain, "Rewards do not undermine people's intrinsic motivation for dull tasks because there is little or no intrinsic motivation to be undermined." Likewise, when Dan Ariely and his colleagues conducted a performance study with a group of MIT students, they found that when a task called for "even rudimentary cognitive skill," a larger reward "led to poorer performance." But "as long as the task involved only mechanical skill, bonuses worked as they would be expected: the higher the pay, the better the performance."

This is extremely important. Although advanced economies now revolve less around those algorithmic, rule-based functions, some of what we do each day—especially on the job—still isn't all that interesting. We have reports to fill out, boring e-mails to answer, and all manner of drudge work that doesn't necessarily fire our soul. What's more, for some people, much of what they do all day consists of these routine, not-terribly-captivating tasks. In these situations, it's best to try to turn work into play—to increase the task's variety, make it more like a game, or use it to help master other skills. Alas, that's not always possible. And this means that sometimes even if-then rewards are an option.

Type I and Type X

Motivation 2.0 depended on and fostered Type X (extrinsic) behavior—behavior fueled more by extrinsic desires than by intrinsic ones and concerned less with the inherent satisfaction of any activity and more with the external rewards to which an activity leads.

Motivation 3.0, the upgrade that's necessary for the smooth functioning of twenty-first-century business, depends on and fosters Type I (intrinsic) behavior. Type I behavior concerns itself less with the external rewards an activity brings and more with the inherent satisfaction of the activity itself. At the center of Type X behavior is the second drive. At the center of Type I behavior is the third drive.

If we want to strengthen our organizations, get beyond our decade of underachievement, and address the inchoate sense that something's gone wrong in our businesses, our lives, and our world, we need to move from Type X to Type I.

For Type X's, the main motivator is external rewards; any deeper satisfaction is welcome but secondary. But for Type I's, the main motivator is the freedom, challenge, and purpose of the undertaking itself; any other gains are welcome, but mainly as a bonus.

A few more distinctions to keep in mind:

- Type I behavior is made, not born. These behavior patterns aren't fixed traits. They are proclivities that emerge from circumstance, experience, and context. Any Type X can become a Type I.
- Type I's almost always outperform Type X's in the long run. Intrinsically motivated people usually achieve more than their reward-seeking counterparts.
- Type I's do not disdain money or recognition. Once compensation meets a baseline level, money plays a different role for Type I's than for Type X's. Type I's like to be recognized for their accomplishments—because recognition is a form of feedback. But for them, unlike Type X's, recognition is not a goal in itself.
- Type I behavior is a renewable resource. It is the motivational equivalent of clean energy: inexpensive, safe to use, and endlessly renewable.
- Type I behavior promotes greater physical and mental well-being. People oriented toward autonomy and intrinsic motivation have higher self-esteem, better interpersonal relationships, and greater general well-being than those who are extrinsically motivated. By contrast, people whose core aspirations are Type X validations, such as money, fame, or beauty, tend to have poorer psychological health.

- Ultimately, Type I behavior depends on three nutrients: autonomy, mastery, and purpose. Type I behavior is self-directed. It is devoted to becoming better and better at something that matters, and it connects that quest for excellence to a larger purpose.

TYPE X VERSUS TYPE I

Type X behavior often holds an entity theory of intelligence, prefers performance goals to learning goals, and disdains effort as a sign of weakness.

Type I behavior has an incremental theory of intelligence, prizes learning goals over performance goals, and welcomes effort as a way to improve something that matters.

Begin with one mind-set, and mastery is impossible. Begin with the other, and it can be inevitable.

Part Two: The Three Elements

In the 1980s, researchers Deci and Ryan moved from categorizing behavior as either extrinsically motivated or intrinsically motivated to categorizing it as either controlled or autonomous. "Autonomous motivation involves behaving with a full sense of volition and choice," they write, "whereas controlled motivation involves behaving with the experience of pressure and demand toward specific outcomes that comes from forces perceived to be external to the self."

A sense of autonomy has a powerful effect on individual performance and attitude. According to a cluster of recent behavioral-science studies, autonomous motivation promotes greater conceptual understanding, better grades, enhanced persistence at school and in sporting activities, higher productivity, less burnout, and greater levels of psychological well-being. Those effects carry over to the workplace.

In 2004, Deci and Ryan, along with Paul Baard of Fordham University, carried out a study of workers at an American investment bank. The three researchers found greater job satisfaction among employees whose bosses offered "autonomy support." These bosses saw issues from the employees' point of view, gave meaningful feedback and information, provided ample choice about what to do and how to do it, and encouraged employees to take on new projects. The resulting enhancement in job satisfaction, in turn, led to higher performance on the job. What's more, the benefits that autonomy confers on individuals extend to their organizations. For example, researchers at Cornell University studied 320 small businesses, half of which granted workers autonomy and the other half of which relied on top-down direction. The businesses that offered autonomy grew at four times the rate of the control-oriented firms and had one-third the turnover.

Autonomy

Our "default setting" is to be autonomous and self-directed. Unfortunately, circumstances—including outdated notions of "management"—often conspire to change that default setting and turn us from Type I to Type X. To encourage Type I behavior, and the high performance it enables, the first requirement is autonomy. People need autonomy over task (what they do), time (when they do it), team (whom they do it with), and technique (how they do it). Companies that offer autonomy, sometimes in radical doses, are outperforming their competitors.

Mastery

Research has shown that the highest, most satisfying experiences in people's lives are when they are in "flow," a state identified by psychologist Mihaly Csikszentmihalyi. In flow, goals are clear: reach the top of the mountain, hit the ball across the net, or mold the clay just right. Feedback is immediate: The mountaintop gets closer or farther away, the ball sails in or out of bounds, the pot you're throwing comes out smooth or uneven.

Most important, in flow, the relationship between what a person has to do and what he can do is perfect. The challenge isn't too easy, nor is it too difficult. It is a notch or two beyond his current abilities, which stretches his body and mind in a way that makes the effort itself the most delicious reward. That balance produces a degree of focus and satisfaction that easily surpasses other, more everyday, experiences. In flow, people live so deeply in the moment, and feel so utterly in control, that their sense of time, place, and even self melts away. They are autonomous, of course. But more than that, they are engaged.

The Three Laws of Mastery Flow is essential to mastery. But flow doesn't guarantee mastery—because the two concepts operate on different horizons of time. One happens in a moment; the other unfolds over months, years, sometimes decades. You and I might reach flow tomorrow morning—but neither one of us will achieve mastery overnight.

So how can we enlist flow in the quest for something that goes deeper and endures longer? What can we do to move toward mastery, one of the key elements of Type I behavior, in our organizations and our lives? A few behavioral scientists have offered some initial answers to those questions, and their findings suggest that mastery abides by three somewhat peculiar laws:

1. Mastery is a mind-set: It requires the capacity to see your abilities not as finite but as infinitely improvable.

2. Mastery is a pain: It demands effort, grit, and deliberate practice.

3. Mastery is an asymptote: It's impossible to fully realize, which makes it simultaneously frustrating and alluring.

Purpose

The first two legs of the Type I tripod, autonomy and mastery, are essential. But for proper balance we need a third leg—purpose, which provides a context for its two mates. Autonomous people working toward mastery perform at very high levels. But those who do so in the service of some greater objective can achieve even more. The most deeply motivated people—not to mention those who are most productive and satisfied—hitch their desires to a cause larger than themselves.

Beyond a Profit Motive "As an emotional catalyst, wealth maximization lacks the power to fully mobilize human energies," says strategy guru Gary Hamel. Today's staggering levels of worker disengagement have a companion trend that companies are only starting to recognize: an equally sharp rise in volunteerism, especially in the United States. These diverging lines—compensated engagement going down, uncompensated effort going up—suggest that volunteer work is nourishing people in ways that paid work simply is not.

We're learning that the profit motive, potent though it is, can be an insufficient impetus for either individuals or organizations. An equally powerful source of energy, one we've often neglected or dismissed as unrealistic, is what we might call the "purpose motive." This is the final big distinction between the two operating systems. Motivation 2.0 centered on profit maximization. Motivation 3.0 doesn't reject profits, but it places equal emphasis on purpose maximization.

Three Places for Purpose We see the first stirrings of this new purpose in three realms of organizational life:

- Goals that use profit to reach purpose
- Words that emphasize more than self-interest
- Policies that allow people to pursue purpose on their own terms

We know that we're not designed to be passive and compliant but to be active and engaged. And we know that the richest experiences in our lives aren't when we're clamoring for validation from others but when we're listening to our own voice—doing something that matters, doing it well, and doing it in the service of a cause larger than ourselves.

So in the end, repairing the mismatch and bringing our understanding of motivation into the twenty-first century is more than an essential move for business. It's an affirmation of our humanity.

The Type I Toolkit

Type I's are made, not born. Although the world is awash in extrinsic motivators, there's a lot we can do to bring more autonomy, mastery, and purpose into our work and life. Here are two exercises to get you on the right track.

Give Yourself a Flow Test Csikszentmihalyi did more than discover the concept of flow. He also introduced an ingenious new technique to measure it. Csikszentmihalyi and his University of Chicago team equipped participants in their research studies with electronic pagers. Then they paged people at random intervals (approximately eight times a day) for a week, asking them to describe their mental state at that moment. These real-time reports proved far more honest and revealing than previous methods.

You can use Csikszentmihalyi's methodological innovation in your own quest for mastery by giving yourself a "flow test." Set a reminder on your computer or mobile phone to go off at forty random times in a week. Each time your device beeps, write down what you're doing, how you're feeling, and whether you're in flow. Record your observations, look at the patterns, and consider the following questions:

Which moments produced feelings of flow?

Are certain times of day more flow friendly than others?

How might you increase the number of optimal experiences and reduce the number of moments when you feel disengaged or distracted?

If you're having doubts about your job or career, what does this exercise tell you about your true source of intrinsic motivation?

Move Five Steps Closer to Mastery One key to mastery is what Florida State University psychology professor Anders Ericsson calls "deliberate practice"—a "lifelong period of . . . effort to improve performance in a specific domain." Follow these steps—over and over again for a decade—and you just might become a master:

Remember that deliberate practice has one objective: to improve performance. Ericsson has said, "Deliberate practice is about changing your performance, setting new goals and straining yourself to reach a bit higher each time."

Repeat, repeat, repeat. Repetition matters.

Seek constant, critical feedback. If you don't know how you're doing, you won't know what to improve.

Focus ruthlessly on where you need help. Ericsson says, "[T]hose who get better work on their weaknesses."

Prepare for the process to be mentally and physically exhausting. That's why so few people commit to it, but that's why it works.

Three Ways to Improve Your Company

Here are three ways to begin pulling your organization out of the past and into the brighter world of Motivation 3.0:

Try "20 Percent Time" with Training Wheels You've read about the wonders of "20 percent time"—where organizations encourage employees to spend one-fifth of their hours working on any project they want. But for all the virtues of this Type I innovation, putting such a policy in place can seem daunting. How much will it cost? What if it doesn't work?

If you're feeling skittish, here's an idea: Go with a more modest version: 20 percent time . . . with training wheels. Start with, say, 10 percent time. That's just one afternoon of a five-day workweek. And instead of committing to it forever, try it for six months. By creating this island of autonomy, you'll help people act on their great ideas and convert their downtime into more productive time.

Encourage Peer-to-Peer "Now That" Rewards Kimley-Horn and Associates, a civil engineering firm in Raleigh, North Carolina, has established a reward system that gets the Type I stamp of approval: At any point, without asking permission, anyone in the company can award a fifty-dollar bonus to any of his or her colleagues.

"It works because it's real-time, and it's not handed down from any management," the firm's human resources director told *Fast Company*. "Any employee who does something exceptional receives recognition from their peers within minutes." Because these bonuses are noncontingent "now that" rewards, they avoid the seven deadly flaws of most corporate carrots. And because they come from a colleague, not a boss, they carry a different (and perhaps deeper) meaning. You could even say they're motivating.

Promote Goldilocks for Groups Almost everyone has experienced the satisfaction of a Goldilocks task—the kind that's neither too easy nor too hard, that delivers a delicious sense of flow. But sometimes it's difficult to replicate that experience when you're working in a team. People often end up doing the jobs they always do because they've proven they can do them well, and an unfortunate few get saddled with the flow-free tasks nobody else wants. Here are a few ways to bring a little Goldilocks to your group:

Begin with a diverse team.
Make your group a "no competition" zone.
Try a little task shifting.
Animate with purpose; don't motivate with rewards.

The Zen of Compensation

The more prominent salary, perks, and benefits are in someone's work life, the more they can inhibit creativity and unravel performance. As Edward Deci explained, when organizations use rewards like money to motivate staff, "that's when they're most de-motivating."

The better strategy is to get compensation right—and then get it out of sight. Effective organizations compensate people in amounts and in ways that allow individuals to mostly forget about compensation and instead focus on the work itself.

Here are three key techniques:

1. Ensure internal and external fairness. The most important aspect of any compensation package is fairness. And here, fairness comes in two varieties— internal and external. Internal fairness means paying people commensurately with their colleagues. External fairness means paying people in line with others doing similar work in similar organizations.

2. Pay more than average. Nobel Laureate George Akerlof and his wife, Janet Yellen, who is also an economist, discovered that paying great people a little more than the market demands could attract better talent, reduce turnover, and boost productivity and morale.

3. If you use performance metrics, make them wide-ranging, relevant, and hard to game. When metrics are varied, they're harder to finagle. Using a variety of measures that reflect the totality of great work can transform often counterproductive if-then rewards into less combustible "now that" rewards.

Three Business Thinkers Who Get It

The following three business thinkers offer some wise guidance for designing organizations that promote autonomy, mastery, and purpose.

Theory X Versus Theory Y Douglas McGregor, a social psychologist, was one of the first professors at MIT's Sloan School of Management. His landmark 1960 book, *The Human Side of Enterprise*, gave the practice of management a badly needed dose of humanism.

McGregor described two very different approaches to management, each based on a different assumption about human behavior. The first approach, which he called Theory X, assumed that people avoid effort, work only for money and security, and therefore need to be controlled. The second, which he called Theory Y, assumed that work is as natural for human beings as play or rest, that initiative and creativity are widespread, and that if people are commit-ted to a goal, they will actually seek responsibility. Theory Y, he argued, was the more accurate—and ultimately more effective—approach.

Self-management

The most influential management thinker of the twentieth century, Peter F. Drucker wrote an astonishing forty-one books, influenced the thinking of two generations of CEOs, received a Presidential Medal of Freedom, and taught for three decades at the Claremont Graduate University business school that now bears his name.

Drucker coined the term "knowledge worker," foresaw the rise of the non-profit sector, and was among the first to stress the primacy of the customer in business strategy. Toward the end of his career, Drucker predicted the next frontier: self-management. With the rise of individual longevity and the decline of job security, he argued, individuals have to think hard about where their strengths lie, what they can contribute, and how they can improve their own performance.

Self-motivation and Greatness One of the most authoritative voices in business today, Jim Collins is the author of *Built to Last* (with Jerry Porras), *Good to Great*, and *How the Mighty Fall*. A former professor at the Stanford Graduate School of Business, he now operates his own management lab in Boulder, Colorado.

"Expanding energy trying to motivate people is largely a waste of time," Collins wrote in *Good to Great*. "If you have the right people on the bus, they will be self-motivated. The real question then becomes: How do you manage in such a way as not to de-motivate people?"

TALENT IS OVERRATED

by Geoff Colvin

I t's easy to spot greatness. There is a circle of elite individuals who inhabit the upper echelon of any pursuit: business, athletics, the arts. These are select individuals whose performance exceeds the era in which they make their achievements. Think of names such as Michelangelo, William Shakespeare, Wolfgang Amadeus Mozart, or, in contemporary life, Warren Buffett and Tiger Woods. These individuals so far outdistance even the greatest in their respective fields that their abilities are often described as "God-given talent." Is this the case? Was there a secret combination of amino acids in the DNA of Buffett that enabled him to become the most successful (and consistent) investor of the past hundred years? Did the Fates and Muses secretly conspire and distill the vast reaches of musical talent into the singular body of a young boy in Salzburg, Austria?

Despite the temptation to place extreme abilities in the realm of the mystical, even Mozart's prodigious compositional abilities were not birthed from the ether. Geoff Colvin, senior editor at large of *Fortune* magazine, examines the secrets of high performance in his book *Talent Is Overrated: What Really Separates World-Class Performers from Everybody Else*. In one of the most entertaining yet informative guides to performance, Colvin debunks the myth of natural talent. Instead, he uses clever and extensive research to argue that there is, in fact, a path that can lead to earth-shattering achievement.

One of the best aspects of *Talent Is Overrated* is Colvin's determination to paint a true picture of extraordinary ability. Readers at one point or another have probably expressed a desire to possess the abilities of a certain individual. Whether it be the ability to drive a golf ball like Woods or the skill to revolutionize a business the way Jack Welch transformed General Electric, the ends are the result of arduous, painstaking means. Furthermore, Colvin reveals the truth about why so few achieve this level of skill; it's a lonely existence that only a select few have the fortitude to bear.

Colvin describes the unique path to extraordinary achievement as the result of what he calls "deliberate practice." This focused, hyperintense method builds the essential skills and jettisons anything that wastes time or energy. Readers will marvel at the way in which individuals in vastly different professions all demonstrate telltale signs of "deliberate practice" in their journeys to greatness. Colvin's own abilities as a creator of an engaging narrative will lead readers to speculate about his own path to the heights of his field. While he keeps the focus squarely on others, it's obvious that the subject of extraordinary performance mystified Colvin. There is every reason to believe that *Talent Is Overrated* will do the same for its readers. The well-worn expression states, "It's lonely at the top." This book demonstrates that the entire journey to extreme greatness is one of solitude as well.

TALENT IS OVERRATED
What Really *Separates World-Class Performers from Everybody Else*
by Geoff Colvin

CONTENTS

THE SUMMARY IN BRIEF

Few people are truly great at what they do. But why aren't they? Why don't they manage businesses like Jack Welch or play golf like Tiger Woods?

Asked to explain why a few people truly excel, most of us offer one of two answers. The first is hard work. Yet hard workers aren't always great. The other possibility is that the elite possess an innate talent for excelling in their field. The trouble is, scientific evidence doesn't support the notion that specific natural talents make great performers.

So what's the real solution to the mystery of high performance? According to author Geoff Colvin, both the hard work and natural talent camps are wrong. What really makes all the difference is a highly specific kind of effort called "deliberate practice."

Based on extensive research, *Talent Is Overrated* shares the secrets of extraordinary performance and shows us how to apply these principles to our lives and work. Colvin explains cutting-edge research and eye-opening facts that debunk the myth of innate talent. Most profoundly, Colvin shows that great performance isn't reserved for a preordained few. The price may be high, but it is available to us all.

In addition, you will learn the following:

Why innate abilities are not necessarily predictive of great performance

The true role of intelligence and memory in high achievement

Why "deliberate practice" is the real method for achieving great performance

How to apply the principles of great performance in your life

How to apply the principles of great performance in your organization

THE COMPLETE SUMMARY

The Mystery

The odds are that few if any of the people around you are truly great at what they do—awesomely, amazingly, world-class excellent.

Why—exactly why—aren't they? Why don't they manage businesses like Jack Welch or play golf like Tiger Woods or play the violin like Itzhak Perlman? The hard truth is that virtually none of them has achieved greatness or even come close, and only a tiny few ever will.

This is a mystery so commonplace that we scarcely notice it, yet it's critically important to the success or failure of our organizations, the causes we believe in, and our own lives.

Extensive research in a wide range of fields shows that many people not only fail to become outstandingly good at what they do but don't even get any better than they were when they started.

Hundreds of research studies have converged on some major conclusions that directly contradict most of what we think we know about great performance. Specifically:

> The gifts possessed by the best performers are not at all what we think they are.
>
> Even the general abilities that we typically believe characterize the greats are not what we think.
>
> The factor that seems to explain the most about great performance is something the researchers call "deliberate practice." Exactly what that is and isn't turns out to be extremely important.

Understanding where extraordinary performance comes from is crucial. The nineteenth-century humorist Josh Billings famously said, "It ain't so much the things we don't know that get us into trouble. It's the things we know that just ain't so." The first step in understanding the new findings on great performance is using them to help us identify what we know for sure that just ain't so.

Talent Is Overrated

If it turns out that we're all wrong about talent, that's a big problem. Our views about talent, which are extremely deeply held, are extraordinarily important for the future of our lives, our children's lives, our companies, and the people in them. Understanding the reality of talent is worth a great deal.

A number of researchers now argue that giftedness or talent means nothing like what we think it means, if indeed it means anything at all.

When researchers have looked at large numbers of high achievers, at least in certain fields, they have found that most of them did not show early evidence of gifts.

No specific genes identifying particular talents have been found. If genes exert any influence, it seems to be much less than the whole explanation for achievement of the highest levels of performance.

How can one possibly account for staggering immortal achievement except as a mysterious divine gift? In fact, when first presented with the logic of the antitalent thesis, a great many people respond immediately with two simple counterarguments: Mozart and Tiger Woods.

The facts are worth examining a little more closely. Mozart's father was Leopold Mozart, a famous composer and performer in his own right. He was also a domineering parent who started his son on a program of intensive training in composition and performing at age three.

What About Tiger?

Researchers on great performance sometimes call Tiger Woods the Mozart of golf, and the parallels do seem striking. Woods's father, Earl, was a teacher, specifically a teacher of young men, and he had a lifelong passion for sports.

Here's the situation: Tiger was born into the home of an expert golfer and confessed "golf addict" who loved to teach and was eager to begin teaching his new son as soon as possible. Earl gave Tiger his first metal club, a putter, at the age of seven months. Before Tiger was two, they were at the golf course playing and practicing regularly.

Neither Tiger nor his father has suggested that Tiger came into this world with a gift for golf. Tiger has repeatedly credited his father for his success. Asked to explain Tiger's phenomenal success, father and son always give the same reason: hard work.

In Search of Business Talent

The overwhelming impression that comes from examining the early lives of business greats is that they didn't seem to hold any identifiable gift or give any early indication of what they would become.

Jack Welch showed no particular inclination toward business, even into his midtwenties. He majored not in business or economics but in chemical engineering and earned a master's and a PhD in that field. At twenty-five, he accepted an offer to work in a chemical development operation at General Electric.

If anything in Welch's history to that point suggests that he would become the most influential business manager of his time, it's tough—in fact, impossible—to spot it.

Bill Gates is a more promising prospect for those who want to explain success through talent. He became fascinated by computers as a kid and says he wrote his first piece of software at age thirteen: It was a program that played tic-tac-toe.

It's clear that Gates's early interest led directly to Microsoft. The problem is that nothing in his story suggests extraordinary abilities.

In surveying the world's business titans we find Welch-like stories more often than Gates-like stories, lacking even a hint of inclination toward the fields or traits that would one day lead to fame and riches.

For most of us, the critical point is that, at the very least, these talents are much less important than we usually think. They seem not to play the crucial role that we generally assign to them, and it's far from clear what role they do play.

How Smart Do You Have to Be?

Everywhere we see hypersuccessful companies seemingly filled with people who got perfect scores on their SATs.

So it's definitely surprising, at least at first, to find that research doesn't support the view that extraordinary natural general abilities are necessary for high achievement. In fact, in a wide range of fields, including business, the connection between general intelligence and specific abilities is weak and, in some cases, apparently nonexistent. As for memory, the whole concept of a powerful memory is problematic, because it turns out that memory ability is very clearly created rather than innate.

A wide range of research shows that the correlations between IQ and achievement aren't nearly as strong as the data on broad averages would suggest, and in many cases there's no correlation at all.

Many of the most successful people do seem to be highly intelligent. But what the research suggests very strongly is that the link between intelligence and high achievement isn't nearly as powerful as we commonly suppose. Most important, the research tells us that intelligence as we usually think of it—a high IQ—is not a prerequisite to extraordinary achievement.

How's Your Memory?

The evidence is similar when it comes to that other general ability we often associate with hypersuccessful people, an amazing memory. A large mass of recent evidence shows that memory ability is acquired and can be acquired by pretty much anyone.

The widespread view that highly accomplished people have tremendous memories is in one sense justified—they often astound us with what they can remember. But the view that their amazing ability is a rare natural gift is not justified. Remarkable memory ability is apparently available to anyone.

It may seem surprising that off-the-charts general abilities, especially intelligence and memory, are not necessary for extraordinary achievement, but it becomes less surprising when we consider the qualities that highly successful companies and business leaders look for in employees, or rather what they don't look for. It's striking to notice companies that don't put extreme cognitive abilities at the top of the list, or sometimes even on the list.

The message from these companies raises an important question: Even if superior intelligence and memory aren't the critical factors for success, are the traits the companies seek—team orientation, humor, confidence, and so on—reliably related to success across companies, and if so, are they innate traits that you either have or don't? Research suggests that some personality dimensions do match up with success at certain types of work.

At this point you can't help but wonder if there's anything at all (a) that makes a significant difference in whether you achieve extraordinary performance and (b) that you can't do anything about. The answer is yes, of course there is.

What's surprising is that when it comes to innate, unalterable limits on what healthy adults can achieve, anything beyond basic physical constraints is in dispute.

That fact is profoundly opposed to what most of us believe. We tend to think that we are forever barred from all manner of successes because of what we were or were not born with.

But what we'd really like to know is not what does or doesn't stop us but what makes some people go so much further than others. And what we have discovered so far is not what makes some people excel but rather what doesn't. Specifically:

It isn't experience.
It isn't specific inborn abilities.
It isn't general abilities such as intelligence and memory.

In short, we've nailed down what doesn't drive great performance. So what does?

A Better Idea

Consider a critically important and highly rigorous scientific study conducted in the early 1990s in Berlin that examined music. The objective of the study was to figure out why some violinists are better than others.

There were three groups of test subjects—we'll call them best, above average, and good. All three groups were spending the same total amount of time on music-related activities.

The violinists were quite certain which activity was most important for making them better: practicing by themselves. They all knew it, but they didn't all do it. Though the violinists understood the importance of practice alone, the amount of time the various groups actually spent practicing alone differed dramatically.

The advantage of practice was cumulative. All the research subjects were asked to estimate their weekly practice hours for each year of their violin-playing lives. The results were extraordinarily clear. By age eighteen, the violinists in the first group had accumulated 7,410 hours of lifetime practice on average, versus 5,301 hours for violinists in the second group and 3,420 hours for those in the third group.

What the authors of the research study called "deliberate practice" makes all the difference. Or as they stated it with stark clarity in their scholarly paper, "The differences between expert performers and normal adults reflect a lifelong period of deliberate effort to improve performance in a specific domain."

This position was highly significant for two reasons. First, it explicitly rejected the you've-got-it-or-you-don't view. Second, it resolved the huge contradiction in the body of scholarly research on performance and high achievement as well as in our everyday experience. On the one hand, we see everywhere that years of hard work do not make most people great at what they do. On the other hand, we see repeatedly that the people who have achieved the most are the ones who have worked the hardest. How can both sets of observations be true?

The problem, observed the researchers, is that "the current definition of practice is vague." Their framework is not based on a simplistic "practice makes perfect" observation. Rather, it is based on their highly specific concept of "deliberate practice."

Precisely what this means turns out to be critically important. An understanding of it illuminates the path to high achievement in any field, not just by individuals but also by teams and organizations.

What Deliberate Practice Is and Isn't

The concept of deliberate practice is quite specific.

It isn't work and isn't play; it is something entirely unto itself. What we think of as practice frequently isn't what the researchers mean by deliberate practice.

Deliberate practice is characterized by several elements, each worth examining. It is activity designed specifically to improve performance, often with a teacher's help; it can be repeated a lot; feedback on results is continuously available; it's highly demanding mentally, whether the activity is purely intellectual or heavily physical; and it isn't much fun.

What we generally do at work is directly opposed to the first principle: It isn't designed by anyone to make us better at anything. Usually it isn't designed at all; we're just given an objective that's necessary to meeting the employer's goals and are expected to get on with it.

As for the second principle, the activities that would make us better are usually not highly repeatable. Even in jobs where we do the same few things, we face few (if any) incentives to get better at them by exceeding our limits and discovering what we can't do well.

Feedback? At most companies this is a travesty, consisting of an annual performance review dreaded by the person delivering it and the one receiving it.

Work is often not fun, because getting anything accomplished in the real world is a grind.

If that's life in most companies, then the opportunities for achieving advantage by adopting the principles of great performance, individually and organizationally, would seem to be huge. In fact they are. Indeed, what's especially surprising about the cluelessness of most organizations with regard to deliberate practice is that the principles are not counterintuitive or hard to grasp.

What We Need to Know Next

Deliberate practice does not fully explain high achievement—real life is too complicated for that. We're all affected by luck. But more significantly, a person's circumstances, especially in childhood, can powerfully affect his or her opportunities to engage in deliberate practice.

It turns out that deliberate practice can extend one's ability to perform at higher levels far longer than most people believe. In addition, even though a wide range of research studies have shown performance improving with increased deliberate practice, the relationship cannot be simple and direct in every case.

Regardless of how well practice is designed, another important variable is how much effort a person puts into it.

Frequently when we see great performers doing what they do, it strikes us that they've practiced for so long, and done it so many times, they can just do it automatically. But in fact, what they have achieved is the ability to avoid doing it automatically.

Great performers never allow themselves to reach the automatic, arrested-development stage in their chosen field. The essence of practice, which is constantly trying to do the things one cannot do comfortably, makes automatic behavior impossible. Ultimately the performance is always conscious and controlled, not automatic.

How Deliberate Practice Works

What makes deliberate practice work? It turns out the answer is the same whether we look at business or sports or any other field, and it isn't what you might expect.

Indeed, the most important effect of practice in great performers is that it takes them beyond—or, more precisely, around—the limitations that most of us think of as critical. It enables them to perceive more, to know more, and to remember more than most people.

Perceiving More

Top performers can figure out what's going to happen sooner than average performers by seeing more. Sometimes excellent performers see more by developing a better and faster understanding of what they see.

The superior perception of top performers extends beyond the sense of sight. They hear more when they listen and feel more when they touch.

When excellent performers look further ahead than average performers do, they are literally looking into their own future. Knowing what lies ahead for them, they prepare for it and thus perform better. They may be looking only one second ahead, but for them that extra moment makes all the difference.

Much of the power of looking further ahead comes from the simple act of raising one's gaze and getting a new perspective—and doing it not once or occasionally but using practice principles to do it often and get better at it.

Knowing More

Top performers in a wide range of fields have better organized and consolidated their knowledge, enabling them to approach problems in fundamentally different and more useful ways.

Many of the best-performing companies explicitly recognize the importance of deep knowledge in their specific field, as opposed to general managerial ability.

Building and developing knowledge is one of the things that deliberate practice accomplishes. Constantly trying to extend one's abilities in a field requires amassing additional knowledge, and staying at it for years develops the critical connections that organize all that knowledge and make it useful.

Remembering More

How can great performers in every realm recall more than would seem possible? Researchers find that excellent performers in most fields exhibit superior memory of information in their field. What's the explanation?

All these people have developed what we might call a memory skill, a special ability to get at long-term memory in a fast, reliable way.

Top performers understand their field at a higher level than average performers do and thus have a superior structure for remembering information about it.

Practice exerts an additional, overarching influence that in a way is even more impressive: It can actually alter the physical nature of a person's brain and body.

Endurance runners have larger-than-average hearts, an attribute that most of us see as one of the natural advantages with which they were blessed. But no, research has shown that their hearts grow after years of intensive training.

We've all had the powerful feeling, when watching or contemplating an extraordinary performer, that in some deep way this person is simply not like us. Great performers really are fundamentally different. Their bodies and brains are actually different from ours in a profound way. But we're wrong in thinking, as many do, that the exceptional nature of great performers is some kind of eternal mystery or preordained outcome. It is, rather, the result of a process the general elements of which are clear.

Applying the Principles in Our Lives

Step one in applying the principles in our lives is knowing what we want to do. Because the demands of achieving exceptional performance are so great over so many years, no one has a prayer of meeting them without utter commitment. The first challenge in designing a system of deliberate practice is identifying the immediate next steps. In a few fields those steps are clear. But in the great majority of careers, and in the advanced stages of all of them, there is no published curriculum, no syllabus of materials that must be studied and mastered.

From this perspective we can see mentors in a new way—not just as wise people to whom we turn for guidance but as experienced masters in our field who can advise us on the skills and abilities we need to acquire next and can give us feedback on how we're doing.

The skills and abilities one can choose to develop are infinite, but the opportunities to practice them fall into two general categories: opportunities to practice directly and opportunities to practice as part of the work itself.

Practicing Directly

What separates the great musicians from the rest is how well they perform music. In business we find many analogous situations. The most obvious involve presentations and speeches, and these form the one element of corporate life that is commonly practiced. Yet for most people, practice consists of perhaps a few run-throughs.

Many other important elements of business life can be practiced. One of the most dreaded tasks for many managers is giving job evaluations to their direct reports. The message can be broken down into pieces and each piece analyzed for intent, then practiced repeatedly with immediate feedback from a coach or by video.

The chess model has been used widely in business education for eighty years, but under a different name: the case method. You're presented with a problem, and your job is to figure out a solution. The process of focusing on the problem and evaluating proposed solutions is powerfully instructive.

The practice of top athletes falls into two large categories. One is conditioning. The other is working on specific critical skills.

Conditioning in business means getting stronger at the underlying cognitive skills that you probably already have. It can mean reviewing the fundamental skills that underlie your work.

Specific skill development is based on focused simulation, and that concept can be applied widely in business. Try to improve a specific aspect of your performance, achieve high repetition, and get immediate feedback.

Practicing the Work

We all face a different way to practice business skills, and that is by finding practice in the work itself. These activities, called self-regulation, are done before, during, or after the work activity itself.

Self-regulation begins with setting goals. The best performers set goals that are not about the outcome but about the process of reaching the outcome. The next prework step is planning how to reach the goal. The best performers make the most specific, technique-oriented plans. The best performers also go into their work with a powerful belief in their ability to perform.

During the work, the most important self-regulatory skill that top performers use is self-observation. They are in effect able to step outside themselves, monitor what is happening in their own minds, and ask how it's going. Researchers call this metacognition—knowledge about your own knowledge, thinking about your own thinking.

The practice opportunities that we find in work won't do any good if we don't evaluate them afterward. Excellent performers judge themselves differently from the way other people do. They're more specific, just as they are when they set goals and strategies.

As you add to your knowledge of your domain, your objective is not just to amass information. You are building a mental model—a picture of how your domain functions as a system. This is one of the defining traits of great performers: They all possess large, highly developed, intricate mental models of their domains.

For anyone, a rich mental model contributes to great performance in three major ways:

It forms the framework on which you hang your growing knowledge of your domain.

It helps you distinguish relevant information from irrelevant information.

Most important, it enables you to project what will happen next.

APPLYING THE PRINCIPLES OF GREAT PERFORMANCE IN OUR ORGANIZATIONS

*O*rganizations that apply the principles of great performance follow several major rules:

Understand that each person in the organization is not just doing a job but is also being stretched and grown.

Find ways to develop leaders within their jobs.

Encourage leaders to be active in their communities.

Understand the critical role of teachers and of feedback.

Identify promising performers early.

Understand that people development works best through inspiration, not authority.

Invest significant time, money, and energy in developing people.

Make leadership development part of the culture.

Applying the Principles to Teams

Turning groups of great individuals into great teams is a discipline in itself, which also operates on the principles of great performance. That's why the best organizations follow one additional rule: Develop teams, not just individuals. The organizations that are the most successful at building team performance are especially skilled at avoiding or addressing potential problems that are particularly toxic to the elements of deliberate practice, such as the following:

Picking the wrong team members
Low trust
Competing agendas
Unresolved conflicts
Unwillingness to face the real issues

Performing Great at Innovation

The greatest innovators in a wide range of fields all have at least one character-istic in common: They spent many years in intensive preparation before making any kind of creative breakthrough.

The most eminent creators are consistently those who have immersed them-selves utterly in their chosen field, devoted their lives to it, amassed tremendous knowledge of it, and continually pushed themselves to the front of it.

Making Organizations Innovative

Since organizations are not innovative—only people are innovative—it follows that the most effective steps an organization can take to build innovation will include helping people expand and deepen their knowledge of their field. Creat-ing innovation networks within the organization is one step.

Organizations can take two other steps that are especially effective in light of how innovation really happens: telling people what's needed and giving them freedom to innovate.

Great Performance in Youth and Age

Becoming world-class great at anything seems to require thousands of hours of focused, deliberate practice. For an adult facing the responsibilities of a family and a career, devoting that kind of time to purely developmental activities would be exceedingly tough. Only in childhood and adolescence will the time typically be available.

That reality creates another advantage to starting early. In any field where people can start early, starting late may put one in an eternal and possibly hope-less quest to catch up.

Should We Create Business Prodigies?

Early training can produce high achievers who are surprisingly young. Tradition-ally, however, training in business skills doesn't start early. There isn't intensive, focused development of business skills in young people that's anything like what happens with swimmers, artists, and mathematicians, for example. The ques-tion then arises whether it's even possible.

The answer is clearly yes. Beyond general-domain knowledge, it would be possible to train quite young people in more specific business skills.

Our society has very little problem with children being directed toward fields other than business at early ages. If similar techniques were applied to early training in business, and similar results were produced, would the same effect follow?

Continued deliberate practice enables top performers to maintain skills that would otherwise decline with age and to develop other skills and strategies to compensate for declines that can no longer be avoided. We've seen business-people performing at the highest levels at advanced ages. Warren Buffett continues to run Berkshire Hathaway brilliantly in his late seventies.

The perspectives of both youth and age raise a profound question about great performance. If it's all about the punishing demands of deliberate practice, the continual, painful pushing beyond what's comfortable, then why does anyone do it?

Where Does the Passion Come From?

The central question about motivation to achieve great performance is whether it's intrinsic or extrinsic. Most of us believe the drive must ultimately be intrinsic. Much of the research supports this view.

The consistent finding reported by many researchers examining many domains is that high creative achievement and intrinsic motivation go together.

The great majority of the research in business motivation has focused on what motivates employees generally, not on what drives the top performers. The drivers are almost never extrinsic. Long after executives and entrepreneurs have accumulated more money than they could ever use and more fame than anyone could hope for, they keep working and trying to get better.

Yet that can't be the whole story. Intrinsic motivation may dominate the big picture, but everyone, even the greatest achievers, has responded to extrinsic forces at critical moments.

The Multiplier Effect

In our search for the source of the motivation that sustains people through the trials of getting better, the evidence pushes in a clear direction. The passion doesn't accompany us into this world, but rather, like high-level skills themselves, it develops. World-class achievers are driven to improve, but most of them didn't start out that way.

If the drive to excel develops, rather than appearing fully formed, then how does it develop? Several researchers have separately proposed "the multiplier effect." The concept is simple. A very small advantage in some field can spark a series of events that produce far larger advantages. This multiplier effect accounts not just for improvement of skills over time but also for the motivation that drives the improvement.

The concept of the multiplier effect is embedded in the fundamental theory of deliberate practice. A beginner's skills are so modest that he or she can manage only a little bit of deliberate practice, since it's highly demanding. But that little bit of practice increases the person's skills, making it possible to do more practice, which increases the person's skill level more.

What Do You Believe?

We've seen that the passion develops, rather than emerges suddenly and fully formed. We've also seen hints that childhood may be especially important in how the drive's development gets started.

What would cause you to do the enormous work necessary to be a top performer? It depends on your answers to two basic questions: "What do you really want?" and "What do you really believe?"

What you want—really, deeply want—is fundamental because deliberate practice is a heavy investment. What would you want so much that you'd commit yourself to the necessary hard, endless work, giving up relationships and other interests, so that you might eventually get it? Whatever it is that the greatest performers want, that's how much they must want it.

The second question is more profound. What do you really believe? Belief is tragically constraining. Everyone who has achieved exceptional performance has encountered terrible difficulties along the way.

What you really believe about the source of great performance becomes the foundation of all you will ever achieve. Regardless of where our beliefs in this matter originated, we all have the opportunity to base them on the evidence of reality.

The evidence offers no easy assurances. It shows that the price of top-level achievement is extraordinarily high. Perhaps it's inevitable that not many people will choose to pay it. But the evidence shows also that by understanding how a few become great, anyone can become better. Above all, what the evidence shouts most loudly is striking, liberating news: that great performance is not reserved for a preordained few. It is available to you and to everyone.

HOW ORGANIZATIONS BLOW IT

*M*ost organizations seem to be managed brilliantly to prevent people from performing at high levels.

How often is feedback at most companies constructive, nonthreatening, and work focused rather than person focused? Evaluations at most companies are exactly the opposite. As for rewards, at most companies they almost always entail more responsibilities and less freedom. Extrinsic motivators may be, by definition, the only type that a company can offer employees, but most companies do it about as poorly as they can.

LINCHPIN

By Seth Godin

I n the 1950s and 1960s, the average worker dreamed of a position that could be labeled a "job for life." During this same time period, working the length of one's career for a single organization was still a distinct possibility and, in the hiring arms of many corporations, an expectation. The most blessed union in that era's working world was the marriage of a "company man" to the firm that bestowed the "job for life." As suits and ties gave way to casual Friday, observers pointed to the steady decline in the existence of job security.

Author and CEO Seth Godin argues that job security never went away. It simply shifted the responsibility for its creation to the employee. After observing thousands of organizations, Godin noticed the emergence of a new group of employees. The existing world of management and labor was now sharing the stage with a passionate, empowered set of workers known as linchpins. In *Linchpin: Are You Indispensable?* Godin argues that though linchpins may not bathe in the limelight, this group achieves a rare triple feat: They hold key positions in an organization. They enjoy freedoms that inspire envy in their colleagues. Best of all, they aren't constantly looking over their shoulders in fear of being part of the next staff reduction.

Lasting success in the workplace is generated by the ability to differentiate oneself and make unique, powerful contributions. Godin views this set of skills as belonging to artists. As he notes, "Artists are people with a genius for finding a new answer, a new connection or a new way of getting things done." *Linchpin* provides readers with an outline to help them break the mentality of assembly-line obedience. The mind-set created by corporate manufacturing practices has so dominated the human condition, Godin argues, that we are unable to see it is a recent development. It has become one of the most common hindrances to success, attaching itself to what Godin describes as the lizard brain. *Linchpin* pushes readers to lull the lizard brain to sleep and allow the forces of genius to create innovation and artistry on the job.

Linchpin is written with the same flair that makes Godin one of the most successful bloggers in the business blogging community. He tears down old models of work. In their place, he envisions a nobler worker entering a workplace that befits his or her unique abilities. Godin identifies seven abilities possessed by all linchpins and demonstrates that success in today's marketplace is built on a culture of making connections and giving gifts. Godin's passion for his subject matter resonates on every page of *Linchpin*, and readers will appreciate his honesty about the tremendous effort required to become a linchpin. The reward, as he indicates throughout the book, is the ability to make a gratifying contribution that sustains both the linchpin and the world in which he or she exists, a true measure of success if ever one existed.

LINCHPIN
Are You Indispensable?
by Seth Godin

CONTENTS

THE SUMMARY IN BRIEF

There used to be two teams in every workplace: management and labor. Now there's a third team, the "linchpins." These people invent, lead (regardless of title), connect others, make things happen, and create order out of chaos. They love their work, pour their best selves into it, and turn each day into a kind of art.

Author Seth Godin, CEO of Squidoo.com, explains that linchpins are the essential building blocks of great organizations. Like the small piece of hardware that keeps a wheel from falling off its axle, they may not be famous, but they're indispensable. And in today's world, they get the best jobs and the most freedom.

Have you ever found a shortcut that others missed? Seen a new way to resolve a conflict? Then you have what it takes to become indispensable by overcoming the resistance that holds people back.

The world has changed (again) and the stakes are higher than ever. Now we're facing a full-fledged revolution—a hypercompetitive world involving arts and gifts and fear and the ability for you (or anyone) to make an indispensable contribution to something you care about. If you're not indispensable (yet) it's because you haven't made that choice. Linchpin will help you see that the choice is yours.

In addition, you will learn the following:

How to focus on the things that really matter

How to get your dream job without a résumé

How to see every customer interaction as a chance to give a gift

How to become a linchpin in your organization

THE COMPLETE SUMMARY

Introduction

Where does average come from?

It comes from two places:

1. You have been brainwashed by school and by the system into believing that your job is to do your job and follow instructions. It's not—not anymore.

2. Everyone has a little voice inside his or her head that's angry and afraid. That voice is the resistance—your lizard brain—and it wants you to be average (and safe).

If you're not doing as well as you had hoped, perhaps it's because the rules of the game were changed and no one told you.

The rules were written just over two hundred years ago; they worked for a long time, but no longer.

Developing Indispensability

You weren't born to be a cog in the giant industrial machine. You were *trained* to become a cog.

There's an alternative available to you. Becoming a linchpin is a stepwise process, a path in which you develop the attributes that make you indispensable. You can train yourself to matter. The first step is the most difficult, the step where you acknowledge that this is a skill, and as with all skills, you can (and will) get better at it. Every day, if you focus on the gifts, art, and connections that characterize the linchpin, you'll become a little more indispensable.

The New World of Work

The first chapter of Adam Smith's *Wealth of Nations* makes it clear that the way for businesses to win is to break the production of goods into tiny tasks, tasks that can be undertaken by low-paid people following simple instructions. Smith writes about how incredibly efficient a pin-making factory is compared to a few pin artisans making pins by hand. Why hire a supertalented pin maker when ten barely trained pin-making-factory workers using a machine and working together can produce a *thousand* times more pins, more quickly, than one talented person working alone can?

For nearly three hundred years, that was the way work worked. What factory owners want is compliant, low-paid, replaceable cogs to run their efficient machines.

Our society is struggling because during times of change the very last people you need on your team are well-paid bureaucrats, note takers, literalists, manual readers, TGIF laborers, map followers, and fearful employees. The compliant masses don't help so much when you don't know what to do next.

We Need Artists

What we want, what we need, what we must have are indispensable human beings. We need original thinkers, provocateurs, and people who care. We need marketers who can lead, salespeople able to risk making a human connection, passionate change makers willing to be shunned if it is necessary for them to make a point. Every organization needs a linchpin—the one person who can bring it together and make a difference. We need artists.

Artists are people with a genius for finding a new answer, a new connection, or a new way of getting things done.

That would be you.

Average Is Over

Our world no longer fairly compensates people who are cogs in a giant machine.

It turns out that what we need are gifts and connections and humanity—and the artists who create them.

Leaders don't get a map or a set of rules. Living life without a map requires a different attitude. It requires you to be a linchpin.

The only way to get what you're worth is to stand out, to exert emotional labor, to be seen as indispensable, and to produce interactions that organizations and people care deeply about.

Thinking About Your Choice

Can you become indispensable?

Yes, you can.

The linchpins among us are not the ones born with a magical talent. No, they are people who have decided that a new kind of work is important and are training themselves to do it.

It's not about what you're born with; it's about what you do.

Teaching Remarkable

A great school experience won't keep you from being remarkable, but it's usually not sufficient to guarantee that you will become so. There's something else at work here.

Great schools might work; lousy schools definitely stack the deck against you. Why is society working so hard to kill our natural-born artists? When we try to drill and practice someone into subservient obedience, we're stamping out the artist that lives within.

Why are you working so hard to bury your natural-born instincts? Everyone has art in them, though it's buried sometimes. Markets are crying out, "We need you to stand up and be remarkable. Be human. Contribute. Interact." Take the risk that you might make someone upset with your initiative, innovation, and insight—it turns out that you'll probably delight that person instead.

Consumers say that all they want are cheap commodities. Given the choice, though, most of us, most of the time, seek out art. We seek out experiences and products that deliver more value, more connection, and more experience and those that change us for the better. You can learn how to do this if you want to.

The New American Dream

Do you remember the old American Dream? It struck a chord with millions of people (in the United States and in the rest of the world too). Here's how it goes:

Keep your head down.
Follow instructions.
Show up on time.
Work hard.
Suck it up.

. . . And you will be rewarded.

As we've seen, that dream is over.

The new American Dream, though, the one that markets around the world are embracing as fast as they can, is this:

Be remarkable.
Be generous.
Create art.
Make judgment calls.
Connect people and ideas.

. . . And we have no choice but to reward you.

THE SKILL OF LEADING

L eading is a skill, not a gift. You're not born with it; you learn it. And schools can teach leadership as easily as they figured out how to teach compliance. Schools can teach us to be socially smart, to be open to connection, to understand the elements that build a tribe. While schools provide outlets for natural-born leaders, they don't teach leadership. And leadership is now worth far more than compliance is.

Indoctrination: How We Got Here

We've been taught to be a replaceable cog in a giant machine.

We've been taught to consume as a shortcut to happiness.

We've been taught not to care about our jobs or our customers.

And we've been taught to fit in.

None of these things helps you get what you deserve.

Mediocre Obedience It seems "natural" to live the life so many of us live, but in fact it's quite recent and totally man-made. We exist in a corporate manufacturing mind-set, one so complete that anyone off the grid seems like an oddity. In the past few years, though, it's become clear that people who reject the worst of the current system are actually more likely to succeed.

Evolutionary biologist Stephen Jay Gould wrote, "Violence, sexism and general nastiness are biological since they represent one subset of a possible range of behaviors. But peacefulness, equality and kindness are just as biological—and we may see their influence increase if we can create social structures that permit them to flourish."

Mediocre obedience is certainly something we're capable of, but if we take initiative and add a little bravery, artistic leadership is equally (or more) possible and productive. We've been trained to believe that mediocre obedience is a genetic fact for most of the population, but it's interesting to note that this trait doesn't show up until after a few years of schooling.

In Search of Great Teachers

Great teachers are precious. Lousy teachers cause damage that lasts forever.

We need to reorganize our schools to free the great teachers from tests and reports and busywork and to expel the lousy teachers. When schools were organized to produce laborers, lousy teachers were exactly what we needed. Now lousy teachers are dangerous.

Don't blame the teachers. Blame the corporate system that is still training compliant workers who test well.

Becoming the Linchpin

A linchpin is an unassuming piece of hardware, something you can buy for sixty-nine cents at the local hardware store. It's not glamorous, but it's essential. It holds the wheel on the wagon.

Every successful organization has at least one linchpin; some have dozens or even thousands. The linchpin is the essential element, the person who holds part of the operation together. Without the linchpin, the thing falls apart.

Is there anyone in an organization who is absolutely irreplaceable? Probably not. But the most essential people are so difficult to replace, so risky to lose, and so valuable that they might as well be irreplaceable. Entire corporations are built around a linchpin or, more likely, a scattering of them, essential individuals who are worth holding on to.

1. Your business needs more linchpins. It's scary to rely on a particular employee, but in a postindustrial economy, you have no choice.

2. You are capable of becoming a linchpin. And if you do become one, you'll discover that it's worth the effort.

The easiest linchpin examples are CEOs and entrepreneurs, because they're the ones who get all the press. Steve Jobs at Apple or Jeff Bezos at Amazon or Ben Zander at the Boston Philharmonic or Anne Jackson at FlowerDust.net. We look at these leaders and say, "Of course they're the linchpin. The organization wouldn't be the same without them."

Create a Magical Experience

What about the way you feel when you walk into an Anthropologie store, unwrap a piece of Lake Champlain chocolate, or send a package using FedEx's Web site? The experience could have been merely ordinary, merely another bit of "good enough." But it's not. It's magical. It was created by someone who cared, who contributed, who did more than he or she was told. A linchpin.

Anthropologie has a buyer, Keith Johnson, who spends six months a year traveling the world, visiting flea markets and garage sales, looking for extraordinary things. Not to sell, perhaps, but to beautify a store. It's not easy to hire a Keith Johnson, which is precisely why his work is so essential to the company's success.

If your organization would get out of the way, and if you would step up, there'd be a slot like that available. For anyone.

Is It Possible to Do Hard Work in a Cubicle?

Emotional labor is the task of doing important work, even when it isn't easy.

It turns out that digging into the difficult work of emotional labor is exactly what we're expected (and needed) to do. Work is nothing but a platform for art and the emotional labor that goes with it.

The Gift of Emotional Labor

When you do emotional labor, you benefit.

Not just the company, not just your boss, but you.

The act of giving someone a smile, of connecting to a human, of taking initiative, of being surprising, of being creative, of putting on a show—these are things that we do for free all our lives. And then we get to work and we expect to merely do what we're told and get paid for it.

This gulf creates tension. If you reserve your emotional labor for when you are off duty, but you work all the time, you are deprived of the joy you get when you do this labor. You're not giving gifts on duty, but you're not off duty much at all. Spend eight or ten or twelve hours a day at work (not only in the office but online or on the phone or in your dreams) and there's not a lot of time left for the very human acts that make you who you are and who you want to be.

So bring that gift to work.

And what do you get in return? There are companies that now value this sort of labor and encourage it. More organizations are embracing this idea and hiring for it and rewarding for it.

In most cases, though, you get little in return. At least, little in terms of formal entries in your permanent file or bonuses in your year-end pay. But you do benefit.

First, you benefit from the making and the giving. The act of the gift is in itself a reward. And second, you benefit from the response of those around you. When you develop the habit of contributing this gift, your coworkers become more open, your boss becomes more flexible, and your customers become more loyal.

The Resistance

Your mind, the thing that drives you crazy and makes you special, has two distinct sections: the "daemon" and the resistance.

The daemon is the source of great ideas, groundbreaking insights, generosity, love, connection, and kindness.

The resistance spends all its time insulating the world from the daemon. The resistance lives inside the lizard brain.

"Daemon" is a Greek term (the Romans called it genius). The Greeks believed that the daemon was a separate being inside each of us. The genius living inside of us would struggle to express itself in art or writing or some other endeavor. When the genius felt like showing up, great stuff happened. When it didn't, you were sort of out of luck.

Every time you find yourself following the manual instead of writing the manual, you're avoiding the anguish and giving in to the resistance.

How the Resistance Evolved

The first part of our brain, the part that shows up first in the womb, the part that was there a million years ago—that's our lizard brain. The lizard brain is in charge of fight or flight, of anger and survival. That's all we used to need, and even now, when there's an emergency, the lizard brain is still in charge.

There are several small parts of your brain near the end of your spinal cord responsible for survival and other wild-animal traits. The whole thing is called the basal ganglia, and there are two almond-shaped bits in everyone's brain. Scientists call these the amygdala, and this minibrain apparently takes over when you are angry, afraid, aroused, hungry, or in search of revenge.

It's only recently that our brains evolved to allow big thoughts, generosity, speech, consciousness, and, yes, art. When you look at a picture of the brain, the new part is what you see: the neocortex. That's the wrinkly gray part on the outside. It's big, but it's weak. In the face of screaming resistance from the amygdala, the rest of your brain is helpless. It freezes and surrenders. The lizard brain takes over and tries to protect itself.

The challenge is to create an environment where the lizard brain snoozes. You can't beat it, so you must seduce it. One part of your brain worries about survival and anger and lust. The rest of it creates civilization.

The lizard brain is here to keep you alive; the rest of your brain merely makes you a happy, successful, connected member of society.

So the two parts duke it out. And when you're put on alert, the lizard brain wins every time unless you've established new habits and better patterns—patterns that keep the lizard brain at bay.

The Powerful Culture of Gifts

In the beginning, there was the culture of potlatch and gifts. Caveman culture has a long tradition of reciprocity, and as Marcel Mauss wrote, this reciprocity was used to build relationships and power. In the Pacific Northwest, Native American tribe leaders established their power by giving *everything* away. They could afford to give everyone a gift because they were so powerful, and the gifts were a symbol of that power. Any leader who hoarded saw his power quickly diminish.

Then, quite suddenly, this ancient tradition changed. Money and structured society flipped the system, and now you get, you don't give. Power used to be about giving, not getting.

In the linchpin economy, the winners are once again the artists who give gifts. Giving a gift makes you indispensable. Inventing a gift, creating art—these are what the market seeks out, and the givers are the ones who earn our respect and attention.

Giving, Receiving, Giving

Part of the reason for this flip is the digital nature of our new gift system. The Internet makes it possible for a gift to spread everywhere, quite quickly, at no cost. Digital gifts, ideas that spread—these allow the artist to be far more generous than he could ever be in an analog world.

Thomas Hawk is the most successful digital photographer in the world. He has taken tens of thousands of pictures on his way to his goal of taking a million in his lifetime. The remarkable thing about Hawk's rise is that his pictures are licensed under the Creative Commons license and are freely shared with anyone, with no permission required for personal use. Hawk is both an artist and a giver of gifts. The result is that he leads a tribe, he has plenty of paid work, and he is known for his talents. In short, he is indispensable.

There Is No Map

What does it take to lead?

The key distinction is the ability to forge your own path, to discover a route from one place to another that hasn't been paved, measured, and quantified. So many times we want someone to tell us exactly what to do, and so many times that's exactly the wrong approach.

Diamond cutters have an intrinsic understanding of the stone in their hands. They can touch and see exactly where the best lines are; they know.

The greatest artists do just that. They see and understand the challenges before them without carrying the baggage of expectations or attachment. The diamond cutter doesn't imagine the diamond he wants. Instead, he sees the diamond that is possible.

Seeing, Discernment, and Prajna

You can't make a map unless you can see the world as it is. You have to know where you are and where you're going before you can figure out how to go about getting there.

No one has a transparent view of the world. In fact, we all carry around a personal worldview—the biases and experiences and expectations that color the way we perceive the world.

The loyal employee has a worldview shaped by experience. She wants a stable place to work and she believes in you. So when you show her your plan, her worldview changes her feelings and her analysis of your plan.

And the lawyer and the competitor and the skeptic and the mother-in-law each have their own worldviews, biases, and expectations. None of us knows the absolute truth, of course, but the goal is to approach a situation with the least possible bias.

So the manager and the investor seek out an employee with discernment, the ability to see things as they truly are. A Buddhist might call this prajna.

A life without attachment and stress can give you the freedom to see things as they are and call them as you see them. If you had this skill, what an asset you would be to any organization.

Making the Choice

You can either fit in or stand out. Not both.

You are either defending the status quo or challenging it: playing defense and trying to keep everything "all right" or leading and provoking and striving to make everything better.

Either you are embracing the drama of your everyday life or seeing the world as it is. These are all choices; you can't have it both ways.

Heads, You Win

Perhaps the biggest shift the new economy has brought is self-determination. Access to capital and appropriate connections aren't nearly as essential as they were. Linchpins are made, not born.

There's no doubt that environment still plays a huge role. The right teacher or the right family support or the accidents of race or birth location are still significant factors. But the new rules mean that even if you've got all the right background, you won't make it unless you choose to.

These are internal choices, not external factors. How we respond to the opportunities and challenges of the outside world now determines how much the outside world values us.

How Does a Linchpin Work?

In a world with only a few indispensable people, the linchpin has two elegant choices:

1. Hire plenty of factory workers. Scale like crazy. Take advantage of the facts that most people want a map, most people are willing to work cheaply, most people want to be the factory. You win because you extract the value of their labor—the labor they're surrendering too cheaply.

2. Find a boss who can't live without a linchpin. Find a boss who adequately values your scarcity and your contribution, who will reward you with freedom and respect. Do the work. Make a difference.

If you are not currently doing either of these, refuse to settle. You deserve better.

The Culture of Connection

Most psychologists agree that there are five traits that are essential in how people look at us: openness, conscientiousness, extroversion, agreeableness, and emotional stability.

Here's the thing: These are also the signs of the linchpin. Work—great work—has been transformed in just one hundred years from doing things that involve heavy lifting to leveraging and enhancing your personality. If you hope to succeed because you are able to connect and work with other people, then that will require you to improve your personality in each of these five elements.

Do you know someone who is more open to new ideas or more agreeable than you are? More stable or extroverted? More conscientious? If so, then you better get moving. It's so easy to fall into the trap of focusing on using a spreadsheet or a time clock to measure your progress, but in fact, it's the investment you make in your interactions that will pay off.

Creating a Culture of Connection

Think about business-to-business sales. The key point of distinction between vendors calling on a company is rarely price. It's the perceived connection between the prospect and the organization.

Now consider job satisfaction. The key point of distinction between places to work is rarely the work you'll be asking the employee to do. It's the perceived connection between the employee and the people he or she works with.

Thus, the individual in the organization who collects, connects, and nurtures relationships is indispensable. This isn't about recording the information in a database somewhere. This is about holding the relationships as sacred as they deserve to be.

The Seven Abilities of the Linchpin

Linchpins do two things for the organization. They exert emotional labor and they make a map. Those contributions take many forms. Here is one way to think about the list of what makes you indispensable:

1. Providing a unique interface among members of the organization. A linchpin helps lead and connects people in the organization, actively and with finesse. This takes emotional labor, and it can't be done by following the instructions in a manual.

2. Delivering unique creativity. Creativity is personal, original, unexpected, and useful. Unique creativity requires domain knowledge, a position of trust, and generosity to actually contribute. "Unique" implies that the creativity is focused and insightful.

3. Managing a situation or organization of great complexity. When the situation gets too complex, it's impossible to follow the manual, because there is no manual. Linchpins make their own maps and thus allow the organization to navigate more quickly than it ever could if it had to wait for the paralyzed crowd to figure out what to do next.

4. Leading customers. The new model of commerce is interactive, fluid, and decentralized. That means that organizations need more than a tiny team. It means that every person who interacts with a consumer (or a business being sold to, or a donor to a nonprofit, or a voter) is doing marketing as leadership. There's no script for leadership.

5. Inspiring staff. You can't say, "Get more excited and insightful or you're fired." Actually, you can, but it won't work. The front-desk worker at a hotel who runs out in the middle of the night to buy gym shorts for a guest isn't doing it out of fear of being reprimanded. He does it because he was inspired to do so by a leader who wasn't even in the hotel when the clerk decided to contribute.

6. Providing deep domain knowledge. Having deep domain knowledge by itself is rarely sufficient to becoming indispensable. Combining that knowledge with smart decisions and generous contributions, though, changes things.

7. Possessing a unique talent. If you want to be a linchpin, the power you bring to the table has to be very difficult to replace. Be bolder and think bigger. If you're not the best in the world (the customer's world) at your unique talent, you have only two choices: Develop the other attributes that make you a linchpin or get a lot better at your unique talent.

When It Doesn't Work

What happens when the conversation doesn't happen, the product doesn't sell, the consumer is not delighted, your boss is not happy, and the people aren't moved?

Make more art.

Give more gifts.

Learn from what you did and then do more.

The only alternative is to give up and to become an old-school cog. Which means failing. Trying and failing is better than merely failing, because trying makes you an artist and gives you the right to try again.

Pulitzer Prize Fighting: You Might Not Be Good Enough

There's no guarantee that anyone who sets out to win a Pulitzer is going to win it. There's no guarantee that merely because you're passionate about Web design, your site is actually going to be popular.

The vivid truth is this: Now that we have the freedom to create, we must embrace the fact that not all creations are equal and some people aren't going to win.

That doesn't mean you're a loser. It might mean that you're making the wrong art, drawing the wrong map. If you're not winning as a stockbroker, perhaps your art lies somewhere else.

The challenge lies in knowing your market and yourself well enough to see the truth.

Two Tactics That Can Help You

The system we work in is changing, but it's an evolutionary change, not a revolutionary one. Organizations rarely give linchpins all the support and encouragement they deserve. Which means that your efforts won't always get what they need to succeed.

There are two tactics that can help you.

1. Understand that there's a difference between the right answer and the answer you can sell. Too often, heretical ideas in organizations are shot down. They're not refused because they're wrong; they're refused because the person doing the selling doesn't have the stature or track record to sell them. Your boss has a worldview too. When you propose something that triggers his resistance, what do you expect will happen?

2. Focus on making changes that work down, not up. Interacting with customers and employees is often easier than influencing bosses and investors. Over time, as you create an environment where your insight and generosity pay off, the people above you will notice and you'll get more freedom and authority.

Don't ask your boss to run interference, cover for you, or take the blame. Instead, create moments where your boss can happily take credit. Once that cycle begins, you can be sure it will continue.

Summary

Every successful organization is built around people. Humans who do art. People who interact with other people. Men and women who don't merely shuffle money but interact, give gifts, and connect.

All these interactions are art. Art isn't only a painting; it's anything that changes someone for the better, a nonanonymous interaction that leads to a human (not simply a commercial) conclusion.

Art can't be bought and sold. It must contain an element that's a gift, something that brings the artist closer to the viewer, not something that insulates one from the other. So we need to remember how to be artists.

Artists, at least the great ones, see the world more clearly than the rest of us do. They have prajna, a sense of what actually is, not simply the artist's take on it. That honest sight allows them to see the future over the cloudy horizon. As our world changes faster and faster, it is these honest artists who will describe our future and lead us there.

Last Word

The only thing keeping you from being one of these artists is the resistance: the loud voice of the lizard brain telling you that you can't possibly do it, that you don't deserve it, that people will laugh at you. Anyone who makes the choice to overcome the resistance and has the insight to make the right map can become a successful linchpin.

You can't fake it, though, because human beings are too talented at sensing when a gift is not a gift, when we're being played or manipulated. And sometimes our art isn't enough. It's not enough to get us a sale or even make us a living. But we persist because making art is what we do.

The result of this art, these risks, the gifts, and the humanity coming together is both wonderful and ironic. Getting back in touch with our precommercial selves will actually create a postcommercial world that feeds us, enriches us, and gives us the stability we've been seeking for so long.

POWER

by Jeffrey Pfeffer

In the aftermath of the 2008 global financial crisis the job market was flooded with more applicants than open positions. Line workers, middle managers, and even C-level executives were suddenly left floating in the deep end of the talent pool. A single job opening produced ten times the number of applicants that it had a year or two earlier. With every résumé boasting of corporate achievement and a scholastic pedigree, a special quality set apart the lone individual whose hand was shaken as the new employee. According to author and professor Jeffrey Pfeffer, that defining characteristic is power. In his book *Power: Why Some People Have It—and Others Don't*, Pfeffer trains the reader to step up and grab the world by its collar.

The advice in Pfeffer's book is the equivalent of a secret handshake among an elite group of individuals. While the party line states that fairness and hard work are the bricks that pave the path to success, *Power* discusses the real-world methods that help individuals get noticed in a group of high achievers. *Power* delivers honest impressions of the modern workplace without resorting to cruelty. A reader can achieve what he or she desires if he or she has the commitment to follow through on Pfeffer's rules. In short, action-oriented strategies, he helps professionals create resources, build influence, expand their networks, and get noticed by the people who matter.

One aspect of *Power*'s success program to which readers should pay close attention is Pfeffer's repeated emphasis on objectivity. He writes that the construction of a more powerful person depends on his or her ability to honestly examine weaknesses and receive constructive criticism. Whether it's negative feedback or a professional setback, Pfeffer reminds readers not to take it personally. These things are to be used as building blocks in the climb to success. He reminds readers that the best way to alleviate the embarrassment that accompanies failure is to talk about the setback with others. It removes the stigma and increases one's appearance of candor and self-control.

There is an expression that successful individuals "make their own luck." Pfeffer's own bold moves in academia helped him become the Thomas D. Dee II

Professor of Organizational Behavior at Stanford University's Graduate School of Business. He does an excellent job of giving readers the tools necessary to open more doors and create more opportunity. *Power* is intended to help readers break the chains of stagnation and discover new heights of their potential. Pfeffer illustrates his principles with stories of individuals in business who exemplify the meaning of power. As Pfeffer writes, "There is a lot of zero-sum competition for status and jobs. Most organizations have only one CEO." Pfeffer's regimen of success-building secrets gives an individual the necessary boost to be the last person standing.

POWER
Why Some People Have It—and Others Don't
by Jeffrey Pfeffer

CONTENTS

THE SUMMARY IN BRIEF

Over decades of consulting with corporations and teaching MBA students the nuances of organizational power, Jeffrey Pfeffer has watched numerous people suffer career reversals even as others prevail despite the odds.

He explains that our most common mistake is not having a realistic understanding of what makes some people more successful than others. By believing that life is fair, he writes, we tend to subscribe to the "just-world phenomenon," which leaves us unprepared for the challenges and competition of the real world.

In *Power* Pfeffer brings decades of insights to a wider audience. Brimming with counterintuitive advice, examples from various countries, and surprising findings based on his research, this groundbreaking guide reveals the strategies and tactics that separate winners from losers.

Power, Pfeffer explains, is not something that can be learned from those in charge: Their advice often puts a rosy spin on their ascent and focuses on what should have worked rather than what actually did. Instead, *Power* reveals the true paths to power and career success. Iconoclastic and grounded in real human interaction, this summary is an essential organizational survival manual and a new standard in the field of leadership.

In addition, you will learn the following:

How working in underexploited niches can help you develop leverage
How power can be used and harnessed not only for individual gain but also
     for the benefit of others
How well-established principles can help you obtain more influence
How to succeed and wield power in the real world

THE COMPLETE SUMMARY

Introduction: Be Prepared for Power

Being politically savvy and seeking power are related to career success and even to managerial performance. For instance, one study investigated the primary motivations of managers and their professional success. One group of managers were primarily motivated by a need for affiliation—they were more interested in being liked than in getting things done. A second group were primarily motivated by a need for achievement—goal attainment for themselves. And a third group were primarily interested in power. The evidence showed that this third group, the managers primarily interested in power, were the most effective, not only in achieving positions of influence inside companies but also in accomplishing their jobs.

In another example, Gerald Ferris of Florida State University and colleagues have developed an 18-item political skills inventory. Research on 35 school administrators in the midwestern United States and 474 branch managers of a national financial-services firm showed that people who had more political skill received higher performance evaluations and were rated as more effective leaders.

The Real World

So welcome to the real world—not necessarily the world we want but the world that exists. It can be a tough world out there, and building and using power are useful organizational survival skills. There is a lot of zero-sum competition for status and jobs. Most organizations have only one CEO. There is only one managing partner in professional-services firms, only one school superintendent in each district, only one prime minister or president at a time—you get the picture. With more well-qualified people competing for each step on the organizational ladder all the time, rivalry is intense and only getting more so as there are fewer and fewer management positions.

Some of the individuals competing for advancement bend the rules of fair play or ignore them completely. Don't complain about this or wish the world were different. You can compete and even triumph in organizations of all types, large or small, public or private sector, if you understand the principles of power and are willing to use them. Your task is to know how to prevail in the political battles you will face.

It Takes More Than Performance

People in power are busy with their own agendas and jobs. Such people, including those higher up in your own organization, probably aren't paying that much attention to you and what you are doing. You should not assume that your boss knows or notices what you are accomplishing and has perfect information about your activities. Therefore, your first responsibility is to ensure that those at higher levels in your company know what you are accomplishing. And the best way to ensure they know what you are achieving is to tell them.

For you to attain a position of power, those in power have to choose you for a senior role. If you blend into the woodwork, no one will care about you, even if you are doing a great job.

Beyond Visibility

In advertising, one of the most prominent measures of effectiveness is ad recall—not taste, logic, or artistry—simply "Do you remember the ad and the product?" The same holds true for you and your path to power. That's because of the importance of what is called "the mere exposure effect." As originally described by the late social psychologist Robert Zajonc, the effect refers to the fact that people, other things being equal, prefer and choose what is familiar to them—what they have seen or experienced before. Research shows that repeated exposure increases positive effect and reduces negative feelings, that people prefer the familiar because this preference reduces uncertainty, and that the effect of exposure on liking and decision making is a robust phenomenon that occurs in different cultures and in a variety of different domains of choice.

The simple fact is that people like what they remember—and that includes you. In order for your great performance to be appreciated, it needs to be visible. But beyond visibility, the mere-exposure research teaches us that familiarity produces preference. Simply put, in many cases, being memorable equals getting picked.

The Personal Qualities That Bring Influence

Ron Meyer, the president and chief operating officer of Universal Studios since 1995, is the longest-serving head of a major motion picture company. A powerful figure in the film industry, Meyer also provides an example of a life transformed. Ron Meyer dropped out of high school when he was fifteen, and a couple of years later he joined the U.S. Marines. After leaving the Marines he got a job at a talent agency as a chauffeur, a position that permitted him to learn a lot about the entertainment business as he listened to the conversations of clients. After working as an agent at the William Morris Agency, Meyer, with some friends, founded the Creative Artists Agency, a position that helped establish him as a power broker in Hollywood.

Meyer, like many successful people, profoundly changed over the course of his life. He developed qualities that permitted him to obtain and hold on to influence. If you are going to do likewise, you need to successfully surmount three obstacles.

First, you must come to believe that personal change is possible; otherwise, you won't even try to develop the attributes that bring power—you will just accept that you are who you are rather than embarking on a sometimes difficult path of personal growth and development.

Second, you need to see yourself and your strengths and weaknesses as objectively as possible. This is difficult because in our desire to self-enhance—to think good things about ourselves—we avoid negative information and over-emphasize any positive feedback we receive.

And third, you need to understand the most important qualities for building a power base so you can focus your inevitably limited time and attention on developing those.

Change Is Always Possible

People often think that whatever qualities are needed for building a path to power, either you have them or you don't, at least by the time you're an adult. But the biographies of Ron Meyer and scores of other figures in political and business life belie that idea.

Choosing Where to Start

Where you begin your career affects your rate of progress as well as how far you go. At two University of California campuses, the speed at which professors moved up a civil service–type salary ladder reflected the power of their academic department—those in more powerful departments moved up the salary scale more quickly. A study of 338 managers who began their career in a 3,500-employee public utility found that the power of the unit where people began their careers affected their rate of salary growth, with people starting in more powerful units moving up more rapidly. That study also found that managers who began their careers in higher-powered departments (such as operations, distribution, and customer service) were more likely to remain in high-powered units as they changed jobs.

Prior to AT&T's breakup by the government, the road to its CEO position was through the Illinois Bell subsidiary. If you wanted to be CEO of Pacific Gas and Electric, the legal department was the best place to build your career. The shift in power at PG&E from engineers to lawyers was visible over time: In 1950, only three of the company's most senior positions were occupied by attorneys; by 1980, the number was eighteen. For many years, finance was the route to the top at General Motors. At the University of Illinois, senior university positions were often filled with people from the physics department.

Path to Power

We intuitively know that not all career platforms are equal as a path to power, and research supports that intuition. But people often err in choosing where to start building their power base. The most common mistake is to locate in the department dealing with the organization's current core activity, skill, or product—the unit that is the most powerful at the moment. This is not always a good idea because the organization's most central work is where you are going to encounter the most talented competition and also the most well-established career paths and processes. Moreover, what is the most important function or product today may not be in the future.

So if you want to move up quickly, go to underexploited niches where you can develop leverage with less resistance and build a power base in activities that are going to be more important in the near future than they are today.

Getting In: Standing Out and Breaking Some Rules

The late Reginald Lewis was a successful African American corporate lawyer and founder of a buyout firm, TLC Group. TLC bought the McCall Pattern Company in the early 1980s and, under Lewis's turnaround efforts, returned investors ninety times their money. TLC later bought Beatrice Foods, creating the first black-owned company with revenues of over one billion dollars and making Lewis one of the wealthiest people in the United States.

But back in 1965, Lewis wasn't someone with a prominent place in African American business history. He didn't have an international law program at Harvard and an African American history museum in Maryland named after him. He was just a young man from a tough Baltimore neighborhood who was graduating from Virginia State University and had set his sights on Harvard Law School. During that summer he was in a Rockefeller Foundation–funded program at Harvard Law School for high-potential college students designed to interest them in careers in the law and help them prepare for the application process. There was just one problem—one of the rules of the program was that no one who participated could even be considered for admission to Harvard Law School. Moreover, Lewis had not taken the Law School Aptitude Test or even applied to Harvard Law, and he wanted to start the program that fall.

Even as he was doing well in the summer program by expending enormous effort and standing out in the mock trial to such an extent that thirty years later professors still talked about his performance, Lewis met with a Harvard Law professor and then with the dean of admissions. With these faculty members he pressed his case by forcefully arguing "the myriad ways an association between Reginald Lewis and the law school would be mutually beneficial." At the end of the summer, Reggie Lewis matriculated at Harvard Law School, becoming the only person in the history of the school to be admitted before he filled out an application.

What's the Worst That Could Happen?

Reginald Lewis understood that the worst that could happen from asking for something would be getting turned down. And if he was turned down, so what? He would not be any worse off than if he had not asked in the first place. If he didn't ask or if he was refused, he would not receive what he sought, but at least in asking there was some hope. Some people do believe that worse things could occur: that their bold behavior could offend those exposed to it and they could develop a "bad reputation." Probably not, and the risk of standing out is well worth taking.

Making Something Out of Nothing: Creating Resources

Resources are great because once you have them, maintaining power becomes a self-reinforcing process.

There are two simple but important implications of resources as a source of power. The first is that in choosing among jobs, it's best to choose positions that have direct control of more resources such as budget or staff. That generally means preferring line to staff positions, since line positions typically control more staff hiring and have more budgetary authority.

Most headhunters will tell you that when they seek candidates for senior general management positions, including the CEO job, they look to people who have had responsibility running operations, and the larger the division or operation the potential candidate has run, the better, other things being equal. Job analyses (such as the Hay system) used to determine salary ranges consider your number of direct and indirect reports, as well as the amount of budget you can spend without higher-level authorization, measures of your responsibility and consequently the economic value of your job. Getting control of resources is an important step on your path to power.

The second implication is that your power comes in large measure from the position you hold and the resources and other things you control as a consequence of holding that position. It is easy for people, motivated by self-enhancement, to believe that the deference and flattery of others is due to their inherent intelligence, experience, and charm. This may be the case, but not often. When you retire or otherwise leave a position in which you once had control over substantial amounts of resources, people will pay you much less heed and give you less attention.

Building Efficient and Effective Social Networks

Two German professors, Hans-Georg Wolff and Klaus Moser, offer a good definition of networking: "Behaviors that are aimed at building, maintaining and using informal relationships that possess the (potential) benefit of facilitating work-related activities of individuals by voluntarily gaining access to resources and maximizing . . . advantages." Their study of more than two hundred people in Germany developed some scales of networking behaviors that demonstrate what actions are required. These included:

1. Building internal contacts (e.g., "I use company events to make new contacts.")

2. Maintaining internal contacts (e.g., "I catch up with colleagues from other departments about what they are working on.")

3. Using internal contacts (e.g., "I use my contacts with colleagues in other departments in order to get confidential advice in business matters.")

4. Building external contacts (e.g., "I accept invitations to official functions or festivities out of professional interest.")

5. Maintaining external contacts (e.g., "I ask others to give my regards to business acquaintances outside of our company.")

6. Using external contacts (e.g., "I exchange professional tips and hints with acquaintances from other organizations.")

The networking behaviors they describe entail making some incremental effort to build, maintain, and use social ties with people. The people targeted are not necessarily in your sights if you are focused just on your immediate job and company.

Networking Jobs

In general, jobs high in networking content require bridging separate organizations, brokering deals, and building relationships to influence decision making.

JACK VALENTI'S POLITICAL POWER

When in 1966 Jack Valenti left his position as a White House aide to become head of the Motion Picture Association of America, he could provide political access for the movie studios, which needed help staving off censorship and dealing with foreign governments on commercial issues, including the repatriation of funds. At the same time, he could provide an entrée to Hollywood and its enormous fund-raising potential for the Democratic Party and his patron, Lyndon Johnson.

Acting and Speaking with Power

We choose how we will act and talk, and those decisions are consequential for acquiring and holding on to power. Harriet Rubin was, for eleven years, the editor of a line of books, called Currency, devoted to understanding leadership. During that time she at once occupied a position of leadership and published leaders' autobiographies and books on leadership. Her experience suggested that the secret of leadership was the ability to play a role, to pretend, to be skilled in the theatrical arts. Rubin was right. The ability to convey power through how we talk, appear, and act matters in our everyday interactions, from seeking a job to attempting to win a vital contract to presenting a company's growth prospects to investment analysts.

Speaking Powerfully

The language people use and how they construct presentations and arguments help determine their power. Great orators move masses—Martin Luther King

Jr.'s famous "I Have a Dream" speech and the speeches of Barack Obama in his campaign for the presidency being two notable examples. But power gets created in private interactions and small meetings, not just on a huge stage. There are some well-established principles that can help you subtly obtain more influence as you speak with power.

Interruption One source of power in every interaction is interruption. Those with more power interrupt; those with less power get interrupted. Interrupting others in conversation, although not polite, can indicate power and be an effective power move.

Contesting the Premises of the Discussion In most companies, the strategy and market dynamics are taken for granted. If someone challenges these assumptions—such as how the company is competing, how it is measuring success, what the strategy is, who the real competitors are now and in the future—this can be a very potent power play.

Persuasive Language Language that influences is able to create powerful images and emotions that overwhelm reason. Such language is evocative, specific, and filled with strong words and visual imagery.

Building a Reputation: Perception Is Reality

For more than a decade, John Browne served as CEO of British Petroleum; under his aegis, BP bought Amoco and ARCO and made numerous smaller acquisitions. Browne was named to the British House of Lords and was voted the country's most admired business leader numerous times. But as many observers point out, Browne is not necessarily the most obvious leader: He is short, less than five feet six inches tall; soft-spoken and awkward in social settings, essentially an introvert; and an intellectual in an industry known for brash, bold leaders who take big chances. Browne's rise to power and his consolidation of his position were based in part on his ability to build an image that served him well.

Three Dimensions of John Browne's Reputation

Although Browne's reputation is multifaceted, three dimensions stand out: hard work and dedication, intelligence, and intimidation of others. Browne was at BP throughout his working life, spending over thirty years in the company. He moved around the world—his postings included Anchorage, New York, Cleveland, and London, among others. He worked enormous hours. It is helpful to be seen as someone devoted to the company above all else.

Browne's intelligence is legendary. Trained in physics, he always emphasized first principles and asked inquisitive questions. His analytical training permitted him to do well in his jobs in both finance and exploration. But what comes across most in his story is how he used his intelligence and memory to build his reputation as being supersmart.

The specifics of a useful reputation will obviously vary depending on the context and your own personal strengths and weaknesses. What is important is that you think carefully about the dimensions of the reputation you want to build and then do everything in your power—from deciding how you spend your time to choosing what organizations and people to associate with—to ensure that is the image that you project.

Overcoming Opposition and Setbacks

Because people come from different backgrounds, seek different rewards, and see different information, they are going to see the world differently. Consequently, disagreements are inevitable in organizations. Unfortunately, many people are conflict averse, finding disagreement disagreeable and avoiding raising differences of opinion or engaging in difficult conversations with their adversaries.

As school leader Rudy Crew has said, "Conflict is just an opportunity for another person's education," for exploring why people think the way they do, and for sharing perspectives so the parties to the conflict can learn about and from each other.

Here are some ideas to make you more successful in surmounting opposition:

Try a little tenderness and leave people a graceful out. Treat opponents well and leave them a way to retreat with dignity.

Don't cause yourself unnecessary problems. Conflict arouses strong emotions, including anger, and these interfere with our ability to think strategically about what we are really trying to do.

Don't take things personally—make important relationships work.

Be persistent. Persistence works because it wears down the opposition.

Advance on multiple fronts. Leverage power from one setting to get influence in another.

Move first—seize the initiative. If you move quickly, you can often catch your opponents off guard and secure victory before they even know what is happening.

Coping with Setbacks

Most successful people have encountered setbacks along the way and survived. Reed Hastings, the highly successful founder and CEO of Netflix, had a much less successful experience with his first software start-up, Pure Software, where he tried to fire himself twice. Bad things sometimes happen to good people. The issue becomes whether and how they recover.

If you are going to persevere and recover, you need to stop blaming yourself, letting your opponents dominate the discussion of what happened, and feeling bad about your complicity in your demise.

The best way to overcome embarrassment is to talk about what happened to as many people as possible. Making what happened less emotionally fraught is absolutely essential to your being able to think strategically about your next moves.

The Price of Power

The late Nobel Prize–winning economist Milton Friedman famously said, "There is no free lunch"—nothing comes without cost—and that is certainly true of power. As you chart your course and make decisions about what you will and will not do to acquire power, consider carefully what you are striving for and whether you really want it. People who seek and attain power often pay some price for the quest, for holding on to their positions and confronting the difficult but inevitable transitions out of powerful roles. Here are some of the costs incurred by those who successfully pursue a path to power:

Cost 1: Visibility and Public Scrutiny An important lesson: If you are going to misbehave in any way, do so before you achieve a high-level position that makes you the object of constant attention by peers, subordinates, superiors, and the media.

Cost 2: Loss of Autonomy Many CEOs and other senior leaders block out time for themselves and the activities that they want to do. But all of them talk about the loss of control over how they spend their time as one of the big costs of being in a position of power.

Cost 3: The Time and Effort Required Building and maintaining power requires time and effort; there are no two ways about it. Time spent on your quest for power and status is time that you cannot spend on other things, such as hobbies or personal relationships and family. The quest for power often exacts a high toll on people's personal lives.

Cost 4: Trust Dilemmas The higher you rise and the more powerful the position you occupy, the greater the number of people who will want your job. The constant vigilance required by those in power—to ensure they are hearing the truth and to maintain their position vis-à-vis rivals—is yet another cost of occupying a job that many others want.

Cost 5: Power as an Addictive Drug The addictive quality of power makes it tough to leave powerful positions. But everyone eventually has to step down, and the druglike nature of power makes leaving a powerful position a truly wrenching experience for some.

How—and Why—People Lose Power

Studies of the effects of power on the power holder consistently find that power produces overconfidence and risk taking, insensitivity to others, stereotyping, and a tendency to see other people as a means to the power holder's gratification.

In a study all too reminiscent of what goes on in workplaces every day, David Kipnis put research participants in a simulated work situation with a subordinate. Some people in the managerial role had little formal control over resources and had to influence through persuasion, while others were given the power to reward and punish those working for them. The more control participants had over levers of power such as pay increases or decreases, the more attempts they made to influence their subordinates. Moreover, those with more power came to see their subordinates' job performance as resulting more from their control and less from the efforts or motivation of those they were supervising. And because the supervisors with power saw themselves as superior to those they were supervising, they evidenced less desire to spend time with their subordinates and wanted to distance themselves from those less powerful—even though who was a supervisor and how much power that person had was randomly determined and temporary.

A Power Mind-set

One lesson from the growing number of studies on the effects of power is how little it takes to get people into a power mind-set where they engage in disrespectful and rude behavior. Giving them even modest control over meaningless rewards in temporary groups of strangers seems to be sufficient.

Overconfidence and insensitivity lead to losing power, as people become so full of themselves that they fail to attend to the needs of those whose enmity can cause them problems. Conversely, not letting power go to your head and acting as if you were all-powerful can help you maintain your position.

Power Dynamics: Good for Organizations, Good for You?

Research confirms what common sense suggests is true: Political struggles are more likely to occur and to be more fierce, and power is used more often, when resources are scarcer and there is more struggle over their allocation. Studies of budget allocations in universities found that when money was tighter, the relationship between departmental power and amount of the budget obtained was stronger.

The lesson is clear: You should always watch your back, but be particularly wary and sensitive to what is occurring during times of economic stress. That is when political turmoil and the use of power are likely to be at their peak.

The employer-employee relationship has profoundly changed over the past several decades, not just in the United States but in many countries. In ways big and small, both implicitly and explicitly, employers and their leaders have told employees that they are responsible for their own careers and, in many instances, their own health care and retirement.

So don't worry about how your efforts to build your path to power are affecting your employer, because your employer is probably not worrying about you. Neither are your coworkers or "partners," if you happen to have any—they are undoubtedly thinking about your usefulness to them, and you will be gone, if they can manage it, when you are no longer of use. You need to take care of yourself and use whatever means you have to do so—after all, that has been the message of companies and business pundits for years. Take those admonitions seriously.

It's Easier Than You Think

It's important for you to find the right place given your aptitude and interests.

Although it is possible and desirable to develop your power skills, few people are comfortable changing their likes and dislikes. Yes, you can evolve and change, but only within limits. Therefore, the first step in building a path to power is to pick an environment that fits your aptitudes and interests—one where you can be successful in both the technical and political aspects, if any, of the work.

Finding the right place for you requires several steps.

First, you must be brutally honest about your strengths, weaknesses, and preferences—and because of the self-enhancement motive, not many people are as objective about themselves as they need to be.

Second, you can't get trapped into following the crowd and doing something just because everyone else is.

Third, to pick the right place for yourself, you must be objective not only about yourself but also about the job and its risks and opportunities.

Take Care of Yourself—Don't Expect Justice

It's not just that the world is not always fair so you should stop counting on the triumph of your merit. People align with who they think is going to win. If you don't stand up for yourself and actively promote your own interests, few will be willing to be on your side. Since observers will see you as not trying to triumph and therefore losing, they will either not join your side or desert you, making your organizational demise more certain. Therefore, although self-promotion and fighting for your interests can seem unattractive, the alternative scenario is invariably much worse.

Not only can you survive, but you can even succeed if you learn the principles and rules and are willing to implement them in your daily organizational life.

So don't complain that life isn't fair or that your organizational culture isn't healthy or that your boss is a jerk. You have both the responsibility and the potential to change your situation, either in your present job or in some new place. Stop waiting for things to get better or for other people to acquire power and use it in a benevolent fashion to improve the situation. It's up to you to find—or create—a better place for yourself. And it's up to you to build your own path to power.

THE DARK SIDE OF POLITICS

*O*ne dominant perspective in the research literature on organizations is that *"politics is associated with the 'dark side' of workplace behavior and researchers have described political behavior as inherently divisive, stressful and a cause of dissent and reduced performance." The empirical evidence supports this view. Higher levels of perceived politics inside organizations are associated with reduced job satisfaction, morale, and organizational commitment and with increased intentions to quit.*

MOJO

by Marshall Goldsmith
with Mark Reiter

Think of the average person's reaction to his or her alarm going off on a Monday morning. It usually signals the start of five consecutive days where the only thing that changes is the date on the calendar. The drudgery of "eat, work, sleep" numbs the minds of workers trapped in a cocoon of e-mails and text messages. Picture this same scenario repeating as months become years and years fade into decades. Is this terrifying vision the natural human condition? According to author and executive coach Marshall Goldsmith, humans are predisposed to float in a state of inertia. He suggests, "Our default response in life is not to experience happiness . . . not to experience meaning." What's missing is the passion and spirit needed to smash open the tomb of inertia. In his book *Mojo: How to Get It, How to Keep It, How to Get It Back if You Lose It,* Goldsmith gives readers the fuel to rejuvenate their personal and professional lives.

Goldsmith's book is a cure for the ills created by the last vestiges of the nine-to-five world. While technology has all but eliminated the era of working by the clock, many workers have yet to let go of the idea that a job is little more than a path to a paycheck and a retirement plan. Mojo forces individuals to become current with the business world while letting go of the crutches that prevent them from achieving higher levels of success. Goldsmith's discussion of "mojo killers" presents six common mistakes that, while easy to spot in others, may prove hard for an individual to recognize in himself. Drawing on his years of experience as a coach, Goldsmith successfully walks the fine line between praise and constructive criticism with advice that helps a reader arrive at moments of personal revelation. The source of mojo is inside the individual. Goldsmith's role is to help people harness their internal mojo and direct it toward their lives inside and outside the office.

The structure of *Mojo* is one of the reasons for the book's success. Goldsmith constructs a "mojo tool kit" of personal empowerment objectives. The tools are spread across four major areas: identity, achievement, reputation, and acceptance. In each section, Goldsmith provides readers with action items that focus solely on achieving results. He injects the tools with a level of passion that demonstrates his own mojo and gives the text an infectious dose of enthusiasm. At the outset of the book he gives readers a simple challenge: Using a scale from one to ten, rate your day's activities based on their long-term and short-term satisfaction. By following the concepts outlined in *Mojo*, readers will see their scores climb the charts until even the alarm clock on a Monday morning rates an eight or a nine on Goldsmith's scale.

MOJO
How to Get It, How to Keep It, How to Get It Back if You Lose It
by Marshall Goldsmith with Mark Reiter

CONTENTS

THE SUMMARY IN BRIEF

Mojo comes from the moment we do something that is purposeful, powerful, and positive and the rest of the world recognizes it. Mojo is about that moment— and how we can create it in our lives, maintain it, and recapture it when we need it.

Top executive coach Marshall Goldsmith lays out the ways that we can get— and keep—our mojo. He explains how our professional and personal mojo is impacted by four key factors and the questions they raise: identity (Who do you think you are?), achievement (What have you done lately?), reputation (Who do other people think you are—and what have you done lately?), and acceptance (What can you change—and when do you need to just "let it go"?).

Mojo is that positive spirit—toward what we are doing now—that starts from the inside and radiates to the outside. Mojo is at its peak when we are experiencing both happiness and meaning in what we are doing and communicating this experience to the world around us. This summary provides practical tools that can help anyone achieve both happiness and meaning, not only in business but also in life.

In addition, you will learn the following:

How to integrate and focus your life and work
How to contribute to the world
How to find more meaning for your life through self-realization and self-actualization
How to deal with human behavior in your business and personal life

THE COMPLETE SUMMARY

You and Your Mojo

The word "mojo" originally referred to a folk belief in the supernatural powers of a voodoo charm, often in the form of a piece of cloth or a small pouch.

Over time, the word has evolved to describe a sense of positive spirit and direction, especially in the shifting tides of sports, business, and politics.

To some people, mojo is a more elusive sense of personal advancement through the world. You're moving forward, making progress, achieving goals, clearing hurdles, passing the competition—and doing so with increasing ease. Sports people call this being "in the zone." Others describe it under the umbrella term "flow."

A new definition of "mojo" spins off from the great value attached to finding happiness and meaning in life. Mojo plays a vital role in our pursuit of happiness and meaning because it is about achieving two simple goals: loving what you do and showing it. These goals govern an operational definition: Mojo is that positive spirit toward what we are doing now that starts from the inside and radiates to the outside.

Our mojo is apparent when our positive internal feelings about what we are doing are evident to others.

Four vital ingredients need to be combined in order for you to have great mojo: identity, *achievement*, *reputation*, and *acceptance*.

Measuring Your Mojo

How much mojo do you have? How can you measure your mojo?

There are people who by all external measures—money, respect, power, status—are "winning." They are outpacing their peers and competition quite handily. And yet inside they derive little satisfaction or meaning from their job or achievements.

Mojo is not merely about the rush we feel when we're on a winning streak. It's not only about the direction we're heading in, nor is it about the pace of change we're creating around us. Mojo is an expression of the harmony—or lack of harmony—between what we feel inside about whatever we are doing and what we show on the outside.

The Mojo Paradox

As much as we all claim to want happiness and meaning in our lives, there's a paradoxical catch that thwarts us at every turn. It is called the Mojo Paradox and it states: Our default response in life is not to experience happiness. Our default response in life is not to experience meaning. Our default response in life is to experience inertia.

In other words, our most common, everyday process—the thing we do more often than anything else—is continue to do what we're already doing.

Once you appreciate the Mojo Paradox, you become aware of its paralyzing effect on every aspect of your life, not just the mindless routines of eating or watching TV but also things that really matter—such as the level of happiness and meaning in your life—and you become more thoughtful about turning things around.

How do we break the cycle of inertia? All that's required is the use of a simple discipline.

As you go through your day, evaluate every activity on a one to ten scale (with ten being the highest score) on two simple questions: How much long-term benefit or meaning did I experience from this activity? How much short-term satisfaction or happiness did I experience in this activity?

Simply record the activities that make up your day, both at work and at home, and then evaluate each activity by applying these two questions. At the end of the day you will have a chart that tracks your experience of happiness and meaning.

If you journey through life knowing that all of your activities will be evaluated on these two simple questions, you will tend to experience more happiness and meaning in each activity and, in the aggregate, you will have a happier and more meaningful life.

The Building Blocks of Mojo

Before you can assess your mojo, you have to determine who "you" are. How do you define yourself?

The first building block is identity. Identity is a complicated subject, and we make it even more complicated when we're not sure where to look for the best answer. Many people hurtle back to their past—to signal events, memorable triumphs, painful disasters—to define themselves. Some rely on the testimony of others—a boss's or teacher's good review—as a means of defining themselves. Still others project themselves into the future, defining themselves as who they would like to be rather than who they actually are.

How do we know who we are? Our identities are remembered, reflected, programmed, and created. First review the various components of your current identity. Where did they originate? If your present identity is fine with you, just work on becoming an even better version of who you are. If you want to make a change in your identity, be open to the fact you may be able to change more than you originally believed that you could.

Assuming that you do not have incurable or unchangeable limitations, you can create a new identity for your future without sacrificing your past.

Your Mojo is that positive spirit toward what you are doing now that starts on the inside and radiates to the outside. To understand how you are relating to any activity, you need to understand your identity—who you are. To change your mojo, you may need to create a new identity for yourself.

WAITERS AND MOJO

What is interesting about waiters, at least in terms of mojo, is the wide variety of attitudes that people bring to a narrowly defined job that ends with a monetary tip.

The best ones appreciate the process. They realize that the more engaging and positive they are, the bigger their tip. So no matter how they feel about their circumstances, they radiate a positive spirit (high mojo).

The worst ones make it a point of honor to let you know that they find the job demeaning (low mojo), that they are really more interesting in their other life (with more mojo).

Finally, there are the career waiters. There's a professional snap to how they do their job, and they never hint that they would rather be doing something else. They are committed to doing the task well and they are capable of mining personal satisfaction from it. If they have a bad day, they don't take it out on their customers.

Achievement: What Have You Done Lately?

Our achievements are the second component in creating our mojo.

We tend to gauge our achievements using two differing criteria. On the one hand, there are the accomplishments that make others aware of our ability and result in their recognizing us. This is what most people think about when they discuss achievement. On the other hand, there are the accomplishments that only we are aware of, related to our own abilities, that make us feel good about ourselves. Both are legitimate in their own way.

In the best of all worlds, the two types of achievement would be the same—what we do that impresses others would make us feel great about ourselves. But it doesn't always work out that way. Sometimes we perform magnificently at work, to great acclaim, but it doesn't elevate how we feel about ourselves. Sometimes we do something wonderful for the world and no one else is impressed.

False Assumptions Chip away at the false assumptions that distort your achievements and you'll get a much clearer picture of what you've done lately. Without it, you'll never be able to envision everything else you can do.

By increasing our understanding of achievement—what it means to us and what it means to the world—we can increase our mojo. We can look at ourselves more objectively. We can determine what really matters in our lives. We can strive for achievement that really matters to us—and let go of achievement that does not create happiness or meaning in our lives. If we want to increase our mojo, we can either change the degree of our achievement (how well we are doing) or change the definition of our achievement (what we are trying to do well).

Reputation: Who Do People Think You Are?

Reputation is the third element in establishing your mojo. It's where you add up who you are (identity) and what you've done (achievement) and toss the combined sum out into the world to see how people respond. Your reputation is people's recognition—or rejection—of your identity and achievement. Sometimes you'll agree with the world's opinion. Sometimes you won't. But many times you may not even be aware of it. You cannot create your reputation by yourself (the rest of the world, by definition, always has something to say about it). But you can influence it.

How to Change Your Reputation The truth is, reputation doesn't happen overnight. In the same way that one event can't form your reputation, one corrective gesture can't reform it either. You need a sequence of consistent, similar actions to begin the rebuilding process.

It's doable, but it requires personal insight and, most of all, discipline.

You have to be consistent in how you present yourself—to the point where you don't mind being guilty of repeating yourself. If you abandon that consistency, people will get confused. The reputation you're trying to form will get muddied by conflicting evidence and eventually lose its sharp focus.

By impacting our reputation we can impact our mojo. Having a reputation that others find bothersome can make keeping your mojo as easy as pushing a big rock up a steep hill. It is theoretically possible but practically challenging. Having a great reputation—in an area that matters in your life—makes mojo maintenance more of a joy than a chore.

Acceptance: When Can You Let Go?

Worrying about the past and being anxious about the future can easily destroy our mojo. It upsets us emotionally, it clouds our judgment, it fills us with regret, and it can lead to self-punishment.

When we cannot accept a situation for what it is and refuse to forgive people for causing that situation, whom do we ultimately hurt? The answer is always the same: ourselves. By carrying around anger and negative baggage, we weigh ourselves down. We limit our opportunities to find meaning and happiness. We kill our mojo.

That's what makes acceptance as important as identity, achievement, and reputation in building our mojo. It's the element that liberates us from toxic emotions. When everything around us seems confusing, acceptance reminds us what really matters.

Try it the next time you find yourself filled with anger at someone who has disappointed or hurt you. Ask yourself who is making you feel upset, angry, or crazy. Then set aside every thought, every argument, and every image about the people who are upsetting you. Block all of it out, and focus on these people as they are in your life now. Not on what they did in the past. Not on what you want to happen to them in the future. They're being who they are. (If you had their parents, their genes, their résumé, you might be them too.) You don't have to like them, agree with them, or even respect them. Just accept them for being who they are.

When you can do that, you can forgive them for being who they are—and forgive yourself for being who you are.

Change what you can and let go of what you cannot change.

Mojo Killers

When people lose their mojo, it's usually because of a series of simple, hard-to-spot mistakes that lead up to the humiliating result—mistakes like these:

Overcommitting Before replying with an enthusiastic "yes" to that next request, think of the long-term impact on your mojo.

Waiting for the Facts to Change When the facts are not to your liking, ask yourself, "What path would I take if I knew that the situation would not get better?" Then get ready to do that.

Looking for Logic in All the Wrong Places If you focus on making a positive difference, instead of just being satisfied with feeling "objective," you will benefit both your company and your career.

Bashing the Boss The next time you start to bash the boss, think about what you may be doing to your own mojo and the mojo of the people around you. If you really have a problem with the boss, talk to him about it. If you feel that you cannot talk with him, leave. If you cannot talk with him and cannot leave, accept him and make the best of it.

Refusing to Change Because of "Sunk Costs" Are your decisions based on what you might lose or what you have to gain? If it's the former, your devotion to sunk costs might be costing you more than you know. It may be costing you your mojo.

Confusing the Mode You're In If you look around your company, you'll see that the executives you most admire tend to be those who, with consistent discipline, never drift out of professional mode. They have clear ideas about their identity, achievement, and reputation. They have chosen a role for themselves and they rarely go off script. That's why they have mojo.

Four Pointless Arguments

Arguing can put our mojo at risk by needlessly creating enemies who could have been allies. Many of our arguments fall into classic patterns that, if looked at from a distance, would seem silly and beneath our dignity.

It is worth arguing over true injustice in the workplace or the world. But it is pointless to argue about perceived injustices that usually say more about our own egos than the "cause" we are championing.

By recognizing classic argument traps, we can better determine which battles to fight—and which to avoid.

1. *Let Me Keep Talking.* When we keep fighting after the bell has rung, we can start damaging our reputation and, ultimately, our mojo. In the end we will not win more arguments; we will win fewer. Our arguing will be viewed more as our own stubborn need to prove we are right than as a sincere commitment to help our organization.

2. *I Had It Rougher Than You.* You end up looking foolish when you try to glorify your past for all its deficiencies and all the suffering it brought upon you. All you're doing is creating a contest of competing memories.

3. *Why Did You Do That?* We never really know other people's motives for doing something that affects us. People do things that annoy or enrage us, and it's almost impossible to get to the bottom of why they did them, yet we waste hours trying.

4. *It's Not Fair.* Great influencers are like great salespeople. When the customers don't buy, they don't whine and blame the customers. They focus on what they can learn to do a better job next time. Great influencers keep their mojo. Poor influencers lose it.

That Job Is Gone!

Many jobs don't exist anymore. They've been exported beyond our borders. And even if they've stayed inside the United States, many of the long-term benefits that made them so attractive have been stripped away by cost cutting and global competition. What's even harder to accept is that those jobs are not coming back.

The forces that created this new high-stress environment are not mysterious.

The biggest factor is globalization. Westerners must compete for the best jobs not only with other Americans and Europeans but also with smart, highly motivated candidates from India, China, and Eastern Europe.

Another factor is the dramatically increased gap in compensation between the top people in an organization and everyone else.

A third factor is decreased job security. The shortage of midlevel jobs has only widened the gap between society's economic winners and losers.

Another factor is the steady erosion in the past twenty years of company-funded, guaranteed health care and retirement security. This affects professionals as well as wage earners, meaning that everyone worries more about long-term security.

A fifth factor is the global financial crisis that began in 2008. It has heightened the already present fear in the workplace—fear of losing a job or home or of ever finding high-quality professional work again.

The sixth and most lethal factor is new technology. New technology, hand in hand with globalization, has created a 24/7 world where work never seems to stop.

In this new world, mojo is both harder to attain and more important to keep. When your competition is already responding to a tough new environment by working harder and longer, you need unique tools to separate yourself from the throng.

Your Mojo Tool Kit

If you step back, you'll discover that you're still in control of your life and destiny. You have the power to create significant positive change.

What can you change? The answer is simple: You can change either You or It.

"You" is how you think, how you feel, what you say—basically everything about you that's under your control.

"It," on the other hand, refers to any influencing forces in your life that are not you. It could be another individual, or a group of people, or a job, or a place, or a relationship, or the results of a choice you made in the past that needs undoing. It is everything that's not You.

Changing You is not inherently preferable or easier than changing It (and vice versa). The best approach depends on the situation.

Once you're aware of this You-or-It dichotomy, you'll begin to see manifestations of it everywhere and to realize its impact on mojo. You'll see that in all work and personal situations, mojo is a function of the relationship between who you are (i.e., You) and your situation (i.e., It). If you cannot change You, mojo is influenced by your relationship to It. If you cannot change It, mojo is influenced by your relationship to You. It's your choice.

The following fourteen actions can help you attack the challenge of changing You or It. Like tools, they don't work unless you grab them and use them.

These actions are organized into four parts, each corresponding to one of the four building blocks of mojo: identity, achievement, reputation, and acceptance.

Identity: Making Sense of Who You Are

The following four tools can help reshape or refine the "you" that you present to the world.

Tool #1: Establish Criteria That Matter to You. Before you can establish or regain your mojo, you first have to imagine what it looks like and what it takes to get there. If you write it down, that's your criteria. It's a good place to start.

Tool #2: Find Out Where You're "Living." A great way to test your mojo is to consider your life at work—then consider your life outside work. Research shows that people who find happiness and meaning at work tend to be the same people who find happiness and meaning at home! In other words, our mojo is coming from inside ourselves as much as from what we are doing. For the majority of people, the only way to increase overall satisfaction with life is to increase both happiness and meaning.

Tool #3: Be the Optimist in the Room. If you can maintain your optimism in the face of negative forces, you have an enormous advantage over most people.

Optimism is not just a mind-set; it's a form of behavior that guides everything we do. It can be self-fulfilling. And it's contagious. The optimist in the room always has more influence than anyone else. People pick up on optimism and gravitate toward it.

Tool #4: Take Away One Thing. The untapped power of subtraction is within your grasp. It's as easy as saying to yourself, "My life might actually be better if I took away _____," and filling in the blank. Subtract something from your life that is a "big deal." There are so many things we can lose in our daily lives without harming our mojo that it's inexcusable if we can't identify one item to toss away to increase our mojo.

Achievement: Making It Easier to Get Things Done

The following tools offer courses of action that put our achievements in sharper relief.

Tool #5: Rebuild One Brick at a Time. Here are some rules to consider so you finish what you've started and people take note:

First rule: Stop trying to be an oracle. Stop waiting for more information or better circumstances before you get started.

Second rule: Move quickly. You're constructing a sequence of successes, and you might as well do it quickly.

Third rule: Say two no's for every yes. Be more ruthless about saying no, especially when other people try to steer you off course.

Fourth rule: It pays to advertise. People have preconceptions about you. They not only filter everything you do through those preconceptions, but they are constantly looking for evidence that confirms them.

Tool #6: Live Your Mission in the Small Moments Too. Mission statements are now regarded as overbaked relics of the 1980s—a faddish buzzword of the same vintage as "excellence" and "quality." That may be true, but the fact that a concept is no longer the newest fad does not mean it doesn't have value. What turned mission statements into a corporate joke was how quickly companies broadcast their embracing of a concept and then didn't follow up on it with consistent action. You don't write a mission statement. You live it and breathe it. A lot of organizations never did that.

When you have a mission, you give yourself a purpose—and that adds clarity to all the actions and decisions that follow.

There's an underestimated value to articulating your mission: It focuses you, points you in a new direction, alters your behavior, and, as a result, changes other people's perception of you.

Tool #7: Swim in the Blue Water. It's dangerous to extrapolate a personal strategy from a corporate competitive strategy. We are human beings, not strategic business units. But there's some appeal in the idea that we can find a "blue water" alternative (an uncontested space) as we shape our personal aspirations. Our identities and reputations are made in small, incisive moments. We can't all be transformative geniuses who see the world in a paradigm-shifting light. But we can all find a way to differentiate ourselves, however minimally, from the thundering herd—and in doing so, we achieve a small slice of singularity in our world.

If you want to enhance your mojo, you can do worse than pursue an achievement that has everyone wondering, Why didn't I think of that?

Reputation: Taking Control of Your "Story"

The following tools operate in that space where our identity and achievements intersect with the world and shape our reputation.

Tool #8: Know When to Stay, When to Go. Can you find more happiness and meaning by changing the situation? Can you find more happiness and meaning by changing yourself? What are your real alternatives? Conduct a mojo analysis that clarifies what you need to change. Make your decision, accept the trade-offs, and get on with life.

Tool #9: Hello, Good-bye. No matter how you dress up a dismissal, you still have to deal with the perception that something went wrong, you came up short, and you may not be all that you're cracked up to be.

But it doesn't have to be quite that bad, not if you have a preexit strategy; leave the company (on positive terms) before the company leaves you (on negative terms); accept that your identification with your vanished job is pointless and move quickly to transfer your affections to something else; and ask yourself, "How solid is my reputation? And is it solid because of what I've done or who I work for?"

Tool #10: Adopt a Metrics System. We all employ personal metrics to measure our progress during the day. If we're on a diet, our metric is stepping on the bathroom scale each morning. Applying personal metrics when the numbers may be depressing tells us not only where we're failing but also how to change our luck.

Once you have your personal metric, no matter how alarming the data, you'll know what to do next.

Tool #11: Reduce This Number. How much of our interpersonal communication is spent on pointless, negative, nonproductive topics?

What percentage of people's interpersonal communication time is spent talking about how smart, special, or wonderful they are (or listening while someone else does this) or talking about how stupid, inept, or bad someone else is (or listening while someone else does this)? Reducing this number costs nothing, it will save you time, and it will make your work and home life more positive.

WHY BLUE WATER?

*T*he blue/red water metaphor comes from the Blue Ocean Strategy, in which W. Chan Kim and Renée Mauborgne, two professors at INSEAD, France's leading business school, divided the marketing universe into Red Oceans (the known market space, comprising all the markets in existence today), where companies outperform rivals by grabbing a greater share of existing demand, and Blue Oceans (the unknown market space, untainted by competition, comprising all the markets not in existence today), where demand is created rather than fought over and growth potential is limited only by one's imagination.

Acceptance: Change What You Can, Let Go of What You Can't

The following tools will help you deal with some elements of life that you may not be able to directly control.

Tool #12: Influence Up as Well as Down. Every decision in the world is made by the person who has the power to make that decision—in most cases not you. If you influence the decision maker, you will make a positive difference. If you do not influence this person, you will not make a positive difference. Make peace with this. You will have a better life! And you will make more of a positive difference in your organization and be happier.

Tool #13: Name It, Frame It, Claim It. If you want to improve your understanding of a situation, give it a name.

Naming something lets us organize the action into a coherent shape. It lets us compare the action to what has gone before. It helps us retain it for future purposes, so that we may recognize—and respond to—the action more brilliantly the next time we face it. Naming helps us learn, make sense of things, and take control.

Tool #14: Give Your Friends a Lifetime Pass. When considering the actions of a friend who has offended you, ask one question: Am I better off or worse off because of having this person in my life?

If we can be that forgiving with family members, why can't we extend the same level of acceptance to people who, when all is said and done, have demonstrably made our lives better?

Connecting Inside to Outside

You should not feel obligated to do any of this alone! If you want to improve your performance at almost anything, your odds of success improve considerably the moment you enlist someone else to help you.

Some of us already practice this instinctively, when we enlist a friend to attend yoga class with us or commit to training for a marathon (an inherently lonely sport) the moment a friend agrees to join us. We enjoy the companionship and support, but knowing we're answerable to someone else, even if it's only to schedule a time for a training run, is also motivating. That small obligation keeps us focused. At some point we reach a point of no return where we don't want to disappoint a friend or don't want to be the first to give up. Pairing up provides us with a discipline that we cannot summon as readily working solo.

This "power of two" thinking works well for overt personal objectives, such as quitting smoking or losing weight or athletic training, where we're relying more on moral support, rather than instructive coaching, to reach a clearly marked finish line.

But enlisting someone else to help us isn't our first impulse when we dive into a self-improvement campaign involving our professional lives. Whether it's upgrading the quality of our customer base, landing a big promotion, or executing a career U-turn, our initial impulse is to do it on our own. After all, it's our goal, our effort, our accomplishment, and our payoff if we succeed. How can we share the burden—and glory—with someone else?

Part of the reason behind this is psychic self-preservation on our part; if we fall short of our goal, we want to contain the failure to a circle of one: ourselves. If no one knows what we're striving for, then no one can criticize us for faltering.

Don't let your ego block you from your goals. Start seeing every challenge as a choice between (a) I can do it by myself and (b) I may be able to do it better with help.

Once you accept that you are judged more on the result than on how many hands played a part in achieving it, you'll make the right choice.

Coda: You Go First!

Do you want the people who love you at home to be happy? Do you want the people who respect you at work to be happy? You go first. You be happy. Mojo is that positive spirit toward what you are doing that starts on the inside and radiates to the outside.

Do you want the people whom you love and respect to have mojo? Show them yours! There are good people out there who look up to us. They respect us. They want to be like us. We are role models for them.

What message do we send to the people we love at home when we communicate that we are unhappy and that our lives at home are meaningless? "Being with you does not bring me joy, and my life at home really doesn't matter that much to me."

What message do we send to the people whom we respect at work when we communicate that we are unhappy and that our jobs are meaningless? "I wish that I were not here today. I would rather be doing almost anything than working with you or in this company."

On the other hand, what message do we send to the people—at work and home—when our mojo is high? "I find joy in my life when I am with you. Being with you—in this home or in this workplace—matters to me. You are important, and what I am doing with you is important."

Is there any better message that we can communicate to the people who trust us, respect us, and love us? Having a happier and more meaningful life will help the wonderful people in your life find more happiness and meaning. Don't just do it for you. Do it for them!

THE ART OF WOO

by G. Richard Shell and
Mario Moussa

When peers point to what makes a colleague a success, one quality that is often mentioned is the person's ability to "get things done." The act of accomplishing any task, regardless of size, involves engaging and persuading other people to join the endeavor. This conjures images of the iron-fisted leader whose tough talk and intimidating glare rally the troops to flatten the opposition and achieve the goal. According to authors G. Richard Shell and Mario Moussa, this image could not be more incorrect. While top-down leaders plow headlong into roadblocks, clutching their copies of Sun Tzu's *The Art of War*, Shell and Moussa provide a path of less resistance in *The Art of Woo: Using Strategic Persuasion to Sell Your Ideas*.

Readers will discover the patterns of persuasion the authors uncovered through their extensive research. The art of persuasion isn't intended to be a weapon wielded with a heavy hand. It's a simple, four-step process that can be learned and used in a variety of situations. The result is a reversal of traditional thought on leadership success. Even leaders who appear cut from the cloth of dominance, such as financier J. P. Morgan, are shown to have a deft understanding of the power of restraint. Historical examples provided by the authors reinforce that the masters of the art fall into one of five persuasive styles. Whether delivered as self-oriented or other oriented, a persuasive message works to build relationships.

The person who hopes to achieve success in persuading others must first be self-aware. As Shell and Moussa stress in several sections of *The Art of Woo*, "Woo starts with you." An informed sense of self will provide the confidence and, more important, the competence to establish much-needed credibility with the listener. The book proves that, despite readers' thoughts to the contrary, credibility exists in the mind of the listener, not the speaker. It should be handled with the understanding that miscues, even in a single moment or utterance, can destroy the audience's belief in the presenter. A bullish attitude toward the person on the other side of the table will flatten the persuading party faster than the recipient of the message.

What separates *The Art of Woo* from other books on negotiation is the authors' constant emphasis on the audience rather than the persuader. Shell and Moussa oppose any theory that equates persuasion with simple salesmanship. Audiences are to be treated with respect, honesty, and kindness. It is not enough to want to force another person to stop saying no. The true goal is to provide the other person with enough information and incentive to lead that person to say yes of his or her own accord. As the title suggests, *The Art of Woo* urges readers to treat persuasion with the same emotion that guides the realm of courtship. In romantic relationships, as in business, isn't it better to be wanted by others, rather than have to convince them to want you?

THE ART OF WOO
Using Strategic Persuasion to Sell Your Ideas
by G. Richard Shell and Mario Moussa

CONTENTS
1. Selling Ideas: How Woo Works
2. Start with You
3. Connect Your Ideas to People
4. Build Relationships and Credibility
5. Respect Their Beliefs
6. Give Them Incentives to Say Yes
7. State Your Case
8. Make It Memorable
9. Close the Sale
10. Woo with Integrity

THE SUMMARY IN BRIEF

When Napoléon was a young officer at the siege of Toulon, he established an artillery battery in an extremely exposed, dangerous location. His superiors thought he would never get troops to man it. But instead of ordering or threatening his soldiers, Napoleon created a large placard and placed it next to the cannons: THE BATTERY OF MEN WITHOUT FEAR. The position was manned night and day.

That's woo: the ability to win people over to your ideas without coercion, using relationship-based, emotionally intelligent persuasion. It's the secret of success with colleagues, clients, and customers.

Authors G. Richard Shell and Mario Moussa know what it takes to deal with difficult bosses and drive new initiatives through complex organizations. They have advised thousands of executives and have studied the greatest persuaders in history—Abraham Lincoln, John D. Rockefeller Jr., and Andy Grove, to name only a few. Their four-step process, called woo, is a systematic, repeatable strategy for putting your ideas across.

The Art of Woo does not suggest high-level strategies to defeat opponents in a competitive world. It delivers a process to win people over rather than defeat them.

In addition, you will learn the following:

What makes up the four steps of woo

What the six channels of persuasion are and the appropriate times to use them

How to determine your personal persuasion style

How the eight best practices for managing organizational politics can help ensure that your idea gains the commitment needed

How to use the PCAN (problem, cause, answer, net benefits) model to make a case for your idea

Selling Ideas: How Woo Works

Companies sell their products and services. People in organizations sell their ideas. Your success depends on how well you sell. The president and chairman of the board of a large bank in the Northeast once was asked how he thought about his job. "I am a salesman," he replied. "I have to sell policy changes and new ideas. I sell to the board of directors, the stockholders, the branch managers, the tellers, the cleaning crew, and the customers all at the same time."

But selling ideas—especially the kind that make organizations work—is a skill shrouded in mystery. Classical geniuses from Aristotle to Cicero considered the idea of selling (they called it rhetoric) to be one of the most critical subjects an educated person could learn. Yet two thousand years later, most schools have stopped teaching it. Rhetoric is seen as something practiced by those in the realm of political spin, while selling is viewed as something people can learn once they start work.

The Four Steps

You will discover that relationship-based persuasion follows a distinctive, repeatable four-step process that you can master to achieve your goals:

Step 1: Survey Your Situation

Step 2: Confront the Five Barriers

Step 3: Make Your Pitch

Step 4: Secure Your Commitments

To start using this process, you must master the main influence channels people use at work—and gain a sense of your own biases in communicating in these channels. Are you a soft-spoken relationship manager or a hard-driving taskmaster? Woo starts with a look in the mirror.

Start with You

In persuasion, you are trying to win people over, not defeat them. Where do you start on this journey toward others' perspectives? With self-awareness. Unless you are aware of your own needs, emotions, and communication impulses, you have little chance of seeing other people clearly—much less anticipating their feelings and crafting a message that will appeal to them. Thus, woo starts with you.

The Six Channels of Persuasion

Extensive research on how people influence one another in work settings has revealed that they return over and over again to a relatively small number of persuasion moves. Although communication scholars have labeled as many as sixteen separate and identifiable strategies, there are six main persuasion channels that dominate when people are selling ideas.

1. Interest-based persuasion takes place every time someone frames a sales pitch in terms of the other party's self-interest. The essence of this persuasion channel is inducement, not trading.

2. Authority is usually used in a "top-down" situation, but even a secretary can use this channel if he or she has jurisdiction over expense accounts or other procedures. Effective appeals using authority are almost always accompanied by independent justifications to help persuade the audience that the authority is legitimate.

3. Politics—the use of coalitions, pressure tactics, and other power moves—is not limited to government. You are using the political persuasion channel whenever you acknowledge that appearances may be as important as substance, work through coalitions, or lobby.

4. Rationality-based persuasion tries to influence someone's attitudes, beliefs, or actions by offering reasons and/or evidence to justify a proposal on its merits.

5. Inspiration and emotion (the Vision Channel) includes any appeal to an audience's overriding sense of purpose, values, or beliefs.

6. Relationships, when positive, predispose an audience toward your message. Negative relationships distort almost everything an idea seller says. You are accessing the relationship channel whenever you use similarity, liking, rapport, and reciprocity or rely on your existing network of contacts to open doors.

Personal Persuasion Styles

Some acts of persuasion are specially tailored to appeal to specific audiences, while others are more akin to blunt announcements of the speaker's point of view. The former are called other-oriented persuasion, and the latter are called self-oriented persuasion.

When you are working from the audience's point of view, you are focused more on social considerations—existing relationships, political environment, other people's interests. On the other hand, when you are working from your own frame of reference, you focus on your internal perspective—the authority you want to assert, the need you want to express, or the evidence you want to demonstrate. If your preferences run strongly toward one of these orientations, that can define your overall communication style.

A second important variable that goes into the persuasion styles people display is the "volume" they give to their message. At work, you may have noticed people who speak up right away and others who prefer to listen and quietly give their views when asked. If you have a strong inclination toward communicating one way or the other, this will affect your choice of persuasion roles.

What's Your Personal Style?

Five persuasive styles factor in the self-oriented and other-oriented dimensions. The more other-oriented roles are the Promoter and the Chess Player. The more self-oriented roles are the Driver and the Commander. The Advocate role is a balance of both and involves a moderate tone or "volume." The following chart will give you a sense of how the five roles relate to one another.

Self-Oriented vs. Other Oriented

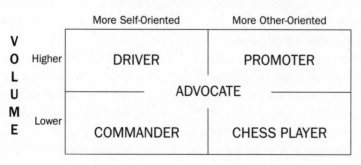

The Driver: Andy Grove

Drivers are fond of saying things like "Do this my way, or you can hit the high-way." In an ineffective persuader, this comes across as overbearing. But if the persuader conveys a sense of self-awareness and shows true dedication to the organization's mission, this strong style can be effective.

As head of Intel, Andy Grove was notorious for his blunt style of communication. But he knew this about himself and compensated by making his style the cultural norm within Intel. An example of how this culture worked comes from an incident between Grove and his secretary, Sue McFarland. During McFarland's first performance review, Grove told her she lacked ambition and deserved no raise. She went home that night and put together an airtight case refuting each of Grove's charges. The next day she confronted Grove and walked out of his office with not only a raise but also permission to hire an assistant.

The Commander: J. P. Morgan

You don't have to be aggressive like the Driver when you want people to know exactly what you think. A quiet, understated demeanor can often be much more effective. People listen when you speak your mind from a position of quiet confidence and credibility.

In 1895, a financial panic set off a run on the gold reserves that served as the basis of the U.S. currency. President Grover Cleveland called a meeting of advisers, including the nation's most powerful financier, J. P. Morgan, to address the crisis. Morgan sat silently as leaders from Congress and Cleveland's cabinet offered plans that Morgan knew would fail. When asked for his suggestion, Morgan laid out a plan to save the Treasury. He offered to repatriate 3.5 million ounces of gold he controlled in Europe and agreed to take, in return, $65 million worth of thirty-year government bonds. Morgan then produced a legal memorandum showing that the government had authority to act as he proposed based on a little-known emergency law passed just after the Civil War.

Morgan's proposal was adopted. His message gained power from the quiet way he communicated both his authority and expertise. Playing the Commander with finesse, he saved both the American and his own financial empire from a fiscal catastrophe.

The Promoter: Andrew Carnegie

In 1883, steel mogul Andrew Carnegie faced one of his first labor crises. He adopted a politically sophisticated negotiation strategy designed for delivery on the Rationality, Interest, and Relationship channels. He and his management team prepared a document that displayed the trade-offs between forcing layoffs and reducing wages. This analysis demonstrated that if wages were reduced 13 percent, the plant could remain in operation without layoffs—a key interest of the unions. He offered to open his books so union leaders could see the financial constraints the steel market was forcing on the business. He mobilized them as his allies. The union leaders accepted the deal and sold it to their members.

The Chess Player: John D. Rockefeller

In 1865, John D. Rockefeller found himself trapped in a partnership with four other men: Maurice, James, and Richard Clark (brothers) and Samuel Andrews. Rockefeller favored leveraging the partnership's assets to invest in the oil business, but the Clarks repeatedly vetoed his ideas. Rockefeller wanted to end the partnership, but the firm could be dissolved only if all partners consented. Therefore, Rockefeller went to work behind the scenes, lining up support from some banks, and then he provoked another quarrel over an oil industry investment. Maurice Clark barked, "If that's the way you want to do business, we'd better dissolve." Catching his partners in their bluff, Rockefeller placed a formal notice in the morning paper stating that he and his partners had unanimously agreed to part ways.

By communicating in a moderate tone and appearing to play to his partners' interests, Rockefeller arranged the situation so that his partners gave him exactly what he wanted.

The Advocate: Sam Walton

As Wal-Mart's founder, Sam Walton could have ordered people to do what he wanted. But part of his genius was that he rarely forced an idea. By protecting the self-esteem and autonomy of his executives, he was able to win their cooperation.

Take the idea of using "greeters." Walton got this idea when visiting a Wal-Mart in Louisiana. He was met by an elderly man who said, "Hi! How are ya? Glad you're here." He discovered the store had experienced a shoplifting problem. Rather than offend the 99 percent of customers who were honest by posting a guard to check bags, the manager placed a friendly looking older man out front to put shoplifters on notice that someone was watching.

Walton went back to Bentonville and told everyone about placing greeters in every store. A lot of people thought he'd lost his mind. Walton immediately gave credit for the greeters program to the people in the field who had conceived it. Through his skilled advocacy, the greeters program has become an enduring signature part of the Wal-Mart shopping experience.

The Problem of Authenticity

The need in persuasion to adapt to audiences raises an important ethical issue: authenticity. Your personal credibility provides the foundation for influence. The authenticity paradox diminishes when you see that you cannot help being a somewhat "different person" depending on whom you are interacting with. And your awareness of these various roles gives you a range of "authentic selves" to display in persuasion.

Connect Your Ideas to People

As you plan your idea-selling strategy, you will need to set persuasion goals for each stage of the process. In some encounters, your goal will be to get introductions to key influencers; in other meetings, you will be looking for endorsements; eventually you will be asking for decisions.

It All Begins with Ideas

Inside or outside an organization, you need to bring lots of energy to the process of developing and promoting new concepts. The Netflix concept got its start one day when Reed Hastings had a huge late fee for a copy of *Apollo 13* he had rented. As he was driving to the gym, he began to think about the video store's business model. The store charged customers by the rental and penalized those who were late returning movies. The gym charged a flat fee and did not keep score on his usage. Would it be possible to run a movie-rental business the way the gym worked? He worked on the idea until he had developed a full-fledged profit model.

From Ideas to Action: Deciding Whom to Woo

Once you have a well-polished idea, you are ready to map the influence you will use to sell it. Even the most unlikely ideas can be pushed through the most difficult environments if you act methodically—one idea, one ally, one e-mail, one conversation, one meeting, and one presentation at a time. And sometimes you can get to the decision maker and make a sale in one move—even with a very big initiative.

Selling ideas in one move can work with lower-level decision makers, provided you have taken the trouble to form good relationships with them. As Peter Drucker once noted, it is a "dangerous mistake" to think that only those at higher levels make important decisions.

Setting Specific Persuasion Goals for Each Encounter

The stepping-stone process for selling ideas requires you to persuade different people to do different things at different stages. Thus, you will need somewhat different goals as you move from one encounter to the next.

Early on, you may simply be trying to introduce your idea and get key people thinking about it by floating "trial balloons." Later, you may be seeking input to help shape your idea into a final product. Finally, you may be asking for specific forms of cooperation as you work through your social network toward the ultimate decision makers.

Build Relationships and Credibility

Managing relationships plays a crucial role in selling ideas. Relationships give people a level of trust and confidence in one another, facilitating communications and making it easier to cooperate.

Three social psychological foundations form the basis for relationships: similarity, liking, and reciprocity. Add these ingredients to a history of positive interactions and you get a crucial idea-selling asset: trust.

Similarity and Liking

Selling ideas is seldom the same as conventional salesmanship. But in the area of relationships, there are common features. First, face time matters. The more you work with people, the more familiar they become with you, laying the groundwork for functioning relationships.

The second trigger for the liking response is a perception of similarity between two people. Even something as elusive as personal style can be enough to strike a chord of similarity. Early in his battle to get a casino license in Atlantic City, Donald Trump needed to hire a local lawyer to help him drive through his application. A young man named Nick Ribis was recommended to him. Ribis won over Trump in their opening conversation by showing he could match Trump ego for ego.

Said Trump after being introduced, "I'm not sure a lawyer as young as you are can handle a big project like this."

Nick did not miss a beat. "To tell you the truth, Mr. Trump, I've never had a client as young as you who could afford my bill." The two men hit it off and worked closely on a successful legal strategy to get the casino license.

Reciprocity

Reciprocity means that we tend to do things for people who do things for us. It can be observed at the bargaining table when people take turns making concessions. Reciprocity can also take the form of mutual exchanges of resources, services, emotional support, status, and information.

You can benefit from the reciprocity system even when nobody owes you any personal favors. All you need are allies and champions who are willing to use their networks and associated reciprocity systems to advance your cause.

Relationship Builders

In the world of electronic communications, you have a dizzying number of choices for building relationships. When practicing the art of woo, there is no substitute for meeting face to face. However, this is bad news because in today's multitasking world, convenience usually trumps judgment when it comes to developing relationships.

When you want to build a relationship with an important person on an idea-selling campaign, take the time to meet face to face. If conflicting schedules or distances make this impossible, spend some time composing a careful message. Research shows that e-mail messages are more likely to be effective if you personalize your note and build some rapport, forecast the agenda, and then get to the heart of your communication. Don't send until you reread your message and edit it with an eye to how it will be seen when received.

Credibility

Credibility comes down to audience perceptions of three key things: competence, expertise, and trustworthiness. Thus, your credibility resides in your audience's mind. This means you can lose it in a single moment of poor judgment, miscalculation, or misconduct.

Whereas people give you competence-based credibility when they think you have accomplished something worthy, they give you expertise-based credibility when they think you have specialized knowledge. If you are respected enough, expertise can overcome even the most socially awkward presentation. But no matter how slick your presentation, you will lose your audience if you show a lack of expertise.

When it comes to data, your credibility will depend on the reliability of your sources as well as your expertise. You should try to find out what sources your audience considers reliable.

By showing reliability and integrity in everything you do—not just when everyone is watching—you build the foundation for people to trust you.

Respect Their Beliefs

The people you are selling your idea to will have their own individual, sometimes quirky way of processing information and concepts. It will help you to gather as much information as you can on the thought processes, values, and preferences of each person in your stepping-stone strategy.

Sometimes you can gain insights into people's preferred language by finding out how they speak when they are selling ideas. Search for the special words that your audience will find familiar and that can convey your idea in the most user-friendly way. Be ready to shift strategies based on your audience's real-time feedback.

Beliefs as Barriers to Persuasion

The very power of your audience's beliefs creates hidden barriers to persuasion. Some people refuse to believe the Holocaust happened, and no amount of historical evidence can shake this conviction. Ideas that violate basic beliefs will simply be rejected.

USING A COMMON LANGUAGE

*B*ono is more than a well-known singer: He is an authentic social activist with a bold agenda for helping the world's poorest people. And he has a gift for turning would-be enemies into fervent allies by selecting the right language and saluting the right values.

On September 20, 2000, Bono walked into the office of archconservative U.S. senator Jesse Helms to recruit allies for a program to get governments to forgive debts faced by African countries so more local resources could be directed at the AIDS epidemic. As Bono launched into his litany of statistics, he saw that he was losing his audience. So he switched to a different language. Bono, himself a student of the Bible, had heard that Helms was a religious man. So he started speaking of Jesus' concern for the poor and afflicted. With Helms's support, Congress appropriated $435 million for Bono's cause.

If you can communicate on the right persuasion channel and show how your idea furthers your audience's core purposes, you are well on the way to successfully wooing any group.

Give Them Incentives to Say Yes

When you approach people in your stepping-stone strategy, you must not only use their language and honor their beliefs—you must also frame your idea in terms of their needs and problems. People tend to favor ideas that benefit them and oppose those that will force them to shoulder significant costs. Here are important questions to help you think about your audience's interests.

1. Why Might It Already Be in the Other Party's Interests to Support My Idea? What problems, hopes, needs, fears, desires, and goals do they face that your idea might help them with?

When Donald Trump was starting off as a New York City real estate developer, one of his projects was to take an old, boarded-up hotel and turn it into the Grand Hyatt. Many people thought lenders would charge extra high interest rates for loans on such a risky property. But his target audience was not lenders. His targets were public officials whom he could address in terms of their interest in rejuvenating the city and their craving for positive publicity. When he got his project approved, he made sure that those involved were seen as the people who had "saved" New York.

2. What Do Other Parties Want That I Can Give Them to Gain Their Support? A key point to remember is that people's self-esteem and pride can be rich sources of low-cost trade-offs. When Andrew Carnegie was a boy, his mother let him keep pet rabbits in the backyard. He persuaded children in his neighborhood to gather food for the rabbits by promising to name baby rabbits after the kids. In today's world, fund-raisers follow this example, selling ideas by promising to place donors' names on them.

3. Why Might the Other Party Say No? When there is a strict conflict of interest that cannot be overcome, you will have to accept that no sale is possible. When you hear unanticipated objections, probe to see if there is any way you can work around them. If the people who will win with your new idea outnumber or outrank the people who will lose, you might still succeed.

State Your Case

In the end, the two most reliable ways to persuade people are the most traditional: Offer them solid reasons to say yes, and back up those reasons with evidence. The soundness of reasons and the depth of evidence required, however, vary with circumstances. When people don't care much about the issue, are unqualified to evaluate it, or are already inclined to agree based on their own beliefs and interests, arguments need not be rigorous. Often the simplest statement, such as "I think this is a good idea because . . ." may be enough to make a sale if you say it with conviction and credibility.

The PCAN Model

One template for making a tight idea-selling case to an involved audience is the PCAN (problem, cause, answer, net benefits) model.

Define the problem. By providing a crisp answer to the question "What is the problem?" you establish the context in which your idea will be evaluated.

Explain the cause of the problem. An investigation into causes usually points toward solutions. You may sometimes need to do this in a way that avoids assigning blame, especially if your audience helped to create the situation.

What is my answer to the problem? Here you outline your proposal, show how it will solve the problem, and demonstrate that it could work in the real world.

Does my answer provide net benefits compared with alternatives? You must prove that your idea is better than the current situation and alternative solutions.

Solid evidence may be hard to come by. Proposals for pilot projects and market tests are popular methods for concluding a good policy-based idea pitch.

Using the PCAN Model with Maximum Credibility

You must balance two important credibility factors: (1) your need to come across as a committed advocate, and (2) your objectivity as an expert who has considered all sides. If you come to an argument with an obvious conflict of interest, address this conflict up front. Better yet, give someone with less of a conflict the starring role in presenting your views.

You gain credibility by acknowledging the possible weaknesses in your own arguments before presenting them, whereas you lose credibility if you present a weak argument and your audience punches holes in it. If you are assuming the audience shares your belief about the nature of a problem, say so. If they do, you get credit as someone who advances his case only with *his audience's* permission.

Make It Memorable

You have two audiences in every persuasion event: your audience's rational calculator and its intuitive decision maker. You must present arguments and evidence to the former, but unless you also make your ideas easily accessible to and actionable by the latter, you will lose the sale.

Pathway No. 1: Make It Vivid. Vividness can trigger belief even when no proof is available. Before grabbing just any visual image, make sure it is an image *your audience* will respond to in the way you intend.

Pathway No. 2: Use Demonstrations and Symbolic Actions. Demonstrations and symbolic activities are an excellent way to make an idea memorable. Asking senior people to take symbolic action can be risky—be sure your audience is ready for such drama.

Pathway No. 3: Put Your Heart into It. People will be more inclined to believe your arguments if you show that you believe in them. Reserve your emotions for your most urgent ideas. But do not be afraid to reveal your feelings when the audience does not seem to be "getting it."

Pathway No. 4: Tell a Story. When you tell a good story, the audience starts wondering what plot twists lie ahead. If you have integrated your idea pitch into the story in a compelling way, the intuitive decision maker will be listening.

Pathway No. 5: Personalize It. Talk about specific things a customer or employee shared with you about the problem your idea addresses. Give people names and place the story in a specific location.

Pathway No. 6: Make It a Puzzle. Look for puzzles embedded within the problems you are trying to help solve. The puzzle device works best when the solution is exactly what you want the audience to remember about the idea you are selling.

Pathway No. 7: Build Bridges with Analogies and Metaphors. When you are talking about something the audience does not know much about, you need to start with something it does know. The simpler and more widely understood the image, the greater its hold on the imagination.

Pathway No. 8: Force Your Audience to Think. You can sometimes get people thinking about old issues in new ways. Ask your audience to consider what an upside-down world might look like. Make a radical assumption and get the audience to explore what the world might look like if it were true. Ask the audience to rethink the purpose or mission as part of your idea sale.

Close the Sale

Your first job in closing a sale is often the hardest: overcoming the natural inertia that keeps people locked into the tried and true. Scientists have a name for this phenomenon: the status quo bias. Change requires effort, so people maintain the status quo, provided it works well enough to satisfy their interests.

Gaining Individual Commitment

Unless you can take an individual's word to the bank, you need to close your sale by asking for performance-based rather than promise-based commitments.

Psychologists claim that to engage the commitment process, you need the other party to take concrete action that requires effort, is freely chosen, and is observed by or known to people other than you. The action the other party takes can be as simple as sending an e-mail to a group list endorsing your idea or as complex as allocating millions of dollars and hundreds of staff to your initiative. Either way, you can count that person as an ally.

Organizational Commitment: Managing Politics

Organizational momentum can carry your idea a fair distance once you get decision makers to take concrete action. Unfortunately, there are also many countervailing forces that can slow or stop this momentum. If you want your idea to succeed, you must remain an active and energetic advocate.

Selling ideas sometimes sparks large-scale disputes between organizational units. When this happens, serious issues of corporate strategy, resources, careers, and turf can stop an initiative. Of course, you can expect people who disagree in good faith over the merits of a proposal to do battle over it. The solution to such disputes lies in your making the best possible case to the most influential people: essentially using the four steps of woo.

But often battles are less about the merits of an idea and more about the effects your idea will have on the existing distribution of power, resources, and status. When this happens, political strategies become paramount.

Best Practices for Managing Politics

Winning political battles within organizations is not all that different from winning traditional political fights. Here are some time-tested tactics that can help you win.

1. Find a simple theme that captures your idea. The bigger the group you need to communicate with, the larger the payoff from having a theme that captures the essence of what you want to get done. To succeed in politics, you need a slogan.

2. Get your idea on the agenda—create a sense of urgency. Deadlines, external threats, and mandates from a higher authority can be useful ways to make your idea a priority.

3. Score small wins early and broadcast them widely. When people see positive results from their actions, their commitment deepens.

4. Form key alliances to broaden your base. Form alliances with the people who have three key powers: to decide, to fund, and to implement.

5. Create a snowball effect. As the number of people who back the idea increases, the pressures build on opponents to get out of the way.

6. Be flexible—respond and adjust. Your ideas will take on a life of their own as more people become involved. When this happens, you need to show flexibility if you and your idea are to survive politically.

7. Lock it in. Once you have generated momentum, you need to lock the idea into the organizational matrix through budget lines, job descriptions, incentives, and other procedures.

8. Secure appropriate credit. The secret to gaining appropriate kudos centers on relationships. If you cannot blow your own horn, you need others to blow it for you.

Woo with Integrity

Like any powerful force, persuasion skills can serve many purposes—some good and some not so good. With these tools now in your hands, you confront the ethical problem of how you will use them. If you could not defend your actions on the front page of the *Wall Street Journal*, then you should rethink your strategy.

You need persuasion skills no matter what kind of organization you work for. And the higher you go the more these skills matter. The typical organization may have many traffic lights and stop signs. The art of woo will provide a road map for working your way through these dangerous intersections to safety and success.

GETTING THINGS DONE

by David Allen

I magine an executive who walks into her office at 8:00 A.M. Regardless of when she woke up this morning, she has probably already waded through several dozen e-mails and responded to only the ones that classify as "five-alarm fire" emergencies. Whether her commute is ten minutes or two hours, she spent that time on the phone and, despite the risk to personal safety, continued checking text messages and social media updates while driving. The only moment of peace in her morning is the forty-eight seconds it takes for her laptop to boot up. If someone were to ask this executive to write down her to-do list for today alone, it would probably take the remainder of her twelve-hour day.

This example typifies the life of millions of successful professionals. What they have in common is life in an environment marked by a relentless pace and constant distraction. Author and executive coach David Allen views this cognitive clutter as the reason so many professionals are unable to increase their productivity. His book *Getting Things Done: The Art of Stress-Free Productivity* is an antidote to life in the high-pressure world of work.

Allen believes that the single most important tool for increased performance isn't a tablet computer or an app for a smart phone. A professional's own mind is the key to getting more done. It just needs a bit of reengineering to increase its output. Allen helps readers gear their minds to a more relaxed method of working in five stages. He believes successful professionals are on par with elite athletes because both achieve greatness through rigorous training. The more devotion an executive has to his or her training regimen, the more automatic Allen's work-flow system becomes. He reveals how to collect, process, organize, review, and do the tasks that produce stress and block the path to achievement.

Getting Things Done helps professionals handle the ad hoc aspect of the workplace. These are the ASAP tasks that randomly appear during the course of a day and draw someone away from his or her set course of action. Allen writes that the use of "horizontal focus" can help brush aside the distractions and give anyone a better method to rank his or her tasks. Allen pushes readers toward a state of relaxed control where projects are clearly defined, including the steps necessary to get the job done. He introduces the unique idea of a dedicated reminder system to help people return to the correct course of action each time they tackle a common task.

Perhaps the most difficult demand Allen makes is for readers to clear forty-eight hours to implement his system. The five steps cannot be administered with a half-hearted effort. While it may seem impossible for anyone to imagine unplugging from the world for even a few minutes, Allen's time-saving strategies are worth the investment of a few hours' silence. It makes reentering the daily workplace fray a less daunting prospect.

GETTING THINGS DONE
The Art of Stress-Free Productivity
by David Allen

CONTENTS

THE SUMMARY IN BRIEF

In today's world, yesterday's workload management methods just don't work.

In Getting Things Done, veteran coach, management consultant, and personal productivity guru David Allen shares his breakthrough methods for stress-free performance, which he has introduced to tens of thousands of people across the country. Allen's premise is simple: Our productivity is directly proportional to our ability to relax. Only when our minds are clear and our thoughts are organized can we achieve effective results and unleash our creative potential. Offering core principles and proven tricks, this summary can transform the way you work and live, showing you how to pick up the pace without wearing yourself down.

Getting Things Done helps readers build the mental skills needed in an age of multitasking and overload. It also shows how to apply these skills for immediate results.

Getting Things Done describes powerful methods that can vastly increase personal organization, efficiency, and creative results—at work and in life. It also brings new clarity to the power of purpose and the essential nature of relaxation and provides deeply simple guidelines for getting things done.

The practical process described in Getting Things Done can help any organization or individual survive in today's business world.

In addition, you will learn the following:

How to master the art of relaxed and controlled knowledge work
How to reassess goals and stay focused in changing situations
How to plan and unstick projects
How to feel fine about what you're not doing

THE COMPLETE SUMMARY

Part 1: The Art of Getting Things Done

Most of the stress people experience comes from inappropriately managed commitments they make or accept. Even those who are not consciously "stressed out" will invariably experience greater relaxation, better focus, and increased productive energy when they learn more effectively to control the "open loops" of their lives.

You've probably made many more agreements with yourself than you realize, and every single one of them—big or little—is being tracked by a less-than-conscious part of you. These are the "incompletes," or "open loops," which are defined as anything pulling at your attention that doesn't belong where it is the way it is.

Managing commitments well requires the implementation of some basic activities and behaviors.

First of all, if it's on your mind, your mind isn't clear. Anything you consider unfinished in any way must be captured in a trusted system outside your mind, or what is called a collection bucket, that you know you'll come back to and sort through regularly.

Second, you must clarify what your commitment is and decide what you have to do, if anything, to make progress toward fulfilling it.

Third, once you've decided on all the actions you need to take, you must keep reminders of them organized in a system you review regularly.

The Process: Managing Action

You can train yourself, almost like an athlete, to be faster, more responsive, more proactive, and more focused in knowledge work. You can think more effectively and manage the results with more ease and control. You can minimize the loose ends across the whole spectrum of your work life and personal life and get a lot more done with less effort. And you can make front-end decisions about all the "stuff" you collect and create standard operating procedures for living and working in this new millennium.

Before you can achieve any of that, you'll need to get in the habit of keeping nothing on your mind. And the way to do that is not by managing time, managing information, or managing priorities.

Instead, the key to managing all of your "stuff" is managing your actions.

What you do with your time, what you do with information, and what you do with your body and your focus relative to your priorities—those are the real options to which you must allocate your limited resources. The real issue is how to make appropriate choices about what to do at any point in time. The real issue is how we manage actions.

Getting Control of Your Life: The Five Stages of Mastering Work Flow

The core process for mastering the art of relaxed and controlled knowledge work is a five-stage method for managing work flow. No matter what the setting, there are five discrete stages that we go through as we deal with our work. We (1) collect things that command our attention; (2) process what they mean and what to do about them; and (3) organize the results, which we (4) review as options for what we choose to (5) do.

When you're getting things done, or "working" in the universal sense, there are three different kinds of activities you can be engaged in.

Doing Predefined Work When you're doing predefined work, you're working off your "next actions" lists—completing tasks that you have previously determined need to be done and managing your work flow.

Doing Work as It Shows Up Often things come up ad hoc—unsuspected and unforeseen—that you either have to or choose to respond to as they occur. When you follow these leads, you're deciding by default that these things are more important than anything else you have to do.

Defining Your Work Defining your work entails clearing up your in-basket, your e-mail, your voice mail, and your meeting notes and breaking down new projects into actionable steps. As you process your inputs, you'll no doubt be taking care of some less-than-two-minute actions and tossing and filing numerous things.

Once you have defined all your work, you can trust that your lists of things to do are complete. And your context, time, and energy available still allow you the choice to do more than one thing.

PROJECTS

A project is any desired result that requires more than one action step. This means that some rather small things that you might not normally call projects are going to be on your "Projects" list.

Getting Projects Creatively Under Way: The Five Phases of Project Planning

The key ingredients of relaxed control are (1) clearly defined outcomes (projects) and the next actions required to move them toward closure, and (2) reminders placed in a trusted system that is reviewed regularly. This is what is called horizontal focus. Although it may seem simple, the process can create profound results.

Horizontal focus is all you'll need in most situations, most of the time. Sometimes, however, you may need greater rigor and focus to get a project under control, to identify a solution, or to ensure that all the right steps have been determined. This is where vertical focus comes in. Knowing how to think productively in this more vertical way and how to integrate the results into your personal system is the second powerful behavior set needed for knowledge work.

When people do more planning, more informally and naturally, they relieve a great deal of stress and obtain better results.

The Natural Planning Model You are actually a planning machine. You're planning when you get dressed, eat lunch, go to the store, or simply talk. Although the process may seem somewhat random, a complex series of steps has to occur before your brain can make anything happen physically. Your mind goes through five steps to accomplish virtually any task:

1. Defining purpose and principles. It never hurts to ask the "why" question.

2. Outcome visioning. This is the "what" instead of the "why." What will this project or situation really be like when it successfully appears in the world?

3. Brainstorming. Once you know what you want to have happen and why, the "how" mechanism comes into play. Asking questions is part of the naturally creative process that happens once you commit to some outcome that hasn't happened yet.

4. Organizing. If you've done a thorough job of emptying your head of all the things that came up in the brainstorming phase, you'll notice that a natural organization is emerging. Organizing usually happens when you identify components and subcomponents, sequences or events, and/or priorities.

5. Identifying next actions. The final stage of planning comes down to decisions about the allocation and reallocation of physical resources to actually get the project moving. The question to ask here is "What's the next action?"

Part 2: Practicing Stress-Free Productivity

Create a block of time to initialize this process and prepare a workstation with the appropriate space, furniture, and tools. If your space is properly set up and streamlined, it can reduce your unconscious resistance to dealing with your stuff and even make it attractive for you to sit down and crank through your input and your work.

An ideal time frame for most people is two whole days, back to back. Implementing the full collection process can take up to six hours or more, and processing and deciding on actions for all the input you'll want to externalize and capture in your system can easily take another eight hours.

Of course, you can also collect and process your stuff in chunks, but it'll be much easier if you can tackle that front-end portion in one fell swoop.

Setting Up the Space

You'll need a physical location to serve as a central cockpit of control. If you already have a desk and office space set up where you work, that's probably the best place to start. If you work from a home office, obviously that will be your prime location. If you already have both, you'll want to establish identical, even interchangeable systems in both places.

A functional workspace is critical. If you don't already have a dedicated workspace and in-basket, get them now. Everyone must have a physical locus of control from which to deal with everything else.

Getting the Tools You'll Need

If you're committed to a full implementation of this work-flow process, there are some basic supplies and equipment that you'll need to get started. As you go along, you're likely to dance between using what you're used to and evaluating the possibilities for new and different gear to work with.

Collection: Corralling Your "Stuff"

The process of getting all your incompletes, all your "stuff," into one place—into "in"—is the critical first step. Just gathering a few more things than you currently have will probably create a positive feeling for you. But if you can hang in there and really do the whole collection process, 100 percent, it will change your experience dramatically and give you an important new reference point for being on top of your work.

The collection phase usually takes between one and six hours. It can take longer than you think if you are committed to a full-blown capture that will include everything at work and everywhere else. That means going through every storage area and every nook and cranny, in every location, including cars, boats, and other homes, if you have them.

In the real world, you probably won't be able to keep your stuff 100 percent collected all of the time. If you're like most people, you'll move too fast and be engaged in too many things during the course of a week to get all your ideas and commitments captured outside your head. But it should become an ideal that keeps you motivated to consistently "clean house" of all the things about your work and life that have your attention.

Ready, Set . . . There are very practical reasons to gather everything before you start processing it:

1. It's helpful to have a sense of the volume of stuff you have to deal with.

2. It lets you know where the "end of the tunnel" is.

3. Once you have all the things that require your attention gathered in one place, you'll automatically be operating from a state of enhanced focus and control.

. . . Go! The first activity is to search your physical environment for anything that doesn't belong where it is, the way it is, permanently, and put it into your in-basket. You'll be gathering things that are incomplete, things that have some decision about potential action tied to them. They all go into "in" so they'll be available for later processing.

Processing: Getting "In" to Empty

When you've finished processing "in," you will have

1. trashed what you don't need;
2. completed any less-than-two-minute actions;
3. handed off to others anything that can be delegated;
4. sorted into your own organizing system reminders of actions that require more than two minutes;
5. identified any larger commitments (projects) you now have, based on the input.

Process Guidelines The best way to learn this model is by doing. But there are a few basic rules to follow.

Process the top item first. Even if the second item down is a personal note from the president of your country and the top item is a piece of junk mail, you've got to process the junk mail first! That's an exaggeration to make a point, but the principle is important: Everything gets processed equally.

Process one item at a time. Put back everything but the one item on top. The focus on just one thing forces the requisite attention and decision making to get through all your stuff.

Never put anything back into "in." The first time you pick something up from your in-basket, decide what to do about it and where it goes. Never put it back in "in."

Once You Decide on the Action Step You have three options once you decide what the next action really is:

Do it (if the action takes less than two minutes).

Delegate it (if you're not the most appropriate person to do the action).

Defer it into your organization system as an option for work to do later.

Organizing: Setting Up the Right Buckets

Creating and maintaining one list of all your projects (that is, every commitment or desired outcome that may require more than one action step to complete) can be a profound experience! You probably have more of them than you think.

If you haven't done so already, make a "Projects" list in a very simple format, similar to the ones you've used for your lists of actions: It can be a category in a digital organizer, a page in a loose-leaf planner or even a single file folder labeled "Projects," with either a master list or separate sheets of paper for each one.

The Projects List(s) The Projects list is not meant to hold plans or details about your projects themselves, nor should you try to keep it arranged by priority or size or urgency—it's just a comprehensive index of your open loops. You actually won't be working off the Projects list during your day-to-day activities; for the most part, your action lists and any ad hoc tasks that come up will constitute your tactical, in-the-moment focus. Remember, you can't do a project; you can only do the action steps it requires.

The real value of the Projects list lies in the complete review it can provide (at least once a week), allowing you to ensure that you have action steps defined for all of your projects and that nothing is slipping through the cracks.

Organizing Nonactionable Data Interestingly, one of the biggest problems with most people's personal management systems is that they blend a few actionable things with a large amount of data and material that has value but no action attached. Having good, consistent structures with which to manage the nonactionable items in our work and lives is as important as managing our action and project reminders. When the nonactionable items aren't properly managed, they can clog up the whole process.

Unactionable items fall into two large categories: reference materials and reminders of things that need no action now but might at a later date.

Reviewing: Keeping Your System Functional

The purpose of this whole method of work-flow management is not to let your brain become lax, but rather to enable it to move toward more elegant and productive activity. In order to earn that freedom, however, your brain must engage on some consistent basis with all your commitments and activities. You must be assured that you're doing what you need to be doing and that it's okay to be not doing what you're not doing. Reviewing your system on a regular basis and keeping it current and functional are prerequisites for that kind of control.

If you have a list of calls you must make, for example, the minute that list is not totally current with all the calls you need to make, your brain will not trust the system and it won't get relief from its lower-level mental tasks. It will have to take back the job of remembering, processing, and reminding, which it doesn't do very effectively.

All of this means your system cannot be static. In order to support appropriate action choices, it must be kept up to date. And it should trigger consistent and appropriate evaluation of your life and work at several horizons.

Two Major Issues There are two major issues that need to be handled at this point:

What do you look at in all this, and when?
What do you need to do, and how often, to ensure that all of it works as a consistent system, freeing you to think and manage at a higher level?

A real review process will lead to enhanced and proactive new thinking in key areas of your life and work. Such thinking emerges from both focused concentration and serendipitous brainstorming, which will be triggered and galvanized by a consistent personal review of your inventory of actions and projects.

Doing: Making the Best Action Choices

Remember that you make your action choices based on the following four criteria, in order:

1. Context. At any point in time, the first thing to consider is what you could possibly do, where you are, with the tools you have.

2. Time available. The second factor in choosing an action is how much time you have before you have to do something else.

3. Energy available. Knowing about everything you're going to need to process and do at some point will allow you to match productive activity with your vitality level.

4. Priority. Given the context you're in and the time and energy you have, the obvious next criterion for action choice is relative priority: "Out of all my remaining options, what is the most important thing for me to do?"

At the end of the day, in order to feel good about what you didn't get done, you must have made some conscious decisions about your responsibilities, goals, and values. That process invariably includes an often complex interplay with the goals, values, and directions of your organization and of the other significant people in your life and with the importance of those relationships to you.

Getting Priority Thinking off Your Mind

Take at least a few minutes, if you haven't already done so, to jot down some informal notes about things that have occurred to you while reading this summary. Whatever popped into your mind at these more elevated levels of your inner radar, write it down and get it out of your head.

Then process those notes. Decide whether what you wrote down is something you really want to move on. If not, throw the note away or put it on a "Someday/Maybe" list or in a folder called "Dreams and Goals I Might Get Around to at Some Point." Perhaps you want to continue accumulating more of this kind of future thinking and would like to do the exercise with more formality. If so, put that outcome on your "Projects" list and decide the next action. Then do it, hand it off to get done, or put the action reminder on the appropriate list.

Getting Projects Under Control

The tricks and methods you need to clear your head and make intuitive choices about what to do and when address the horizontal level—what needs your attention and action across the horizontal landscape of your life. The last piece of the puzzle is the vertical level—the deep digging and pie-in-the-sky thinking that can leverage your creative brainpower. That gets us back to refining and energizing our project planning.

The Need for More Informal Planning Virtually all of us could be doing more planning, more informally and more often, about our projects and our lives. And if we did, it would relieve a lot of pressure on our psyches and produce an enormous amount of creative output with minimal effort.

The biggest improvement opportunity in planning does not consist of techniques for the highly elaborate and complex kinds of project organizing that professional project managers sometimes use (like Gantt charts). Most of the people who need those already have them, or at least have access to the training and software required to learn about them. The real need is to capture and utilize more of the creative, proactive thinking we do—or could do.

Which Projects Should You Be Planning? Most of the outcomes you have identified for your Projects list will not need any kind of front-end planning, other than the sort you do in your head, quickly and naturally, to come up with a next action. The only planning needed for "Get car inspected," for example, would be to decide to check the phone book for the nearest inspection location and to call and set up a time.

There are two types of projects, however, that deserve at least some sort of planning activity: (1) those that still have your attention even after you've determined their next actions and (2) those about which potentially useful ideas and supportive detail just show up.

The first type—the projects that you know have other things about them that must be decided on and organized—will need a more detailed approach than just identifying a next action. For these you'll need a more specific application of one or more of the other four phases of the natural planning model: purpose and principles, vision/outcome, brainstorming, and/or organizing.

The second type—projects for which ideas just show up, ad hoc, on a beach, in a car, or in a meeting—need to have an appropriate place in which these associated ideas can be captured. Then they can reside there for later use as needed.

Part 3: The Power of the Key Principles

It seems that there's a part of our psyche that doesn't know the difference between an agreement about cleaning the garage and an agreement about buying a company. In there, they're both just agreements—kept or broken. If you're holding something only internally, it will be a broken agreement if you're not moving on it in the moment.

The Radical Departure from Traditional Time Management

This method is significantly different from traditional time-management training. Most of those models leave you with the impression that if something you tell yourself to do isn't that important, then it's not that important—to track, manage, or deal with. But that's inaccurate, at least in terms of how a less-than-conscious part of us operates. It is how our conscious mind operates, however, so every agreement must be made conscious. That means it must be captured, objectified, and reviewed regularly in full, conscious awareness so that you can put it where it belongs in your self-management arena. If that doesn't happen, it will actually take up a lot more psychic energy than it deserves.

The reason to collect everything is not that everything is equally important; it's that it's not. Incompletions, uncollected, take on a dull sameness in the sense of the pressure they create and the attention they tie up.

When will you know how much you have left in your head to collect? Only when there's nothing left. If some part of you is even vaguely aware that you don't have it all, you can't really know what percentage you have collected. How will you know when there's nothing left? When nothing else shows up as a reminder in your mind.

This doesn't mean that your mind will be empty. If you're conscious, your mind will always be focusing on something. But if it's focusing on only one thing at a time, without distraction, you'll be in your "zone."

Use your mind to think about things rather than think of them. You want to be adding value as you think about projects and people, not simply reminding yourself they exist.

To fully realize that more productive place, you will need to capture everything. It takes focus and a change of habit to train yourself to recognize and download even the smallest agreements with yourself as they're created in your mind.

Doing the collection process as fully as you can, and then incorporating the behavior of capturing all the new things as they emerge, will be empowering and productive.

The Power of the Next-Action Decision

There is an extraordinary shift in energy and productivity whenever individuals and groups install "What's the next action?" as a fundamental and consistently asked question. As simple as the query seems, it is still somewhat rare to find it fully operational where it needs to be.

One of the greatest challenges you may encounter is that once you have gotten used to "What's the next action?" for yourself and those around you, interacting with people who aren't asking it can be highly frustrating. It clarifies things so quickly that dealing with people and environments that don't use it can seem nightmarish.

We are all accountable to define what, if anything, we are committed to make happen as we engage with ourselves and others. And at some point, for any outcome that we have an internal commitment to complete, we must make the decision about the next physical action required. There's a great difference, however, between making that decision when things show up and doing it when they blow up.

The Value of a Next-Action Decision-Making Standard Many sophisticated senior executives say that installing "What's the next action?" as an operational standard in their organization was transformative in terms of measurable performance output. It changed their culture permanently and significantly for the better.

Why? Because the question forces clarity, accountability, productivity, and empowerment.

Clarity. Too many discussions end with only a vague sense that people know what they have decided and are going to do. But without a clear conclusion that there is a next action, much less what it is or who's got it, more often than not a lot of "stuff" gets left up in the air.

Accountability. The dark side of "collaborative cultures" is the allergy they foster to holding anyone responsible for having the ball. Real togetherness of a group is reflected in the responsibility that all take for defining the real things to do and the specific people assigned to do them, so everyone is freed of the angst of still-undecided actions.

Productivity. Organizations naturally become more productive when they model and train front-end, next-action decision making. Determining the required physical allocation of resources necessary to make something happen as soon as the outcome has been clarified will produce more results sooner and with less effort.

Empowerment. Perhaps the greatest benefit of adopting the next-action approach is that it dramatically increases your ability to make things happen, with a concomitant rise in your self-esteem and constructive outlook.

The Power of Outcome Focusing

The power of directing our mental and imaginative processes to create change has been studied and promoted in thousands of contexts. Applying the principle in terms of practical reality raises several questions: Does it help get things done? If so, how do we best utilize it in managing the work of our lives? Can we really use this information in ways that allow us to produce our desired results with less effort? The answer is a resounding "yes."

These processes really work in the arena of the ordinary things we must deal with daily—in how to deal with the immediate realities and how we tie in the power of positive imagery to practical experiences in our lives. For some, slowing down, getting out of the squirrel cage, and taking care of themselves may be the major change precipitated by this methodology. The bottom line is that it makes you more conscious, more focused, and more capable of implementing the changes and results you want, whatever they are.

Learning to process the details of our work and lives with this clear and consistent system can affect others and ourselves in significant ways we may not expect.

Employing next-action decision-making results in clarity, productivity, accountability, and empowerment. Exactly the same results happen when you hold yourself to the discipline of identifying the real results you want and, more specifically, the projects you need to define in order to produce them.

It's all connected. You can't really define the right action until you know the outcome, and your outcome is disconnected from reality if you're not clear about what you need to do physically to make it happen. You can get at it from either direction, and you must, to get things done.

Only Two Problems

As an expert in whole-brain learning, Steven Snyder, put it, "There are only two problems in life: (1) You know what you want and you don't know how to get it, and/or (2) you don't know what you want." If that's true, then there are only two solutions:

- Make it up.
- Make it happen.

The truth is, our energy as human beings seems to have a dualistic and teleological reality. We create and identify with things that aren't real yet on all the levels we experience; and when we do this, we recognize how to restructure our current world to morph it into the new one and experience an impetus to make it so.

Your life and work are made up of outcomes and actions. When your operational behavior is grooved to organize everything that comes your way at all levels, a deep alignment results and wondrous things emerge. You become highly productive. You make things up and you make them happen.

GOOD TOOLS

Note that good tools don't necessarily have to be expensive. Often, on the low-tech side, the more "executive" something looks, the more dysfunctional it really is.

Conclusion

To consistently stay on course, you'll have to do some things that may not be habits yet: Keep everything out of your head; decide actions and outcomes when things first emerge on your radar, instead of later; and regularly review and update the complete inventory of open loops in your life and work. By now you at least have established a reference point for the value these behaviors create. Don't be surprised, though, if it takes a little while to make them automatic. Be patient and enjoy the process.

Here are some final tips for moving forward.

Get your personal physical organization hardware set up. Get your workstation organized. Get in-baskets. Create a personal filing system—for work and home. Get a good list-management organizer that you are inspired to play with. Give yourself permission to make any changes that you have been contemplating for enhancing your work environment—hang pictures, buy pens, toss stuff, rearrange your workspace. Support your fresh start.

Set aside some time when you can tackle one whole area of your office and then each part of your house.

Share anything of value you've gleaned from this with someone else. (It's the fastest way to learn.)

Review *Getting Things Done* again in three to six months. You'll notice things you might have missed the first time through.

Stay in touch with people who are broadcasting and reflecting these behaviors and standards.

MANAGING BRAND YOU

By Jerry S. Wilson and Ira Blumenthal

The supermarket is the arena for one of the most intense competitions on earth. As a shopper walks its aisles, every step he or she takes offers a panoramic view of products waiting to be purchased. The items that end up in the person's cart are often the dominant brands for their product category. A great brand, according to authors and executives Jerry S. Wilson and Ira Blumenthal, is a combination of a promise and an actual experience. It's a philosophy culled from Wilson's time as senior vice president of the Coca-Cola Company and Blumenthal's experience as a brand consultant for Marriott, Disney, Trump Enterprises, and American Airlines. The principles that apply to building a great consumer product can also be used to boost one's personal success. In *Managing Brand YOU: Seven Steps to Creating Your Most Successful Self*, Wilson and Blumenthal help readers get maximum exposure.

Each of the seven steps in the book helps readers mold their identity, goals, and actions toward a well-crafted, consistent message. The authors are clinical in their dissection and analysis of the creation of a personal brand. It's a method that repeatedly pushes the pain point of honest self-evaluation. *Managing Brand YOU* requires a degree of bravery on the part of the reader. Early in the text, the authors suggest that readers ask ten friends or relatives to list twenty-five words that best describe who the reader is and what he or she represents. As they admit, the result will be an eye-opener. While it's a bit extreme to suggest that building a successful personal brand requires tearing a person down to his or her foundation, the book emphasizes the kind of self-scrutiny that achievers make a part of everyday life.

The connection between famous brands and personal success is the basis of *Managing Brand YOU*. Success stories focus less on individuals and more on familiar names such as Harley-Davidson, Coca-Cola, Wal-Mart, and Volvo. Critics may question the validity of comparing people to consumer goods such as motorcycles and soda, but Wilson and Blumenthal show a clarity of vision for modern life. The members of the generation that is entering today's workplace have been building their personal brands since birth. Through the use of online social technology a recent graduate can give companies (or anyone else) a window into his or her achievements, passions, and talents. The average person in his or her twenties has invested hundreds of hours in carefully cultivating the image that's presented for the world to view. With this in mind, *Managing Brand YOU* is an excellent companion for those who may need to play catch-up.

The book's purpose is for a reader to gain the ability to communicate his or her essence in the span of a moment. Technology has created an environment where attention is microscopic and choice is near infinite. An individual needs an advantage to ensure that he or she isn't lost in the sea of possibilities. *Managing Brand YOU* will help readers leap out and grab the attention they desire while others are left sitting on the shelf.

MANAGING BRAND YOU
Seven Steps to Creating Your Most Successful Self
by Jerry S. Wilson and Ira Blumenthal

CONTENTS

THE SUMMARY IN BRIEF

What do successful consumer-goods companies know that could help transform your life? And how can you use this knowledge to become a more fulfilled person? The answers to these questions lie in the discipline of building strong brands. Successful brands convey a consistent message and create an emotional bond with consumers. Don't we all want to convey a consistent message and create an emotional bond with those important people around us? The process of building such brands is widely used in the commercial world, and now you too can use these techniques build a brand-new you—a Brand YOU.

In *Managing Brand YOU*, nationally respected brand experts Jerry S. Wilson and Ira Blumenthal reveal their proven seven-step process for personal brand building. In a self-paced, step-by-step tutorial, readers will analyze where their personal brand has been and where it currently is and help define where they'd like to be and what they'd like to stand for. The authors provide a road map for conducting a self-analysis, creating a unique identity, defining objectives, discovering passions, creating a plan, putting that plan into action, and monitoring progress.

Managing Brand YOU will help readers identify what it is that makes them unique and communicate it in a way that guarantees success.

In addition, you will learn the following:

How to identify your inner passions and core essence
When to stand up for what is important to you
How to find simplicity in the clutter
How to focus your energy on meeting your top priorities
Why you must stop spending time doing things that do not excite you
How to execute your own personal Brand YOU plan

THE COMPLETE SUMMARY

What Exactly Is a Brand?

There are many different descriptions and definitions of a brand. For our purposes, the concept and definition of a brand is really quite simple. Think of a brand as a promise to a group of specific consumers, or a well-defined audience, combined with the actual experience these individuals have with the brand. This view recognizes that there is a relationship between the brand and the individual. As well as being a promise, a successful brand has a unique personality and, ideally, a competitively advantaged position in the marketplace.

In our daily lives we come in contact with many products, services, and brands. Some of these items have achieved the status of recognized and/or beloved brand, occupying a favored place in our minds, hearts, and lives. Professional branders refer to this as *share of mind*.

Procter & Gamble built its large laundry detergent business with brands like Tide. In 1943, Tide was introduced as a scientific breakthrough to clean clothes

better than the soap flakes of the 1920s and 1930s, combining synthetic surfac-
tant molecules with another element to attack heavy stains. It met with huge
consumer acceptance and within weeks became the top-selling detergent. Its
sales and market share continue to grow today, more than sixty years later.

Procter & Gamble has introduced many different improvements on Tide over
the decades, based on the changing needs of consumers. The company has
established a bond with consumers that has yielded brand loyalty and lasting
success. In short, it makes a promise to consumers that has been delivered on
through daily experience. This customer loyalty, frequently referred to as *brand
insistence*, is testimony to Tide's reputation, well beyond the functional attributes
of the product.

So what is your brand promise and how well do you deliver on this promise?
What is your brand reputation? If you ask ten close friends and relatives to list
twenty-five words that they believe best describe who you are and what your
personal brand represents, it would likely be an eye-opener. Start by asking
yourself what twenty-five words you'd use to describe Brand YOU.

Your Promise to Your Target Audience

As you establish your unique Brand YOU position, it will be important to remain
true to yourself. While you will certainly be judged by others, you must first
judge yourself. Are you comfortable with the promise you have established for
yourself? Can you live it? Is this promise bold, something you can be proud of
achieving? Is it achievable in the time frame you've defined? Are you realistic
about your ability to fulfill your promise?

Once you are comfortable with yourself, then you can identify your target
audiences and your desired effects. Given that you lead so many different lives,
it will be necessary to identify those important groups you wish to influence:
family, friends, coworkers, church members, and so on. These people become
your target audiences. Yet each brand promise you make should be consistent
with the others you make, or you will not be building a cohesive Brand YOU.
The proof points will be reflected in the actual experiences that you deliver to
your audiences.

Successful brands cannot be, and do not try to be, all things to all people. In
fact, a characteristic of well-positioned brands is their narrow focus and specific
expertise. What a great lesson for us all: to be able to focus on our goals and
stand for something, not everything.

Step 1: Do the Brand YOU Audit

The first step of the Brand YOU journey is an honest self-assessment. Consumer
brand companies call this a *brand audit*.

Whether their product is Harley-Davidson motorcycles or Tide laundry detergent, brand managers take a thoughtful approach, stepping back and conducting a thorough assessment of the standing of their brand before revising or enhancing a marketing plan. This step includes what professional marketers refer to as a SWOT analysis—strengths, weaknesses, opportunities, and threats. With the Brand YOU audit you will identify and develop your own SWOT portrait.

You are a function, today, of all the life experiences you have had to date. These include, but are not limited to, your major accomplishments and significant setbacks. Now is the time to chronicle the mile markers in your life that have defined your current brand position.

A Rebranding Success Story

The Harley-Davidson Motor Company produces great products and has established and maintained a stellar reputation. However, the company faced increased competition when Japanese companies entered the American market. Japan's power brands, Honda, Yamaha, and Suzuki, began to challenge Harley-Davidson's market share and hurt Harley brand loyalty. In 1969, Harley-Davidson motorcycles had become expensive and were perceived by consumers as having eroded in quality. This led to a sales decline and put Harley-Davidson in the unenviable position of facing bankruptcy.

In 1981, the company was sold to a group of investors who returned the original Harley look and feel to the product. Also, an important strength surfaced during a thorough brand analysis and audit. Specifically, Harley-Davidson had a group of very loyal Harley owners. Acting on information received from their comprehensive audit, Harley-Davidson managers set up what is called the Harley Owners Group (more affectionately, HOG) in 1983.

The group offered insights about the product and shared honest feedback. For example, they wanted the product to remain absolutely authentic—absolutely "all-American." They wanted it to be an American icon, true to its proud heritage, which included the sound, feel, and power of the engine. As a result, Harley reconfigured its product, marketing, and overall brand image and turned the company around. Today, this group of brand-loyal owners includes more than one million members worldwide. These Harley superfans feel pride in the product and consider Harley an important part of their very life and—just as important—a vital piece of the fabric of American culture.

By returning to the core equity of the Harley-Davidson brand and bringing HOG to life, the brand started growing again. The Harley turnaround demonstrates that almost any corporate or product brand image can be dramatically altered for the better. Remember, though, that the Harley transformation didn't just happen. It was the result of a great deal of analysis (the brand audit) and a step-by-step process to rebuild the brand.

The Five Distinct Phases of Life

Begin your Brand YOU audit by imagining your life as a series of five distinct phases. Each phase is rich with experience and learning that influence your life. By organizing your life into these five phases, you can take stock of your life.

Phase one. Your childhood comprises the years from birth through age twelve. You have certain very distinct memories of this period, and they are happy or sad and involve friends and family because your life at this time is closely linked to these people.

Phase two. Your teen years include the ages from thirteen through seventeen and can best be characterized as the years of change. These high-school years are when you face enormous challenges of acceptance and rejection and certainly include some times of confusion and perhaps even frustration.

Phase three. Your young adult years range from ages eighteen through twenty-two. This part of your life is when you first experience independence. Following high school, people either move to college or take on work, military service, or other activities. Many use this time to experiment with different lifestyles, and dramatic personal growth occurs as a result.

Phase four. When you become an adult, the years from age twenty-three to age thirty, you move into a period of establishing yourself as a real adult, and this is likely very important for you: to be viewed, treated, and respected as an adult. Whether this life is centered on a career, a relationship, travel, or something else, you are engulfed in proving to yourself and others that you can make it in the real world.

Phase five. The longest phase, phase five, encompasses age thirty-one through the present. This entire phase is about adaptation. By now you are a full-fledged, fully functioning adult with all the responsibilities and realities that go along with adulthood. Your ability to survive and thrive now depends on how well you adapt to whatever life throws at you.

The Brand YOU Audit

Now that you understand the phases of life, it is time to get to work on your Brand YOU audit. Take the time to go back to your earliest childhood memories. Log every significant event, every achievement, every affiliation or activity that you can recall. Recognize the times of pride and of disappointment. Prepare this log through your five life phases up to the present day.

Filling out the brand audit is an introspective experience that may reopen old wounds. Whether it's a minor childhood disappointment or a personal failure in an important endeavor, you need to face the music. Ultimately, you will find this cathartic and, in the long term, it will help you come to grips with the injuries that have put you in the place you are now. Facing those lingering problems will provide the long-term relief you need to achieve your new Brand YOU.

Once you have completed this self-assessment, you will have a clear picture of who you are and how you got here. Realize that the most important part of your life lies ahead, not behind you. Yet recognizing the building blocks of your life will help you understand your present situation and provide insight on how to plot a course for the future Brand YOU you're hoping to become.

Step 2: Assess Your Brand YOU Image

A *brand image* is defined as how your brand is currently perceived by those around you. That perception may be very different from your *brand identity*, which is what you would like to stand for and what you'd prefer to project to others.

The brand image is the total picture of how consumers think of a brand. In the case of personal branding, it is how others think of you, if they think of you at all. This perception compares the promise a brand makes with the delivery of that promise. For example, if a brand promises a high-quality experience and then falls short, the image is tarnished. Conversely, if a brand overdelivers on its promise, the image is polished.

The Volvo Brand Image

Volvo has developed a reputation as a reliable and safe car. Its brand image is important to maintaining the company's strong position in the marketplace, and it also serves as a sustainable, discernable point of uniqueness. Passenger safety is the overarching theme that has framed Volvo's image. While Volvo delivers solid vehicle performance, Volvo engineers constantly study features that help contribute to greater automotive safety. From multiple air bags to skid-free braking to better handling and improved visibility, all safety factors must be routinely monitored.

By owning this brand image of safety, Volvo has successfully permeated its product development and consumer messages. The company delivers on its promise, and consumers, especially those looking for safety in a car, are attracted to the brand. Volvo's brand identity and its brand image are seamless and in sync.

Imagine if, for some unforeseen reason, the safety of passengers in a vehicle produced by Volvo was compromised. There would be a material breakdown in the promise and Volvo's image would deteriorate quickly. While it has taken Volvo many years to create this image, it would only take a few days before consumers would lose their trust in the brand. This is why great branders such as Volvo constantly review the "snapshots" through their consumers' lenses; and it's why the company also seeks feedback from outsiders.

All great branders desperately seek to understand consumers' feelings, viewpoints, and perspectives on their brands. You are your personal brand manager; you also need to seek feedback. You need to know what they think of you.

Obtaining Feedback on Your Image

So, how can you go about learning how others perceive you? The first step is to write down the various comments or pieces of feedback you have received from others over the past couple of years. You may be surprised just how reflective these small pieces of feedback might be.

The second step is to call in a few chips from your loved ones and friends. Share with them that you're going through a personal development program designed to audit your life. Share with them your quest for a better Brand YOU. Declaring your commitment to improvement is a positive thing that true loved ones and friends will support. Ask them to write a few sentences or a paragraph about you. Here are some questions to suggest they answer:

How do you perceive me?
How do you think others perceive me?
What kind of image do others have of me?
What kind of image do I project?
What do you believe are my top three personal strengths?
What three areas in my life need improvement or development?

When you discuss your image with a friend or family member, be open to whatever comes out of such a conversation. Do not become defensive or try to rationalize the feedback. Take written notes to refer to later. Listen intently and probe for greater clarity.

The third approach to consider is to use some tools that will help you better understand how you are seen by others. There are many different programs that may aid in self-assessment. For example, the Myers & Briggs Foundation has developed a simple yes/no questionnaire that helps you identify your specific personality type.

THE COCA-COLA BRAND IDENTITY

The Coca-Cola Company has long been recognized as an organization with significant brand equity, with more than four hundred brands available in virtually every nook and cranny of the world. Its flagship brand, the Coca-Cola soft drink, has stood the test of time for more than 120 years. In fact, Coca-Cola alone is recognized as the most valuable brand in the world. The Coca-Cola brand has effectively become a part of modern world culture. Though its advertising campaigns have changed over the years, Coca-Cola ("the Real Thing") has always stood for a "real" cola drink with authenticity. This identity has been built over the decades with consistent values and differentiated elements. Many competitors have taken aim at Coke, but the brand continues to command the number one position globally in rankings of brand equity.

Just as Coca-Cola has remained true to its time-tested identity, you have the opportunity to stand for something that is equally relevant to you. This Brand YOU identity should reflect your own unique equities and core essence. This will ensure you create an identity that is meaningful and sustainable over the long term.

Step 3: Determine Your Brand YOU Identity and Essence

As brand image refers to the current perception of your personal brand, think of brand identity as what you would like your personal brand to stand for in the future. Visualizing your desired Brand YOU identity requires a clear picture of your aspirations, strengths, and core values. Each of us can define and craft a vision of exactly what we want to stand for. That vision is our brand identity.

Clarifying your unique identity is the starting point to developing that brand you would like to become. While being true to yourself, you will envision what you want to represent, based on the values and principles that are such an important part of your life.

You have great strengths that will help you grow to become all you should and could be. You can use your strengths as a conduit to personal fulfillment. These strengths are your personal equities, and they can be leveraged and transferred to different areas of professional development, to community service, and to personal satisfaction.

Strengths and Gaps

Strengths represent areas of success, pride, or skill and anything else that you do well. These are capabilities you have developed over time and that may now come naturally to you. Gaps are areas that could represent potential barriers if left unresolved. Notice that gaps may not be actual weaknesses, unless they get in the way of building your new Brand YOU.

Sometimes people choose to either overlook a gap or avoid dealing with it, reverting to outright denial mode. Any gap that is neglected has the potential to grow and become an issue—or decline and never be a problem. That is important to understand. You should not feel the obligation to become "gapless." In fact, this is the beauty of thinking of yourself as a brand.

Remember, a brand is focused, is targeted, and does not try to be all things to all people. This view of yourself gives you license to live with gaps and be self-actualized. You may find that some gaps represent significant upside potential if they could be minimized or eliminated. Other gaps have absolutely no bearing on where you want to take your new Brand YOU.

Discovering Your Likes and Dislikes

Frequently, people develop a skill or strength in an area in which they have little interest or that they have little passion to pursue. Likes are those things that really excite you and make you happy when you are doing them. Dislikes are those activities or situations that you find distasteful, unexciting, unsatisfying, or any other "dis-" words that come to mind. You hate doing these things.

Now, do not become confused. There are tasks you dislike that you still need to accomplish. Students may not like doing homework, but in order to graduate, they must complete their studies. A talented cook, who takes pleasure in preparing gourmet meals, may not enjoy washing the pots and pans. You will be able to distinguish between those tasks that must be done and the habitual things that you can eliminate because they become distasteful over time.

As you consider your strengths and gaps, take some time also to ask yourself some fundamental questions about your likes and dislikes. Of the elements, which do you truly like and which do you dislike? Remember, there is a correlation between superior performance and enjoying what you do for a living. Passion is an important part of success. Your Brand YOU deserves better than mere accommodation.

Your Brand YOU also has a brand essence. Consider your brand essence the true north on your life's compass.

Step 4: Position Your New Brand YOU

It is important to recognize that brand positioning happens whether companies choose to be proactive or not. In other words, if a company pays no real attention to the space its brands occupy, then it will have abdicated the positioning job and relegated its space in the marketplace to chance (or the consumer) and, possibly worse, to its competitors. Positioning results in a credible and unique image of the product in the minds of customers. It communicates a promise that is delivered through actual experience. So doesn't it make sense to use this same technique to establish a new personal brand identity that will capture and captivate its target as well?

What space do you want to occupy in the minds and hearts of others? Do you want to create a unique identity that reflects what you stand for, or would you prefer to just hope that others will sense your strengths and understand you? Or, even worse, do you want to settle for whatever happens to come your way? Settling is what most people do. They sit on the sideline, going through the motions of the life that materialized around them, with neither rhyme nor reason to their decisions, if they even make any decisions.

The Cycle of Brand Positioning

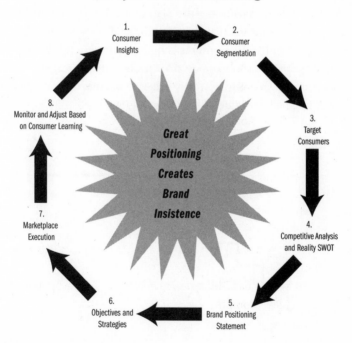

1. Consumer Insights
2. Consumer Segmentation
3. Target Consumers
4. Competitive Analysis and Reality SWOT
5. Brand Positioning Statement
6. Objectives and Strategies
7. Marketplace Execution
8. Monitor and Adjust Based on Consumer Learning

Great Positioning Creates Brand Insistence

Brand Insistence and Brand Loyalty

Companies all vie for the loyalty of their target consumers, but earning that loyalty is not easy. Customers learn about brands in many different ways, whether by word of mouth, from advertising, or through observation. In these encounters, they initiate a mental decision tree for review, evaluation, and consideration. First they become aware of the brand.

Once shoppers find the brand, they determine whether to give it a try. Trial is the first time a consumer experiences a product or service. People in your world go through a similar process as it relates to your personal brand. Once others (e.g., employers, colleagues, family members, friends, neighbors) are aware of you, they are likely to get closer to you and enter a trial acquaintance. A colleague might ask you for assistance, an employer might assign you a difficult task, a neighbor might request a favor—these are crossroad instances where your personal brand is evaluated. The way you produce and perform defines how your brand is perceived, regarded, trusted, and respected.

Should you exceed expectations, your personal brand will be highly respected and you will move to brand loyalty, whereby others will prefer your service for the work, the assignment, the responsibility, the favor because they have learned to trust you.

The definitive brand position—the platinum-level goal of all brands—is brand insistence. This means that there is no substitute and that nothing else will do. In fact, not only are consumers completely loyal to this brand, but they also will become ambassadors among their friends and colleagues. When that customer continues to not buy from any other competitor because you provide more service, more added value—that's brand insistence.

The Stepping-stones to Brand Insistence

Insistence

Loyalty

Acceptance (or Rejection)

Retry

Reflection

Trial

Awareness

Step 5: Set Your Brand YOU Goals

Successful businesses, universities, nonprofit organizations, sports teams, rock bands, military operations—any organization or group, for that matter—have one thing in common. They understand the need to focus on top priorities and have established a set of goals that they plan to achieve. Whether the goal is to win the state football championship or debut as a singer at Carnegie Hall, each sees goal setting as an important step that cannot be taken lightly. Organizations that function without clear goals have perplexed administrators, who are confused about what they are expected to deliver. Besides presenting other problems, deficient goal setting leads to wasted time, energy, and talent.

So we begin by writing down our goals. The act of committing goals to a sheet of paper forces you to think about what it is you are trying to accomplish. And having your goals down in writing helps avoid misinterpretations and memory lapses.

Long-term Brand YOU Goals

The best place to start building Brand YOU goals is to think long term. Regardless of the time line, long-term thinking is an important first phase. What do you want your life to be like in three, five, or ten years? Where would you like to be living? What would you like to be doing with your time and friends? What will you have done with your life by then? From these larger goals will come the smaller, personal targets.

These long-term goals will start your juices flowing. These are legacy questions. What do you want to be remembered for in your life? Setting long-term goals aligned with your priorities will inspire you to action, change, and transformation.

Flexibility is another key element in setting long-term goals. Things will happen along the way that will necessitate your changing and modifying those goals. Adaptability in achieving your goals will be an important capability.

Your long-term personal goals provide direction for setting your short-term goals. In effect, short-term goals can be viewed as objectives, while long-term goals are expectations of something higher in magnitude. Think of objectives more as tactical targets that will direct your short-term activities.

Step 6: Establish Your Brand YOU Strategies

Accomplishing your goals depends on your ability to choose the best strategic options, eliminate personal barriers, and maximize individual strengths. You will now use those short- and long-term goals to build action-backed strategies. Bear in mind that there are many potential paths to your destination.

Now is the time to assess those options and make the strategic choices to best achieve your goals. Whether you call it surveillance, due diligence, situation

analysis, or even market intelligence, you must analyze all the known and anticipated variables, obstacles, and challenges you might face in your quest. And you
will want to understand each of your options before locking in one strategic
plan.

Goals without bona fide support plans or strategies are hollow statements.
That is why organizations go to great lengths to draw detailed road maps during
their strategic planning process. Road maps provide a comprehensive view of the
landscape for any business. They are based on the company's mission statement,
its corporate culture, and its strengths and weaknesses, as well as its opportunities and threats. The strategic planning occurs at the corporate, strategic-business,
and operating-unit levels to ensure alignment through the organization. The
payoff is a decision to allocate people, time, and money to the highest-priority
activities.

This same process applies to individuals developing their personal brands.
Although the high-magnitude resource allocation and focus on shareholder
value don't exist in the Brand YOU process, all the other areas surely do. So when
setting your strategy, ask three key questions:

1. What strategic options are available and should be considered?
2. What are the barriers to capturing these high-leverage opportunities?
3. What strengths do I possess to activate the strategy?

The answers to these questions will drive your strategies to eliminate barriers or pick up the pace to maximize your opportunities.

A BUSINESS EXAMPLE

Wal-Mart is a great example of a brand with a simple and clear goal: to deliver
the lowest prices every day. In fact, its mantra is "National brands at everyday low prices." This global brand has a written goal that is transparent to all
consumers, and by being consistent the brand occupies a strong position in the
marketplace. Wal-Mart maximizes its supply chain and overhead expenses to allow
low prices to prevail. Through its high-volume sales and aggressive price negotiations with suppliers, Wal-Mart is able to achieve its goal.

Step 7: Implement, Monitor, and Adjust Your New Brand YOU

Your personal branding success will not happen by accident. There are five essential factors that ensure the highest level of implementation, whether by a company or by you in your quest for a new Brand YOU:

Clear objectives have been established.
People have been given responsibility for implementation. (In the case of Brand YOU, that means you.)
Expectations are in place and well understood by those who are accountable.
Performance is monitored regularly.
The strategy is flexible enough to accommodate adjustments during implementation.

Successful companies follow these five principles to improve the delivery of their brand promise to target consumers. Remember, the work of brand building does not end when the product is made, advertised, and shipped. Implementation goes all the way to the point of purchase and even to use of the brand by consumers. Failure to think of the retailing obligations leaves the success of brand positioning to chance. The brands that earn consumer loyalty have assigned great time and resources to detailed implementation systems.

Brand YOU Implementation Guidelines

Commitment to your strategic plan is essential if you want to successfully establish the new Brand YOU. You must make a personal promise to achieve the goals you have identified. The implementation plan includes the what, when, where, who, and how that will bring your strategies to life. This will take courage; after all, your new activities will mean being in unfamiliar situations. While the temptation may be to retreat to your comfort zone, be confident in your future.

Monitoring and Adjustment

Even the best-laid plans need some modification along the way. As things progress, you will want to and need to alter your strategy for implementation. These course corrections should be driven by actions that have produced a new perspective on your plans. You may also determine that your learning has shifted your thoughts and a different tactic would be more successful in the short or long run. Regardless of the reason, be prepared to adjust your actions at some point.

Your new Brand YOU is a work in progress. Just because you have a plan and the plan seems to be working, don't take your eye off the ball. You'll constantly be confronting new situations that demand decisions on your part. The Brand YOU process is repeatable, continuous, and worthy of revisiting when things dramatically change in your life—or when you're ready to dramatically change your life again. You should constantly monitor your brand's health. After all, unpoliced brands lose their value. Focus on continuous improvement and plan your life to work your plan.

WINNERS NEVER CHEAT

by Jon M. Huntsman

f one were to judge based on the headlines, it would be easy to believe that the world's moral compass is spinning directionless. Corporate misdeeds that began early in the first decade of the millennium culminated in the global financial crisis that closed it. Athletes stood before Congress to explain away their otherworldly performance on the field. There were times when individuals in academia, media, and politics stood together in a lineup of ethical misbehavior. Business appears to be the segment of society with the broadest allowance for misdeeds in the pursuit of success. There is almost an acceptance of amorality as long as the bottom line grows and a lawyer is only a speed dial away.

One person who stands in complete opposition to the loosening of the globe's moral grip is executive and philanthropist Jon M. Huntsman. He has devoted his life and a generous portion of his personal fortune to helping others. Huntsman embodies the type of success story that was once considered to exemplify life in America. The child of a teacher and a homemaker, Huntsman began his career with an egg-distribution company. Through a series of successes in container manufacturing with various companies, he was able to found Huntsman Corporation, which at one time was the largest privately held chemical company in the world. With each step he took, Huntsman was careful to never stray from the strong ethical code that governed his business and life.

He shares the secrets to his considerable success in *Winners Never Cheat*, a book that returns readers to the simple principles that are learned in childhood but lost along the way. He takes on a tough challenge as he attempts to convince readers that the abilities to deceive and connive are not the twin strengths that win every competition. Huntsman succeeds through an honest presentation of evidence that does not scold or pander. He believes more in the gentle pat on the back than in the wagging of a finger. The author's honesty extends to his willingness to pull back the curtain on his own business practices. One of the critical tales Huntsman tells involves his company's refusal to pay kickbacks to a foreign government to ensure smooth operations. It's easy to acknowledge Huntsman's conviction when one learns that his decision to take the moral high road cost his company three million dollars in 1980.

It's disheartening to admit that the advice in *Winners Never Cheat* needs to be repeated. However, the temptations that occur along any person's road to success require Huntsman's reminders to combat them. He points out time and again that good ethics and strong moral character are irreplaceable business assets. Trust is a quality that can take a lifetime to accrue and a moment to erase. With his lessons on integrity, graciousness, and philanthropy, Huntsman provides a course that will awaken the senses he fears are being deadened by a cynical, cutthroat world. Strengthening one's moral fiber will lead one to make headlines for all the right reasons, and that, as Huntsman indicates, is something everyone will notice.

WINNERS NEVER CHEAT
A Self-Made Billionaire Speaks Out on Honesty and Generosity
by Jon M. Huntsman

CONTENTS

THE SUMMARY IN BRIEF

Jon M. Huntsman started with practically nothing and built a world-class business that carried him to *Forbes*'s list of America's wealthiest people. In this summary, Huntsman, chairman and founder of Huntsman Corporation, presents the principled lessons he has learned and followed throughout his lifetime. He also explains how business can return to the days when your word was your bond, a handshake was sacred, and swarms of lawyers weren't needed to back it up.

Huntsman built his career and fortune on ethical principles—from his refusal to comply with the Nixon administration's corrupt demands to his life-long commitment to charity to the way he approaches his biggest deals. In this summary, Huntsman describes how readers can learn to listen to their moral compass, build teams with the highest values, share success, take responsibility, and earn the rewards that only come from giving back.

This summary also explains that you don't live these principles just to succeed: You live them because they're right. In an age of many business scandals, Huntsman's life proves honesty is more than right: It's your biggest competitive differentiator.

In addition, you will learn the following:

How to win the right way and win for life.

How to compete fiercely and fairly and win without cheating.

How you can lead using risk, responsibility, and reliability.

How to put the lawyers in their place: Your word and your handshake are more powerful than any contract.

How graciousness is next to godliness and how to respect customers, partners, employees, and even competitors.

How to treat the workplace as an extension of the family.

How to give back, return favors, and share your good fortune.

THE COMPLETE SUMMARY

Lessons from the Sandbox

Young children growing up, whether rich or poor, are taught to play by the rules. Be tough, be competitive, give the game all you have—but do it fairly: These are simple values that form the basis for how families, neighborhoods, and communities behave. It is a value system that is learned in homes, sandboxes, playgrounds, classrooms, Sunday schools, and athletic fields.

Those lessons do not lose their value simply because we're involved in the business world, yet they are missing in segments of today's marketplace. Many CEOs enjoy princely lifestyles even as stakeholders lose their jobs, pensions, benefits, investments, and trust in the American way.

Dishonesty in Business

Cooked ledgers, look-the-other-way auditors, kickbacks, and flimflams of every sort have burrowed their way into today's corporate climate. Many outside corporate directors bask in perks and fees, concerned only with keeping Wall Street happy and their fees intact. In the past twenty years, investor greed has become obsessive and a force with which CEOs must deal.

In the 2004 U.S. presidential election, morality issues influenced more votes than any other factor, but a Zogby International poll revealed that the single biggest moral issue in voters' minds was not abortion or same-sex marriage. Greed/materialism was cited as far and away the most urgent moral problem facing America today. (A close second was poverty/economic justice.) The question is, why have lying, cheating, misrepresentation, and weaseling on deals ingrained themselves so deeply in society? What's needed is a booster shot of commonly held moral principles from our childhood.

Although these childhood prescriptions may appear to have been forgotten in the fog of competition, it is more a matter of values being expediently ignored. Whatever the case, it is time to get into ethical shape with a full-scale behavioral workout. Financial ends never justify unethical means. Success comes to those who possess skill, courage, integrity, decency, and generosity. Men and women who maintain their universally shared values tend to achieve their goals, know happiness in home and work, and find greater purpose in their lives than simply accumulating wealth. Nice guys really can and do finish first in life.

Deceivers Seem to Win in Life

Michael Josephson, who heads the Josephson Institute of Ethics in Marina del Rey, California, says one only has to view popular shows such as *The Apprentice* and *Survivor* to get the notion that life's winners are those who deceive others without getting caught. Yet we all know that when we bend or break the rules, what we are doing is not right. Traditional behavioral values will lead us not into temptation but to long-term success. Forget about who finishes first and who finishes last. Decent, honorable people finish races—and their lives—in grand style and with respect.

The principles we learned as children were simple and fair. They remain simple and fair. With moral compasses programmed in the sandboxes of long ago, we can navigate career courses with values that guarantee successful lives, a path that is good for one's mental and moral well-being, not to mention long-term material success.

COMMONLY HELD PRINCIPLES
FROM THE PLAYGROUNDS OF OUR YOUTH

Be fair.
Don't cheat.
Play nicely.
Share and share alike.
Tell the truth.

Check Your Moral Compass

No one is raised in a moral vacuum. Every mentally balanced human being basically recognizes right from wrong. Whether a person is brought up a Christian, Jew, Buddhist, Muslim, Hindu, Unitarian, New Ager, freethinker, or atheist, he or she is taught from toddlerhood on that he or she shouldn't lie and that there are consequences for doing so. There is no such thing as a moral agnostic. An amoral person is a moral person who temporarily and creatively disconnects his or her actions from his or her values. Each of us possesses a compass or conscience programmed by parents, teachers, coaches, clergy, grandparents, uncles, aunts, scoutmasters, friends, and peers.

Some people point out that today's society tolerates too much questionable activity, making it difficult for young people to get a consistent fix on right and wrong. While society is more permissive today, does anyone today truly condone stealing? Does any student not consider cheating intrinsically wrong, no matter how many of his or her friends do it? Does society accept cooking corporate books, embezzlement, fraud, or outlandish perks for corporate executives? The answers, of course, are no. Basic misbehavior is considered as wrong today as it was a hundred years ago.

Ethics Versus Laws

We are not always required by law to do what is right and proper. Decency and generosity, for instance, carry no legal mandate. Pure ethics are optional. Laws define courses that we must legally adhere to or avoid. Ethics are standards of conduct that we ought to follow.

The ingredients for long-term success—courage, vision, follow-through, risk, opportunity, sweat, sacrifice, skill, discipline, honesty—never vary. In the winner-take-all atmosphere of today's marketplace, shortcuts to success are alluring, and lying can often be lucrative. But scammers and cheaters have never lasted for long, and their fall is fast, painful, and lasting.

THE GREAT, GREAT GUYS CLUB

A group of young children formed a special club called the Great, Great Guys Club. Members have to be at least six years old to attend meetings. It's not permissible to fall asleep, wet your pants, or crawl under the table, among other prohibitions. Here are a few standards that the kids established by themselves:

> *Do what you're supposed to when you are told to do it.*
>
> *Kindness and honesty determine heart and character.*
>
> *Never tell lies.*
>
> *Cover your mouth when you cough and sneeze.*

Kids know what proper behavior is even if they don't always show it. Their moral compasses, although still developing, are in working order. Ever notice how little guile youngsters exhibit? How honest they are with observations? How well they play with others? How smoothly they compete when adults aren't present? Sure, there are still squabbles, but kids work them out without a three-hundred-page rule book or a court of law.

Play by the Rules

Which rules we honor and which ones we ignore determine personal character, and it is character that determines how closely we will allow our value system to affect our lives. Character is most determined by integrity and courage. Your reputation is how others perceive you. Character is how you act when no one is watching. These traits, or lack thereof, are the foundation of life's moral decisions. Once dishonesty is introduced, distrust becomes the hallmark of future dealings or associations. The eighteenth-century Scottish philosopher Francis Hutcheson had this in mind when he wrote, "Without staunch adherence to truth-telling, all confidence in communication would be lost."

Bribes and Payoffs

Bribes have a huge cost. Bribes and scams may produce temporary advantages, but they carry an enormous price tag. They cheapen the way business is done, enrich only a few corrupt individuals, and make a mockery of the rules of play.

In 1980, Huntsman Chemical opened a plant in Thailand. Mitsubishi was a partner in this joint venture, called HMT. With about thirty million dollars invested, HMT announced the construction of a second site. One day, Huntsman received a call from a Mitsubishi executive in Tokyo responsible for Thailand operations. He stated that HMT had to pay various government officials kick-backs annually to do business and that Huntsman Chemical's share was $250,000 for that year. Huntsman said it had no intention of paying even five cents toward what was nothing more than extortion.

The next day, Huntsman informed Mitsubishi it was selling its interest. After failing to talk Huntsman out of it, Mitsubishi paid the chemical company a discounted price for its interest in HMT. Huntsman Chemical lost about three million dollars in the short term, but it was a blessing in disguise. When the Asian economic crisis came several years later, the entire industry went down the drain.

Once a company compromises its values by agreeing to bribes or payoffs, it is difficult to reestablish its reputation or credibility. Carefully choose your partners.

Competition is good. Competition is an integral part of the entrepreneurial spirit and the free market. Cheating and lying are not. If the immoral nature of cheating and lying doesn't particularly bother you, think about this: They even-tually lead to failure. Moral shortcuts always have a way of catching up with you.

Make it a point to never misrepresent or take unfair advantage of someone. That way, you can count on second and third deals with companies after suc-cessfully completing the first one. Have as a goal both sides feeling they achieved their respective objectives.

Standards are important. Every family, home, and school classroom has its standards. Children observe their elders so they know how to act. Employees watch supervisors. Citizens eye civic and political leaders. If these leaders and role models set bad examples, those following frequently follow suit. It's that simple. There are no moral shortcuts in the game of business—or life.

There are three kinds of people in business and life: the unsuccessful, the temporarily unsuccessful, and those who become and remain successful. The dif-ference is character.

Setting the Example

"Whatsoever a man soweth, that shall he also reap." That describes leadership responsibility clearly and concisely, the precise spot where the buck stops. The lesson is clear: Careful cultivation pays off. Parents and employers who nurture, praise, and, when necessary, discipline fairly experience happier and more suc-cessful lives for themselves and those in their charge.

Nothing new, you say? We need reminders of this point to help overcome unforeseen or uncontrollable obstacles that cloud end results. What's important is that the person in charge take responsibility for the outcome, be it good, bad, or ugly. Surround yourself with the best people available and then accept responsibility. Anything that happens is your responsibility, even if you don't catch mistakes.

THE CORE ELEMENTS OF LEADERSHIP

Integrity

Courage

Vision

Commitment

Empathy

Humility

Confidence

Genuineness

Energy

Engagement

Characteristics of Good Leadership

Leadership is found in all walks of society: business, political, parental, athletic, military, religious, media, intellectual, entertainment, academic, and so forth. In every instance, leadership cannot exist in a vacuum. Effective, respected leadership is maintained through mutual agreement. Leadership is not meant to be dominion over others. Rather, it is a composite of characteristics that earns respect, results, and a continued following.

Leadership demands decisiveness. That is why it is absolutely critical that leaders know the facts. To ensure that, leaders must surround themselves with capable, strong, competent advisers—and then listen. Unfortunately, many companies and organizations are led by executives who fear bold, candid, and talented subordinates. Leaders must show affection and concern for those they lead. Those who would render loyalty to a leader want to know that they are appreciated. Whether or not they realize it, executives in leadership roles solely for the four Ps—pay, perks, power, and prestige—are on their way out.

Leadership is also about taking risks. If your life is free of failure, you're not much of a leader. Take no risks, and you risk more than ever. A 2004 survey found that three in five senior executives at Fortune 1000 companies have no desire to become a CEO. That's twice the number who said the same in the first survey, conducted in 2001. Why? The risks. The chances of making mistakes increase dramatically with leadership, no matter its nature or level, but never having failed is never having led.

Turn Failure into Opportunity

To succeed, we must attempt new things. Mistakes are not the problem. How one identifies and corrects errors—how one turns failure into a new opportunity—determines the quality and durability of leadership. Those who prefer jeering and ridiculing on the sidelines when the players err or stumble just don't get it. Mistakes and miscues are often transformed into meaningful, successful experiences.

President Teddy Roosevelt made this observation, in which he places the participant and the belittler in perspective:

> It is not the critic who counts; not the man who points out how the strong man stumbles, or where the doer of deeds could have done them better. The credit belongs to the man who is actually in the arena, whose face is marred by dust and sweat and blood; who strives valiantly; who errs, and comes short again and again, because there is no effort without error and shortcoming; but who does actually strive to do the deeds; who knows the great enthusiasms, the great devotions; who spends himself in a worthy cause, who at best knows in the end the triumph of high achievement, and who at worst, if he fails, at least fails while daring greatly, so that his place shall never be with those cold and timid souls who know neither victory nor defeat.

> The greater these attributes, the stronger the leadership. True leaders ought not worry greatly about occasional mistakes, but they must vigilantly guard against those things that will make them feel ashamed.

> Leadership calls for a high degree of confidence, a requirement that keeps many people from wanting to be in charge of problematic situations. There is a great "can do" spirit in each of us, ready to be set free. Leaders are selected to take the extra steps, to display moral courage, to reach above and make it to the end zone.

Humility

In today's what's-in-it-for-me environment, humility is vital for good leadership. Jeroen van der Veer, chief executive of Royal Dutch/Shell Group, says, "The one common value that most leaders lack today, whether in business, politics or religion, is humility."

Leaders need to be candid with those they purport to lead. Sharing good news is easy. When it comes to the more troublesome negative news, be candid and take responsibility. Don't withhold unpleasant possibilities and don't pass off bad news to subordinates to deliver. Level with employees about problems in a timely fashion.

Leadership is a privilege. Those who receive the mantle must also know that they can expect an accounting of their stewardship.

Most people want to be in sync with a leader whom they can both admire and respect, and they will often model their own lives after that person. A good example of this is Mitt Romney, former governor of Massachusetts, who returned integrity to the scandal-ridden 2002 Winter Olympics. That classic show of leadership was infectious all the way through the Olympic organization to the thousands of volunteers. As a result, those games came off the most successful and problem free in recent Olympic history.

Courage

Courage may be the single most important factor in defining leadership. Leaders—whether in families, corporations, groups, or politics—must be prepared to stand against the crowd when their moral values are challenged. They must ignore criticism and taunts if pursuing a right and just route. Leadership is supposed to be daunting. Courage is an absolute requisite. Without it, noted Winston Churchill, other virtues lose their meaning.

Following one's moral compass is not for the faint of heart or cold of feet. Leaders worthy of the name understand and accept that they are chosen every bit as much for their values and courage as for their administrative skills, marketing savvy, or visionary outlook.

Keep Your Word

Shakespeare didn't literally mean it when he said that the first thing we must do is kill all the lawyers, but you can forgive folks for smiling at the thought, given that the legal profession, collectively and with our complicity, is stripping America of personal accountability and trust. Under the guise of legal protection, many corporate lawyers have made it impossible to seal business deals with just a handshake. One's word being one's bond has been replaced by one's word being subject to legal review.

This is a great weakness in our system because most lawyers have little in the way of business experience. They tend to focus on why something should not or cannot be done. As Jeffrey Sonnenfeld, associate dean of executive programs at Yale School of Management, put it in a *BusinessWeek* article, corporate attorneys are considered "the vice presidents of No."

Problems nearly always arise when clients allow lawyers to make business decisions they are not qualified to make. In a recent *Inc.* magazine article, author Norm Brodsky says that smart lawyers understand the boundaries of their expertise and limit themselves to providing legal advice. "Not-so-smart lawyers," he says, "charge ahead and screw things up."

Integrity

There are larger issues of personal integrity, ethics, and human decency that, on occasion, ought to override the traditional standards of professional practices. Integrity is central to all else virtuous. We can avoid much unpleasantness, legal and social, by offering trust, accepting responsibility, and standing by our word, even though it causes some discomfort.

Abraham Lincoln, himself a lawyer, was on target: "Discourage litigation. Persuade your neighbor to compromise whenever you can. As a peacemaker, the lawyer has the superior opportunity of being a good man. There will still be business enough."

Don't misunderstand. It is important that we listen to lawyers, but only for a second opinion. Your opinion ought to be the first—and the last. The CEO is the one who takes the risk and who must determine the personally decent, ethical route.

Great Resolve

Keeping one's word often requires great resolve. In 1986, after lengthy negotiations with Emerson Kampen, chairman and CEO of Great Lakes Chemical Corporation, there was an agreement to buy 40 percent of a division of Huntsman Chemical for $54 million. A handshake sealed the deal. After four months, Great Lakes lawyers called to say they would like to draft some documents. That took three months. In the interim, the price of raw materials had decreased substantially. Kampen called back, saying that the price of Huntsman Chemical had increased greatly during that time and that he would pay half the increase in value. Huntsman's answer was no. Kampen said it wasn't fair to Huntsman, but Huntsman stuck to its handshake agreement. Kampen never forgot this lesson in fairness.

We need to understand how important it is to keep our word. Trust more in one another and in ourselves. As captains of our own character, it is essential we understand the great legacy of trust and integrity. We will be remembered for truthful disclosures and promises kept.

Pick Advisers Wisely

Look for ethical, loyal, talented associates. There are no one-person teams—by either definition or natural law. Success is a cooperative effort; it depends on those who stand beside you.

The first and most important decision in your success is carefully choosing the people who will surround you. Make sure they share your values. Make certain their character defaults to high moral ground in times of stress, ensure they are bright and comprehend results, and be confident of their loyalty.

Although we regularly treat the terms as if they were synonymous, there is a difference between popularity (or admiration) and respect. The former has to do with positive, outward attributes; the latter is a positive recognition of one's inner strength and character. If you must choose one, go for respect every time.

Stand for what is right, not what is popular. Ethicist Michael Josephson says ethics is all about how we meet the challenge of doing the right thing when that act will cost more than we want to pay. That takes courage. Courage comes from deep within one's own being. Courage is not the understanding of what is right or wrong. Rather, it is the strength to choose the right course.

When you hire managers, don't ask to see their GPAs or inquire about their class standing. Instead of being greatly concerned about their academic majors, search for signs of integrity, commitment, and courage. Applicants should get points for holding full- or part-time jobs in high school and college or underwriting part or all of their educational costs in achieving a degree.

THE RULES OF TEAMS

If you don't have knowledge of something, find people who do. You need wonderful men and women of talent, skill, energy, and promise. They should know that team membership requires the following:

Adherence to proper values

Loyalty to the company

Loyalty to the CEO

Competence

Get Mad, Not Even

In the years following the 2000 presidential election, Al Gore always looked mad and upset. He continued to smart over the fact that he had received more popular votes than rival George Bush but the Electoral College vote had gone to Bush after the Supreme Court ruled Bush had won Florida.

Many of us have been injured emotionally at one time or another by family, friends, business colleagues, or news media, and the urge to strike back becomes our first reaction. We want to do what Ensign Pulver did in the movie *Mister Roberts*: He tossed a large homemade firecracker into the ship's laundry room as payback for the ship's captain making Lieutenant Roberts's life miserable.

Put Things Behind You

There's a better way. Put things behind you and move on. Accept what has transpired and move ahead in a positive and dignified way.

Don't hold back emotions. Let your feelings come out. Getting mad for a brief time is far better than a long and costly plan to get even. Make your reaction fast, furious, and finite. Then say to yourself: "There, I feel better. It's over."

Revenge is counterproductive. If a business competitor has caused you emotional injury, channel your energies into earning a bigger market share and making your company more profitable. Doing better is the healthful response to most anything. In any walk of life, a positive, upbeat outlook trumps any adversarial act. It pays to be positive and upbeat around your opposition. Those who plant mean, vengeful, and unjust seeds will reap what they sow. We tend to become what we degrade.

We assume that successful or revered people do not carry around demons as the rest of us do. They do. When it comes to grudges, we all have held on to some too long. What separates winners from losers is how fast we banish those demons. Pay attention to that voice inside you saying: "Life is short. Move on."

Graciousness Is Next to Godliness

Few human traits are as critical to one's relationship with others as graciousness. It embodies love, kindness, sensitivity, and charity—the qualities of people who have great inner faith. One's capacity to be kind, decent, and thoughtful is the manifestation of godliness, a demeanor that has earned respect for men and women of all faiths and backgrounds.

We are taught in our youth to be kind to others as a matter of habit. The lesson doesn't always stick around in adulthood. Decency is lacking in today's highly competitive business world, political arenas, and sporting events. All truly successful people demonstrate a sense of decency. There are those who appear successful on the surface but who really are selfish, unhappy individuals lacking the motivation and capacity to love.

Many would say there is no place for graciousness and the Golden Rule in business, politics, athletics, or other highly competitive settings and that only results count. Hogwash! How you treat others will be your epitaph. Think about what might be said in your eulogy. Businesses too have reputations. Many companies are known for their values, customer and employee relations, innovative spirit, and philanthropic endeavors. The recent downfalls of Enron, Tyco, WorldCom, and others remind us that deception, greed, and indecency are also present in the misty corporate world.

True Fulfillment

The Dalai Lama once observed: "Accumulation of wealth for the sake of wealth alone is self-defeating. Only in seeing one's work as a calling, a means to serve a higher purpose, can we find true fulfillment."

On another occasion he said, "Relate to others with warmth, human affection, honesty and compassion."

Most companies and individuals seek success and respect. To reach these goals requires a sense of compassion for others and a desire to make others happy. Happiness often comes to us when we try to make others happy. Graciousness is catching.

No one lives or dies unto him- or herself. In his day, Andrew Carnegie made thirty-eight other men millionaires. Each of us has a stake in the accomplishments and failures of those around us; each of us holds an interest in the deeds of others. When one person beautifies the neighborhood, the entire community is enhanced. When a CEO trips, stakeholders stumble. Like the tide that raises all ships, no one can lift others without first bettering him- or herself.

Research suggests a link between the lack of civility and violence. Leaders must instill in others a sense of entitlement, appreciation, and loyalty. Watching dreams unfold is one of the great joys of leadership.

Your Name Is on the Door

Business is much the same as families. The wise CEO of a publicly traded company will operate as if his or her last name is on the company marquee.

Where appropriate, the workplace should be an extension of the family, a place where appreciation for decency, respect, and basic values is encouraged and examples of proper moral behavior are the rule.

Jay Kenfield Morley's description of life sums up how critical it is for the workplace to be an extension of the home: "The recipe for happiness is to have just enough money to pay the monthly bills you acquire, a little surplus to give you confidence, a little too much work each day, enthusiasm for your work, a substantial share of good health, a couple of real friends, and a wife and children to share life's beauty with you."

Emphasize in employee meetings that families come first. Insist that your workplace attempt to be an extension of a supportive home. Everyone wants to feel noticed, respected, and valued. Unfortunately, large corporations tend to be run by the book. They frequently are perceived by employees to be sterile and uncaring. Running a business as if you own it prompts a more personal touch. Employees want to be assured the owner or CEO truly cares about them.

Family Businesses

Effective communications are essential. If you run a family business, assure your children, even after most of them are working in the business, that you are a parent first and chairman of the board second. Employees must be treated as equals. When a company is financially successful, it ought to share its bounty with employees, the community, and customers the same as it does with owners or stockholders. Whether one runs a family business or is CEO of a public company, ways must be identified to recognize and give credit to others—at all levels of the organization. The surest path to success is one where others walk with you. Plants and equipment can be replaced easily; hardworking, loyal employees are as valuable as precious gems.

If top executives fail to follow their moral compasses, how can they expect those they lead to adhere to moral values? And if employees in the workplace do not care about ethics or morality, how can they expect their children to be any different? Everyone loses. That's why it is especially critical that employees understand the company's values and follow them.

All companies—public or private—must create a culture in which employees come first and are treated royally. They always return the favor.

THE PROFITABLE GOLDEN RULE

In his book There Is No Such Thing as Business Ethics, *John Maxwell maintains that in today's marketplace, 70 percent of the people who leave their jobs do so because they do not feel valued. That's an indication of how shabbily many executives and directors treat employees. Everyone wants to be valued, to know that he or she counts. People need to be appreciated, trusted, and respected in every segment of their lives. There is a practical side to decent behavior too. Customers, employers, and suppliers are people who understand and appreciate kindness and decency. They normally react in kind, and that can be good for profits. Bottom lines would be better served if we put this philosophy into practice. "How would I like to be treated in this situation?" That's all you need to ask yourself in most instances.*

The Obligation to Give Back

Philanthropy ought to be the preeminent ingredient in everyone's recipe for material gain. No matter what the field, no star of any success story is a totally self-made man or woman. Along the way, all of us received help from others; most of us were also the beneficiaries of lucky breaks. We owe a portion of our success to others, and the only way to repay that assistance is by sharing good fortune.

All religions of the world reserve a high place on their must-do lists for giving to the less fortunate. The more one gives, the better one feels; and the better one feels about it, the easier it becomes to give. It is a wonderfully warm slippery slope. If you require a less altruistic reason to give, try this: Philanthropy is plain good business. It energizes a company. And publicly owned companies are not exempted from the requisite of returning a portion of their profits to worthwhile causes.

Most People Want to Help Others

In almost every human being there is an inner desire to help others. Unfortunately, some of us never quite find the time or the reason. But there is no more important human quality than sharing with others. There is no source of true happiness more complete than an act of charity. It is what life is all about.

It is of little consequence where or how or to whom we give. What really matters is our attitude. Donations don't always have to be money. In many ways, time is more precious than dollars. Giving of one's time, lending one's stature, or providing one's expertise can be as meaningful as money. Leaders ought to set aside time for volunteer or public-service work.

Giving back applies to everyone, but it surely is not optional, at least for the rich or for corporations. It is the moral obligation of any person of wealth or any business worthy of its name to return to the community some of what it has been given. No less a committed capitalist than Andrew Carnegie lectured the well-heeled in his 1889 work "The Gospel of Wealth" to return their "surplus wealth to the mass of their fellows in the form best calculated to do them lasting good."

Giving is a spiritual obligation. Christianity, Judaism, and Islam all make the same point. Yet it is often the wealthiest citizens who find it the most difficult to share, whereas those with little seem to be first in line to give what they have—and usually in greater proportion to their net worth than the rich.

Sharing wealth and kindness, embracing those in need, and creating opportunities for others are a societal duty. All that is required to be a philanthropist is a passion for making a difference. Giving enriches one's heart and soul—and it's contagious.

The Bottom Line

Society is forever remembering the past as the "good old days." The elders of any society frequently view the young as possessing fewer values than they have, but the fact is we all start out the same. Each generation has unique challenges; no generation has a monopoly on values.

There is, today, a need to reaffirm values that help us determine what is right and what is wrong. This process was passed along and infused into our very beings by the previous generation. We had unwritten rules for the playgrounds, sandboxes, homes, and schools of our youth. They spoke to basic fairness, decency, and integrity. These principles have not changed simply because we migrated from boxes full of sand to buildings full of desks. Acceptable moral values are child's play, not rocket science.

There's a memorable quote by John Andrew Holmes, a physician who wrote *Wisdom in Small Doses*. It became the entire text of a university commencement address delivered in 2000—the shortest address in modern history. It said: "No exercise is better for the human heart than reaching down and lifting another up."

THE ADVERSITY PARADOX

by J. Barry Griswell
and Bob Jennings

Imagine a young boy born into poverty in a bustling city in the southern United States. He is raised in surroundings that lead many of his peers to a life of hardship and misery. While other teens his age are running off to football practice after school, he is heading toward the loading dock to work alongside men two and three times his age. Like his coworkers, the teen loads trucks night after night for the sole purpose of helping to feed his family. Despite tremendous disadvantages, this young man goes on to earn a full scholarship to college and achieve great success as president and CEO of a financial company. It's the kind of rags-to-riches story one would find in the novels of Horatio Alger Jr. It's no coincidence that the story's subject, J. Barry Griswell, received the 2003 Horatio Alger Association Distinguished American Award, given to an individual who overcomes humble beginnings to succeed in life.

The defining moments in any success story are the times when the achiever fails but perseveres. Examine the biography of any successful individual and you will find no shortage of valleys to match the more prominent peaks. It's a journey that requires endurance. Griswell could have quit any number of times during the course of his path to success. The same could be said of his coauthor, Bob Jennings, whose career as a commission-based salesperson nearly derailed in its earliest days. The pair joined forces to write *The Adversity Paradox: An Unconventional Guide to Achieving Uncommon Business Success*, a book that serves as a guide for anyone looking to turn misfortune into the ultimate motivator.

Griswell and Jennings write that learning from adversity builds a "business-savvy framework" consisting of five components. As they reveal the five attributes, the authors instruct readers in the way to build "human capital." This combination of character, behavior, and passion will turn "woe is me" into victory through a systematic process of self-evaluation and hard work. The latter trait is a requirement that the authors admit will deter some from pursuing the lessons of *The Adversity Paradox*. However, they suggest that a work ethic, like a muscle, can be strengthened with exercise. They provide examples throughout the book of individuals who pushed themselves through setbacks and disasters to achieve greatness that none believed was possible.

The Adversity Paradox offers a unique combination of practical advice and inspirational narrative. Griswell's willingness to divulge personal details while discussing the components of human capital should erase any doubt a reader has about the authors' applying their own teachings. Griswell and Jennings are true survivors. In a business environment where downsizing, extended unemployment, and job scarcity continue to dominate the landscape, The Adversity Paradox intends to help those who are down to gain their feet again and walk on toward greatness.

THE ADVERSITY PARADOX
An Unconventional Guide to Achieving Uncommon Business Success
by J. Barry Griswell and Bob Jennings

CONTENTS

THE SUMMARY IN BRIEF

Obstacles and setbacks are inevitable parts of life, especially in today's harsh and volatile economy. How can you use these to build success? The answer lies in firsthand knowledge of the "adversity paradox." Working to overcome humble beginnings, lack of knowledge, unexpected setbacks, or any manner of misfortune can be the foundational step in a path to incredible achievement.

Those who have benefited from the adversity paradox all relate similar experiences. The knowledge they gained from overcoming obstacles played such a crucial role in their success trajectories that they now consider adversity to be an invaluable friend.

While you may not experience the extreme forms of adversity described in *The Adversity Paradox*, it's inevitable that each and every one of us will encounter adversity at some point in our careers. The lessons here are practical and inspirational, and they can be applied at any stage of your career.

J. Barry Griswell and Bob Jennings offer concrete steps that can be taken to increase your own business savvy. Their intent is to embolden you to take action or refocus your determination in your career path. The paths to success are diverse, but *The Adversity Paradox* identifies patterns that anyone can study and learn from.

In addition, you will learn the following:

How to handle the Moment of Truth: when the presentation begins
How to take your own business-savvy inventory
How to use the skill of introspection to find your level of moral development
How to ignite your thirst for knowledge
How to have the confidence to do what others see as impossible
How to build endurance of character the same way you build physical strength

THE COMPLETE SUMMARY

What Is Business Savvy, Anyway?

business savvy: n. **1.** proficiency in the realm of business; the unique ability to consistently meet and surpass one's business goals. adj. **1.** those who are proficient in business and consistently achieve outstanding success.

the adversity paradox: n. **1.** the phenomenon of building outstanding success upon the lessons learned in overcoming serious difficulty or misfortune.

You always have a choice. No matter how terrible the setback, you can make the choice to lie back and let adversity consume you, or you can face the situation head-on and work to make adversity your friend. Befriending adversity means not shying from it but learning from it.

The business leaders who've benefited from the adversity paradox are the ones who use the diagnostic skill of introspection to conduct honest self-assessments so as to make trajectory adjustments whenever necessary. These folks have found a purpose they're passionate about and a way to take the work out of work. They're the employees who nurture a thirst for knowledge that keeps them constantly abreast of the ever-changing world of business.

Given such commendable core competencies and practices, it isn't surprising that those who've learned their lessons the hard way often go on to achieve enormous wealth as a result of their prodigious business savvy.

The Individual Human Capital of the Business Savvy

Individual human capital (HC) is an individual's portfolio of assets in which he or she has invested that can produce future positive outputs. Gary S. Becker, the foremost expert on human capital, states, "Economists regard expenditures on education, training, medical care and so on as investments in human capital. They are called human capital because people cannot be separated from their knowledge, skills, health or values in the way they can be separated from their financial and physical assets."

Business leaders who have benefited from the adversity paradox have tended to build their success upon the same five components: introspection, values behavior, work character, purpose and passion, and thirst for knowledge. This is "the business-savvy framework."

The Individual Human Capital Profile

J. Barry Griswell has successfully put all the components of the business-savvy framework together and built a rags-to-riches kind of success. His industry, associates, competitors, company board, employees, and friends see him as a very business-savvy person. To get to this point in his life, he has defied all the odds. When he was a youth his family was poor, his home broken, and learning difficult. As an adult he fought medical issues and the occasional career setback. But he learned early on to persevere despite all the odds, and that ability has facilitated both personal and career success. His comments about each of the individual human capital components are incorporated in the following descriptions.

Introspection: HC Component 1 Introspection is the practice of observing oneself—one's personality, strengths and weaknesses, overall performance, motivations, goals, ideas, and capabilities—and conducting honest self-assessment.

"Introspection allows us to look deep within and analyze our motives and priorities, and to measure our progress toward goals. Most important, introspection allows us to get an accurate measure of purpose, passion, and commitment to dreams and goals. To truly know oneself can be daunting, but it's essential in order to experience one's personal success."

Our self-understanding needs to be 100 percent accurate. We need an accurate read on our weak areas so we can direct our efforts to focused self-improvement and maintaining an upward success trajectory.

Values Behavior: HC Component 2 Values do not have to be compromised to get ahead. Good values and behavior that matches those values are paramount to maintaining a positive trajectory over a long period of time. Compromising values may get someone ahead in the short run but will always bring him or her down in the long run.

"I do not believe for a second that you can be a bad person—a dishonest or cruel person—and have true success. . . . I firmly believe that honesty and integrity are the foundation for any type of success—honesty with others and, more important, honesty with oneself."

Work Character: HC Component 3 In being business savvy there is no substitute for hard work. "If you buy into the theory that success is about reaching your personal potential, about achieving stretch goals and doing it 'right,' there must be hard work."

Purpose and Passion: HC Component 4 If hard work is critical, then we need to find a way to really enjoy our work, so that it's no longer work but rather something we're passionate about. The trick is to view work as a means to far greater benefits or enjoyment.

"I never forgot how badly we needed insurance after my father died suddenly, and how burdensome it was to be left with so much unexpected debt. What a noble cause it was, I thought, to help families protect themselves if the breadwinner were to die prematurely, to have an income should a disability occur, or to help someone plan for a secure retirement. Was selling life insurance boring? No way. I had a strong and exciting purpose."

Purpose can keep you going in the face of any challenge.

Thirst for Knowledge: HC Component 5 The power of knowledge and lifetime learning is transformative.

"While it took me almost 20 years to catch up, my grades in college eventually became good enough to get an academic scholarship to supplement my athletic scholarship. I even managed to get into graduate school and earn an MBA while loading trucks at night. But, I learned the power of knowledge and how to acquire it. . . . Lifetime learning and an ongoing curiosity have been absolutely essential to my success."

The Power of "And Then Some"

Those who choose to make adversity their friend don't enjoy hardships any more than the next person. But there is a world of difference between those who befriend adversity by overcoming it and learning from the experience and those who give up at the first sign of an obstacle.

Adversity is going to happen, and usually in ways you never could have foreseen. Knowing this, make a choice right now to look at adversity in a new light. Realize that adversity is an ally and that it's here to teach you something of crucial importance.

The Key to Befriending Adversity

You are the agent of change. In other words, the power to act, to positively change your own circumstances, lies with you. No matter how difficult the circumstances, relying on and harnessing the power of "and then some" ensures that you're never helpless in the face of adversity. Because "and then some" is a universal principle, you can apply it to any manner of adversity you encounter.

Have you been laid off? Start with the goal of targeting five companies a day, and then find five more, and don't rest until you follow through by contacting the person in charge of hiring or by sending your résumé. Are you weak in a particular area, such as public speaking, making cold calls, team leadership, or even using a software program? Do whatever it takes to gain not just competency but proficiency in whatever area is holding you back from reaching your potential.

If you're truly meeting your goals and then surpassing them, the amazing results you'll achieve will be an extremely powerful motivational force. Success breeds success. If you habitually use the power of "and then some" to build your human capital, you'll find that the positive results will surpass all your expectations.

And if you're lucky enough not to have experienced full-scale adversity, you can start by applying the power of "and then some" to all the setbacks, obstacles, and even daily nuisances that will always arise in business.

To apply the basic principle of "and then some" to everything you do, put in the extra effort above and beyond others at work, and then expand the principle into a full cycle of self-improvement.

Positive thinking is integral to befriending adversity and harnessing the power of "and then some." Face adversity with a relentlessly positive frame of mind, even if at first it feels artificial or unnatural. Allow no other thought to enter your mind than "I will face this adversity head-on and I will learn from it." You can either wallow in self-pity and pessimism or treat adversity as the clarion call to institute needed change.

THE POWER RESIDES IN ALL OF US

*O*ut of high school, Gene Postma gave community college a shot before being lured away by the attractive hourly wages of a construction job. The job became a career and, after ten years, Gene found himself running a crew and remodeling a building in New York City. The remodel included removing several layers of shingles on a steeply pitched roof. Gene was exasperated with his crew's slow progress and uneasiness on the roof, so he decided to demonstrate that there was nothing to worry about.

Starting at the roof's peak, Gene started ripping and tearing, when, all of a sudden, one of his toeholds broke loose, sending him sliding down the steep slope and off the edge into a twenty-five-foot fall. On the way down he shattered his arm on a balcony, and when he landed he incurred compression fractures in his back. The doctors told him he would never be able to swing a hammer or run a trowel again. He was married with a two-year-old son and was unable to continue with his career.

Gene accepted the unexpected turn in his life, went back to school, and put in extra effort with the books, and he and his wife both worked throughout his education. He graduated second in his class in less than four years with an engineering degree. He is now president of Western States Fire Protection Company, which has 1,500 employees and more than two hundred million dollars in annual sales. Like so many, Gene had the power of "and then some" before his fall, but adversity put it to work to grow his human capital well beyond that which he'd originally thought himself capable of.

Just Add Introspection

Most businesses absolutely stink at assisting employee development through formal appraisal processes. It's a major missed opportunity.

Business leaders and managers do have good intentions when implementing appraisal processes. They aim to facilitate honest self-assessment so as to maximize employee potential, but more often than not, their execution thwarts the intent of growing the human capital within their organizations.

Many appraisals are based upon subjective one-to-five rating systems for performance issues like quality of work, cooperation and relationships, and problem analysis. They call for one person's subjective opinion, and if your performance issue doesn't show up on the form, tough luck.

Then there are the not-so-unusual cases where a change in supervisors produces a large change in a person's appraisal score—no change in performance, just a change in who's doing the appraising.

There is no substitute for real introspection, for an honest and critical examination of one's own thoughts, feelings, and motivations and, by extension, one's strengths and weaknesses. Introspection provides an accurate personal appraisal process that enables one to analyze motives and priorities and to measure progress and commitments toward goals. The process of introspection allows one to make constant—and accurate—trajectory adjustments.

Critical to successful introspection is that it is conducted with *frequency* and with *accuracy*. Frequent but inaccurate introspection gets one nowhere and can even be self-destructive. Accurate but infrequent introspection just places a person on a low trajectory, as trajectory corrections don't occur often enough.

Satellites and Mirrors

When we were young, we were surrounded by mirrors that told us what we were doing right, what we were doing wrong, and what we could do differently. Parents, teachers, test scores, coaches, counselors, sports successes and failures all gave us rapid feedback. We could get a pretty accurate read on who we were and in what areas we might be able to excel.

As we age, many of our mirrors disappear; some are replaced, but the average person is left with far fewer means to obtain accurate and frequent reflections. Just as the key to the Global Positioning System (GPS) is having multiple satellites and accurate signals at all times, the key to good introspection is having multiple mirrors and accurate reflections at all times. In both cases, one needs to be able to triangulate.

Harvey Mackay, a successful business owner, may demonstrate the value of multiple mirrors best. To this day he relies on eighteen "coaches" (for various disciplines)—from marathon, writing, and language and speech coaches to a humor coach. He learned the value of multiple mirrors early, when he bought his struggling company when he was twenty-six. Back then he called each of his mirrors "old grizzly," as his lawyer was sixty, his accountant fifty-eight, and his banker over seventy. His was a professional team, but mirrors need not cost money.

"There are a lot of qualified advisers out there," Mackay says, "who are just waiting for us to ask them. Try it sometime." His success has little to do with luck and everything to do with the science of setting up mirrors (satellites) and conducting accurate and frequent introspection (triangulation).

The Mackay approach stands in stark contrast to many in business today. Take the competent businessperson who relies solely on his or her boss as his or her performance and trajectory gauge. Just as a GPS receiver cannot provide an accurate fix on location with a single satellite, neither can the businessperson conduct accurate introspection with only one mirror.

Mentors of all types are extremely important for increasing both the accuracy and frequency of your introspection. The term "mentor" can apply to any person who is offering you feedback for forward thinking and positive adjustments. The more mentors, the better the triangulation and, more often than not, mentoring is free for the asking.

What Does Behavior Have to Do with Values? Everything!

Business savvy isn't just about superior business skills or proficiency in a particular area of business. It's also about having the right values and bringing those values to bear on the way one does business.

Creating and fostering a culture of integrity and ethical behavior is not only the right thing to do; it's critical to business success. The culture of integrity and ethical behavior must start at the top. Leaders need to set and live out the example for their organizations, and it's all too obvious how one corrupt manager can bring an entire company down.

At the end of the day, the most effective tool anyone has is his or her own behavior, and behavior is always ultimately predicated upon an individual choice.

Kohlbergian Theory

Lawrence Kohlberg was a psychologist and professor at the University of Chicago and Harvard University. His research holds that moral reasoning, which is the basis for ethical behavior, has six identifiable stages.

Stage 1 is simply the rules and punishment trade-off. Thinkers using stage 1 moral reasoning believe that there is an external and fixed set of rules and that there is only one right or wrong answer to every moral dilemma.

In stage 2, individuals lock into a "What's in it for me?" perspective. All behavior comes from serving their own needs.

Those in stage 3 base moral choices on the expectations of others in their proximity, such as family, friends, peers, and the community. Likewise, in business an employee bases his or her behavior upon the expectations of superiors, coworkers, and subordinates.

Stage 4, however, brings us into all-new territory. Individuals at this stage have expanded their circle of thinking enough to see the society or the business they are in as a whole. The emphasis is on obeying laws or rules, respecting authority, and handling their duties so that the social order or business rules and processes are maintained.

Stage 5 thinkers want to do what is best for society or for all parties that touch the business. It is crucial for those in a leadership role to reach this level. At stage 5 one must not only be driven by principle but also understand and balance the interests of everyone.

Few people reach the level of stage 6 moral reasoning, but those with prodigious business savvy always strive for it. This is the stage of universal human ethics. Behavior is predicated upon actions and decisions that demonstrate an equal respect for all.

For the long-term growth and health of any business, it is crucial to hire ethically sound people and to foster an environment in which employees can develop morally and only the ethically sound are rewarded.

So how does one climb the hierarchy of moral development, advancing from one stage to the next? One advances in moral reasoning by actually encountering a moral dilemma, finding that one's current level of moral reasoning is inadequate, and then grappling with the dilemma to the point that one comes to a more comprehensive viewpoint. The more comprehensive our viewpoint, the more robust our moral development and the further we advance up the hierarchy of moral development.

The Gray Zone

The truth is that the business world is full of moral dilemmas, and even with sound moral reasoning, matters will arise that fall into the so-called Gray Zone, a space rife with adversity. The Gray Zone encompasses not only those dilemmas that do not have a definitive right answer but also those in which almost all decisions come at the detriment of someone or something else. There's no end to the number of Gray Zone issues businesspeople will face, especially those in leadership positions. Gray Zone dilemmas are rarely published, as they're often troubling or embarrassing, but companies routinely face them.

WHAT WOULD YOU DO IN THE GRAY ZONE?

In one case a leading sales representative got caught falsifying hotel receipts. Imagine that you are his boss. Your recourse is simple, right? You just fire him. Problem is, he is a top producer, and firing him will hurt the bottom line and the stockholders. He is also well liked, so if he goes, you run the risk of losing some key customers. What's more, he's a friend, a company veteran who's been through thick and thin with you. If you fire him, what are you saying to other employees? That you had an unwritten "one strike and you're out" policy? That you don't value years of loyal and trusted service? But if you don't fire him, are you tacitly telling employees that it's okay to cheat? Now take it a step further: It turns out the employee was falsifying the receipts not for the money but to hide an affair he was having in another city. His behavior, while clearly unethical, hasn't cost the company a dime. So is business now to be concerned with and penalize a person for his conduct outside of work? What would you do in the face of this kind of adversity? How do you find your way through the Gray Zone and arrive at the right decision? In this case, the employee was fired, and the outcome was quite costly; some sales were lost, as were some customers. But in the long run making the extremely difficult decision to fire the employee preserved the company's ethical standards, and it showed employees that management would abide by its principles. The long-term gain exceeded the short-term pain, and again we see the adversity paradox in action.

Sorry, but There's No Substitute for Hard Work

People with a fully developed work character are qualitatively different from their peers: Their excellent work habits and the success they earn distinguish them from the pack. The idea of "work character" as used here is rooted in this distinguishing quality and encompasses a person's attitude and ability. People with an outstanding work character habitually work hard, think hard, and lead well—and because they're pursuing what they love, they enjoy their work.

Physical Work Ethic

People with a well-developed physical work ethic have the ability and the willingness to put in the requisite hours and effort to do a job to their fullest potential.

The fact is, any of you who are trying to move up the corporate ladder will be required to put in whatever extra hours and effort are necessary in order to distinguish yourself from the pack. If you're not physically up to the task or if you're operating at half speed, you're going to be at a significant disadvantage from the beginning.

Those in leadership roles may have even more of a responsibility to develop a strong physical work ethic. Good leaders know that their team members will emulate them; it's their job to set the standard for productivity.

Cognitive Work Ethic

A cognitive work ethic is engagement of the mind to learn, solve problems, find opportunities, develop solutions, or successfully execute the tasks a job requires.

The need for a fully developed cognitive work ethic for any type of success is growing more pronounced every day.

Over time, unemployment in America has remained relatively unchanged, but many in the workforce have been required to move from employing their physical work ethic to employing their cognitive work ethic to earn a living.

In today's business world, a robust cognitive work ethic is required simply to stay in the game, let alone excel.

Skills to Lead

Even with the most highly developed physical and cognitive work ethics, one person can only do so much on his or her own. "Skills to lead," the third part of work character, brings us into more specialized territory. It can uniquely combine any number of skills. It can involve things like public speaking, communication, team selection, team building, motivating others, delegation, and vision.

"Skills to lead" is an adaptable concept. That is, one's skills to lead will depend on the people one is leading, the business one is in, and the corporate culture.

Working Not Just Harder but Better

We can have the best of intentions, but if we have no idea how to start or follow through on them, we're stuck at square one. So here are three proven processes that have worked to promote positive change:

1. Motivation/Visualization If you ask most people what gets them out of bed and to the office every morning, they'll have a quick answer: the paycheck. More dollars might bring you a bit more spending power, a few new things, but those are temporary highs. More money isn't likely to be a permanent motivating factor.

A recent Gallup study found that recognition of one's efforts has the largest impact on worker engagement and performance. Other huge motivating factors include a sense of self-worth, a feeling of accomplishment, the satisfaction of taking part in meaningful work, the sense of being a part of a vibrant and accomplished team, and pursuing a more challenging role with greater responsibility.

Maybe your biggest motivating factor is getting out of one job and into another that provides the kind of long-lasting, intangible rewards that have been listed.

What you need is something powerful enough, something meaningful enough, that it gets you working and thinking at such a level that you won't rest until you attain your goal.

The most powerful motivating factor of all arrives when you've found a purpose you can pursue with passion and bring to fruition through your career.

2. Adding "And Then Some" to Everything You Do Apply the power of "and then some" to literally everything you do, and you're guaranteed to get positive results. Set your goals higher than what is expected of you and find ways to achieve them.

If you're completing your tasks *and then some*, if you're putting in the extra effort required to distinguish yourself from your peers, there's no way you can't advance. The trick is to make "and then some" a lifelong habit.

The difference between employing *"enough to get by"* and *"and then some"* may be hardly visible within a given task or in a day's work, but over a lifetime it can be the largest separator between a life of mediocrity and a life of success.

3. Successful Habits The third way you can make positive change is about making hard work not just a short-term means to reach a short-term goal but a lifetime modus operandi.

Whereas forming habits that make you successful may seem like drudgery, once they become habits they are no longer a grind, especially when you start enjoying the rewards of the success you have created with them.

Purpose and Passion: You Really Can Take the Work Out of Work

Recognizing the importance of the connection between purpose and passion, businesses try to foster corporate statements that help develop and engage employee passion. The business leaders who get their mission statements right are the ones who know how to align purpose and passion.

Wal-Mart's mission is "to give ordinary folk the chance to buy the same thing as rich people." Did this mission statement work? Did it foster and cultivate employee passion? The answer is in the results. So many "ordinary folk" purchased Wal-Mart's goods that it's become one of the most profitable businesses in America.

The true measure of a stated business purpose is its ability to get employees excited and engaged. True purpose, no matter where it is found or how modest it may seem from the outside, is immeasurably powerful. Having the right purpose, the specific purpose that works for you and your business, is central to creating passion that impacts results.

Passion is the enthusiasm you feel as a result of your purpose. Your purpose generates your passion. Finding passion in your work doesn't mean everything is perfect, but it means you have the ability and vision to see beyond the imperfections.

Clay Jones: Take Serendipity and Run with It

Clay Jones is the president and CEO of Rockwell Collins, a company engaged in the design, production, and support of communication and aviation electronics worldwide. When asked how he got from zero interest in flying to having a career in aviation and being a leader of one of the most recognized aerospace companies in the world, he said "serendipity."

He didn't mean simple luck. Rather, the Jones application of serendipity is about encountering the numerous forks in the road of life—most of which are entirely unforeseen and many of which come about through no conscious choice of our own—and then making a conscious choice to pursue a direction with vigor and perseverance.

"You find yourself in certain positions in life where you have to make a decision," Jones said, "and the fact is, each of these decisions has a profound effect on your future direction in life, which is something most of us underappreciate at the time. . . . Each of those decisions builds upon a new direction. . . . And that," concludes Jones, "is how I eventually found my purpose."

The Transformative Power of a Lifelong Thirst for Knowledge

What is the value of knowledge and education for the business-savvy professional? Business-savvy professionals absolutely thrive on the thirst for knowledge.

Knowledge enables you to:

- formulate a vision and execute it successfully;
- think on your feet and act quickly and judiciously when problems or opportunities arise;
- switch back and forth from systems to linear thinking, from seeing the big picture to scrutinizing the details;
- synthesize mountains of data into salient, useful information;
- inspire your team's confidence in your leadership;
- select, train, and inspire business-savvy teams;
- see your lack of knowledge.

This fifth and final component of human capital alone has worked wonders in people's success trajectories; added to the full business-savvy framework, it's guaranteed to transform not only your career but your life.

Formal and Informal Learning

We're all familiar with formal learning: It's the learning that takes place within a structured teacher-student relationship. Informal learning, then, encompasses the balance of our learning. Much of informal learning results from what we do and experience in daily life.

What is surprising, and terribly sad, is the statistics about formal learning for the country at large. The U.S. Census Bureau reveals that one in three Americans drops out of college and, according to the latest government figures, more than 50 percent of college freshmen do not receive a degree within six years.

Over a lifetime, most people spend far more time on and gain far more knowledge from informal learning. But while informal learning is clearly critical to success, without the skills the formal learning environment provides, the informal learner has little chance of accumulating the quantity and quality of knowledge needed to gain business savvy and be successful.

So let's review the benefits of a formal education. We've got job qualifications, increased confidence, a way out of humble beginnings, a way out of a stalled career or life situation, and a statistically better chance of greater earning power. The most important advantage—no matter what discipline the business-savvy professional studies—is learning how to learn. If your formal education has taught you how to learn, your path to success will be all the smoother.

Your success is significantly impacted by the foundation of knowledge you have or will possess. If you haven't already found a thirst for knowledge, it's not too late. Enroll in a class, subscribe to a new journal, read as much as possible, and keenly observe successful people and emulate them. You never know when something will ignite your thirst for knowledge.

Using the Adversity Paradox to Triumph over Unexpected Trajectory Changes

Even though the business savvy are recognized for their ability to see around corners, no one can predict the future with 100 percent certainty. The good news is that most adversities or career catastrophes leave a person's human capital substantially intact. Trajectories may be shaken by the unpredictable, but they can be reestablished—sometimes with far superior results.

Practicing the Paradox

So often, the most powerful catalyst for change lies in the place we'd least expect or want to find it, in adverse circumstances. Failure has a way of making us take stock of our careers and our lives—our progress toward dreams and goals, our strengths and weaknesses, our motivation and our daily work habits—in a way that success does not. It can also force us to take quick, decisive action without benefit of the usual safety nets, which can often reveal inner resources and abilities we wouldn't have otherwise known we possessed. At the very least, overcoming difficult circumstances always causes growth and the development of your human capital.

THE 360-DEGREE LEADER

by John C. Maxwell

There are people in every organization who spend the length of their careers staring upward. It's an unfortunate perception that success is possible only at the very top of an organization. This myth is at its strongest when it applies to leadership. There is nothing wrong with striving for career advancement, but the perception that one cannot create success and impact the lives of others while stationed on other rungs of the ladder is untrue. In *The 360 Degree Leader*, author John C. Maxwell strips away the layers of myth that surround successful leadership and proves that great leaders operate at every level of a company.

If the average company's employee base holds the structure of a pyramid, the chances are good that readers will fall somewhere in the wide middle area rather than the tiny peak. Maxwell views this location as the perfect place to increase one's influence. A person in this position has the unique opportunity to "lead up" to his or her managers, "lead across" to his or her peers, and "lead down" to his or her direct reports. This distinction separates *The 360 Degree Leader* from other books on leadership success. The constant push to the top can take away from the job done along the way. Maxwell has led in every direction during his career as an author, consultant, and business founder.

One of Maxwell's strengths as an author is his ability to anticipate and answer the objections that may be made to his teachings. In *The 360 Degree Leader*, Maxwell lists the challenges faced by a leader in the middle of an organization, one of which is the challenge of ego. He understands that the belly of a business is a space in which a person's achievements can get lost. This can damage the confidence of a person seeking success. It can also lead that leader to shortchange his or her current duties in an effort to escape to higher corporate plateaus. Maxwell answers this by reminding readers to take comfort in the support of the team that surrounds them. He also tells them to understand the difference between self-promotion and selfless promotion. This last piece of advice is in tune with Maxwell's documented personal spiritual beliefs. While this summary contains no overt religious references, readers will understand that the principles of *The 360 Degree Leader* can be applied outside as well as inside the office.

Maxwell's goal is to help those who look only up the corporate ladder bring their eyes back to earth. There is too much opportunity around them to miss the chance to make a difference now. The steps outlined by Maxwell in *The 360 Degree Leader* are rooted in the present. Success comes from doing, not dreaming. Perhaps his strongest point is that successful leadership in the middle of an organization is the perfect qualification for advancement. What better way to prove that one can lead at a top level of an organization than by creating success in the middle?

THE 360-DEGREE LEADER
Developing Your Influence from Anywhere in the Organization
by John C. Maxwell

CONTENTS
1. The Myths of Leading from the Middle
2. The Challenges 360-Degree Leaders Face
3. The Principles 360-Degree Leaders Practice to Lead Up
4. The Principles 360-Degree Leaders Practice to Lead Across
5. The Principles 360-Degree Leaders Practice to Lead Down
6. The Value of 360-Degree Leaders

THE SUMMARY IN BRIEF

These are classic pictures of leadership: William Wallace leading the charge of his warriors against the army that would oppress his people. Winston Churchill defying the Nazi threat as much of Europe had collapsed. Mahatma Gandhi leading a two-hundred-mile march to the sea to protest the Salt Act. Mary Kay Ash going off on her own to create the world-class organization Mary Kay Cosmetics. Martin Luther King Jr. standing before the Lincoln Memorial and challenging the nation with his dream of reconciliation.

Each of these people was a great leader. Each made an impact that has touched millions of people. Yet these pictures can also be misleading. The reality is that 99 percent of all leadership occurs not from the top but from the middle of an organization. Usually, an organization has only one person who is the leader. So what do you do if you are not that one person?

You can learn to develop your influence from wherever you are in the organization by becoming a 360-degree leader. You can learn to lead up, lead across, and lead down. Only 360-degree leaders influence people at every level of the organization. By helping others, they help themselves.

Becoming a 360-degree leader is within the reach of anyone who possesses average or better leadership skills and is willing to work at it. You don't have to be the main leader to have a significant impact in your organization. Good leaders are not only capable of leading their followers but also adept at leading their superiors and their peers.

In addition, you will learn the following:

How to overcome the myths believed by many people in the middle of an organization

How to deal with the most common challenges faced by people in the middle of an organization

How to lead your boss, your colleagues, and your followers

How to overcome the setbacks and obstacles you will face on the road to becoming a 360-degree leader

How to quantify the value of 360-degree leadership

THE COMPLETE SUMMARY

The Myths of Leading from the Middle

The Position Myth

The number one misconception people have about leaders is that leadership comes simply from having a position or title. Nothing could be further from the truth. You don't need to possess a position at the top of your group, department, division, or organization in order to lead. If you think you do, then you have bought into the position myth.

The true measure of leadership is influence—nothing more, nothing less. Leadership is dynamic, and the right to lead must be earned individually with each person you meet. Where you are on the "staircase of leadership" depends on your history with that person.

Position has little to do with genuine leadership. Influencing others is a matter of disposition, not position. Leadership is a choice you make, not a place you sit. Anyone can choose to become a leader wherever he or she is. You can make a difference no matter where you are.

The Destination Myth

Those who believe the destination myth might say, "When I get to the top, then I'll learn to lead."

But if you want to succeed, you need to learn as much as you can about leadership before you have a leadership position. Good leadership is learned in the trenches. If you don't try out your leadership skills and decision-making process when the stakes are small and the risks are low, you're likely to get into trouble at higher levels, when the cost of mistakes is high, the impact is far-reaching, and the exposure is greater. Mistakes made on a small scale can be easily overcome. Mistakes made when you're at the top cost the organization greatly and damage your credibility.

Start now to adopt the thinking, learn the skills, and develop the habits of the person you wish to be. Handle today so that it prepares you for tomorrow.

The Influence Myth

Those who believe the influence myth might say, "If I were on top, then people would follow me."

People who have no leadership experience have a tendency to overestimate the importance of a leadership title. You may be able to grant someone a position, but you cannot grant him or her real leadership. Influence must be earned.

A position gives you a chance. It gives you the opportunity to try out your leadership. It asks people to give you the benefit of the doubt for a while. But given some time, you will earn your level of influence—for better or worse. Good leaders will gain influence behind their stated position. Remember, a position doesn't make a leader, but a leader can make a position.

The Inexperience Myth

Although the desire to improve an organization and the belief that you're capable of doing it are often the marks of a leader, without experience being the top person in an organization, you would likely overestimate the amount of control you have at the top. The higher you go and the larger the organization, the more you realize that many factors control the organization. More than ever, when you are at the top, you need every bit of influence you can muster. Your position does not give you total control—or protect you.

The Freedom Myth

Those who believe the freedom myth might say, "When I get to the top, I'll no longer be limited."

But when you move up in an organization, the weight of your responsibility increases. In many organizations, as you move up the ladder, you may even find that the amount of responsibility you take on increases faster than the amount of authority you receive. When you go higher, more is expected of you, the pressure is greater, and the impact of your decisions weighs more heavily. Leaders have more obligations and, because of that, they become more limited in terms of their freedom. It is a limitation they choose willingly, but they are limited just the same.

The Potential Myth

Someone who believes the potential myth would say, "I can't reach my potential if I'm not the top leader."

People should strive for the top of their game, not the top of the organization. Each of us should work to reach our potential, not necessarily the corner office. Sometimes you can make the greatest impact from somewhere other than first place.

The All-or-Nothing Myth

Someone who believes the all-or-nothing myth might say, "If I can't get to the top, then I won't try to lead."

Some people in the middle become frustrated by their position in an organization because they define success as being on top. As a result, they believe that if they are not on top, they are not successful. If that frustration lasts long enough, they can become disillusioned, bitter, and cynical. If it gets to that point, instead of being a help to themselves and their organization, they become a hindrance.

Improve your leadership and you can impact your organization. You can change people's lives. You can be someone who adds value. You can learn to influence people at every level of the organization—even if you never get to the top. By helping others, you can help yourself.

The Challenges 360-Degree Leaders Face

The Tension Challenge

This challenge comes from the pressure of being caught in the middle. It's not enough to merely recognize that leading from somewhere in the middle of an organization can be stressful. You need to learn how to relieve the tension. Here are five suggestions:

- Become comfortable with the middle. Being in the middle can be a great place—as long as you have bought into the vision and believe in the leader.
- Know what to own and what to let go. Nothing frees a person from tension like clear lines of responsibility.
- Find quick access to answers when caught in the middle.
- Never violate your position or the trust of the leader.
- Find a way to relieve stress.

The Frustration Challenge

This challenge results from following an ineffective leader.

Your job isn't to fix the leader; it's to add value. The only time that is not true is when the leader above you is unethical or criminal. If the leader won't change, then change your attitude or your work address.

When you find yourself following a leader who is ineffective, do the following:

- Develop a solid relationship with your leader, find common ground, and build a solid professional relationship.
- Identify and appreciate your leader's strengths. Find them and think about how they might be assets to the organization.
- Commit yourself to adding value to your leader's strengths.

The Multihat Challenge

Leaders in the middle must perform tasks and have knowledge beyond their personal experience. And they often are forced to deal with multiple shifting priorities, often with limited time and resources.

Every role or "hat" you are asked to wear has its own responsibilities and objectives. If you change hats, keep in mind that the context changes. The goal often determines the role and the approach to take. Don't use one hat to accomplish a task required for another hat. When you change hats, don't change your personality. And don't neglect any hat you are responsible to wear.

The Ego Challenge

It's normal for any person to want recognition, and leaders are the same. The fact that leaders in the middle of the pack are often hidden—and as a result don't get the credit or recognition they desire and often deserve—can be a real ego buster. The challenge is to be a team player and remain content while contributing.

Here's how to do that:

- Concentrate more on your duties than on your dreams.
- Appreciate the value of your position.
- Find satisfaction in knowing the real reason for the success of a project.
- Embrace the compliments of others in the middle of the pack.
- Understand the difference between self-promotion and selfless promotion.

The Fulfillment Challenge

The right attitude is absolutely essential to contentment in the middle of an organization. Truly, leadership is more disposition than position. With the right attitude and the right skills, you can influence others from wherever you are in an organization. Here are five ways to develop an attitude of contentment and fulfillment right where you are:

- Develop strong relationships with key people.
- Define a win in terms of the team.
- Engage in crucial communication.
- Gain experience and maturity.
- Put the team above your personal success. Leadership is about helping others win.

The Vision Challenge

Championing the vision is more difficult when you did not create it. The key to successfully navigating the vision challenge is this: The more you invest in the vision, the more it becomes your own. Even though your own vision may excite you more than someone else's, to get the opportunity to pursue your own dreams, you will almost certainly have to succeed in achieving the dreams of others.

The Influence Challenge

Leading others beyond your position is not easy.

Leadership is influence. If you have neither position nor influence, people will not follow you. And the further outside your position they are, the less likely they are to let you lead them. That's why 360-degree leaders work to change their thinking from "I want a position that will make people follow me" to "I want to become a person whom people will want to follow."

People follow leaders they know, leaders who care. If leaders care about each individual as a person, then people respond well to them. The greater the depth of their concern, the broader and longer lasting their influence.

The Principles 360-Degree Leaders Practice to Lead Up

Leading up is the 360-degree leader's greatest challenge. Most leaders want to lead, not be led. But most leaders also want to have value added to them. If you take the approach of wanting to add value to those above you, you have the best chance of influencing them.

Your underlying strategy should be to support your leader, add value to the organization, and distinguish yourself from the rest of the pack by doing your work with excellence. If you do these things consistently, then in time the leader above you may learn to trust you, rely on you, and look to you for advice. With each step, your influence will increase and you will have more and more opportunities to lead up.

Lead Yourself Exceptionally Well

Nothing will make a better impression on your leader than your ability to manage yourself. If your leader must continually expend energy managing you, then you will be perceived as someone who drains time and energy. If you manage yourself well, however, your boss will see you as someone who maximizes opportunities and leverages personal strengths. To become someone your leader turns to when the heat is on, manage your emotions, time, priorities, energy, thinking, words, and personal life.

Lighten Your Leader's Load

If you help lift the load, then you help your leader succeed. When the boss succeeds, the organization succeeds. Lifting shows you are a team player. It shows gratitude for being on the team and makes you part of something bigger. It also gets you noticed and increases your value and influence.

How do you lift your leader's load? Do your own job well first. When you find a problem, provide a solution. Tell leaders what they need to hear, not what they want to hear. Go the second mile and do more than is asked. Also, stand up or stand in for your leader whenever you can.

Be Willing to Do What Others Won't

Successful people do the things that unsuccessful people are unwilling to do. Few things gain the appreciation of a top leader more quickly than an employee with a whatever-it-takes attitude. That means taking the tough jobs. You learn resiliency and tenacity during tough assignments, not easy ones. When tough choices have to be made and results are difficult to achieve, leaders are forged. That means that you will have to sacrifice some personal goals for the sake of others. You will have to do something because it matters, not because it will get you noticed. Good leaders also find a way to succeed with people who are hard to work with by finding common ground and connecting with them.

Do More Than Manage—Lead!

To move beyond management to leadership, you need to broaden your mind-set and begin thinking like a leader. If you are already leading well, then use this as a checklist to see where you need to keep growing:

- Think longer term.
- See the larger context of how something will impact those above and beside you.
- Push boundaries to find a better way.

- Emphasize intangibles such as morale, motivation, momentum, emotions, attitudes, atmosphere, and timing.
- Rely on intuition. As Dr. Joyce Brothers says, "Trust your hunches. They're usually based on facts filed away just below the conscious level."
- Look for good people and invest in them to the point where they can be released and empowered to perform.
- Be an agent of change. Leaders want more than just to see progress—they want to make it happen.

Invest in Relational Chemistry

All good leadership is based on relationships. People won't go along with you if they can't get along with you. That's true whether you are leading up, across, or down.

The key to developing chemistry with our leaders is to develop relationships with them by listening to their heartbeat to understand what makes them tick, knowing their priorities, catching their enthusiasm, supporting their vision, connecting with their interests, conforming to their personality, earning their trust, learning to work with their weaknesses, and respecting their family.

Be Prepared Every Time You Take Your Leader's Time

For all leaders, time is precious. For that reason, you must always be prepared when you take any of your leader's time.

Whether you have unlimited access to your boss or get only a few minutes on rare occasions, you need to think and plan ahead. Don't make your boss think for you, and bring something to the table.

Know When to Push and When to Back Off

Successful leaders make the right move at the right moment with the right motive. Timing is critically important to leadership. When it comes to gaining influence with your boss, timing is equally important.

It's wise to wait for the right moment to speak up. A great idea at the wrong time will be received just the same as a bad idea. Of course, there are times when you must speak up, even if the timing doesn't seem ideal. The trick is knowing which is which.

Become a Go-to Player

Few things elevate a person above his or her peers the way becoming a go-to player does. Everyone admires go-to players and looks to them when the heat is on—not only their leaders but also their followers and peers. Go-to players produce when the pressure is on. They are the people who find a way to make things happen no matter what.

If you adopt the positive tenacity of a go-to player and take every opportunity to make things happen, your leader will come to rely on you. If you have the willingness and the capacity to lift the load of your leaders when they need it, you will have influence with them.

Be Better Tomorrow Than You Are Today

Often, when people get to their desired destination, they stop striving to grow or improve.

There's certainly nothing wrong with the desire to progress in your career, but never try to "arrive." Instead, intend your journey to be open-ended. Most people have no idea how far they can go in life. They aim way too low. The key to personal development is being more growth oriented than goal oriented. There is no downside to making growth your goal. If you keep learning, you will be better tomorrow than you are today, and that can do many things for you.

The Principles 360-Degree Leaders Practice to Lead Across

To succeed as a 360-degree leader who leads peer to peer, you have to work at giving your colleagues reasons to respect and follow you. You can do that by helping your peers win. If you can help them win, you will help not only the organization but also yourself.

Understand, Practice, and Complete the Leadership Loop

If you want to gain influence and credibility with people working alongside you, don't try to take shortcuts or cheat the process. Instead, show people that you care about them by taking an interest in them. Make an effort to get to know them as individuals. You should also strive to see others' unique experiences and skills as resources and try to learn from them.

When you go out of your way to add value to your peers, they understand that you really want them to win with no hidden agenda of your own. Affirm them by praising their strengths and acknowledging their accomplishments.

Put Completing Fellow Leaders Ahead of Competing with Them

In healthy working environments, there is both competition and teamwork. The issue is to know when each is appropriate. When it comes to your teammates, you want to compete in such a way that instead of competing with them you are completing them.

Winning at all costs will cost you when it comes to your peers. If your goal is to beat your peers, then you will never be able to lead across with them. How do you balance competing and completing? First, acknowledge your natural desire to compete and channel it in a positive way. Embrace healthy competition. The whole goal of healthy competition is to leverage it for the corporate win.

Be a Friend

We often consider ourselves to be many things to the people who work along-side us—coworkers, teammates, contributors, competitors—but we often forget to be the one thing that every person wants: a friend. Poet Ralph Waldo Emerson wrote, "The glory of friendship is not in the outstretched hand, nor the kindly smile, nor the joy of companionship; it is in the spiritual inspiration that comes to one when he discovers that someone else believes in him and is willing to trust him."

A great approach to friendship at work is to make it your goal to be a friend, not to find a friend. As you reach out to your coworkers, listen, find common ground not related to work, be available beyond business hours, have a sense of humor, and tell the truth when others don't.

Avoid Office Politics

Playing politics is changing who you are or what you normally do to gain an advantage with whoever currently has power. In work environments, this may mean sucking up to the boss, constantly changing positions to get on the winning side, or using people for personal gain without regard for how it affects them. Political people are fickle and opportunistic, doing what's expedient in the moment to win, regardless of what's best for their peers, their employees, or the organization.

In the long run, integrity, consistency, and productivity always pay off—in better teamwork and a clear conscience. To avoid office politics, avoid gossip; stay away from petty arguments; stand up for what's right, not for what's popular; look at all sides of the issue; don't protect your turf; and say what you mean and mean what you say.

Expand Your Circle of Acquaintances

If you want to expand your influence, you have to expand your circle of acquaintances.

Expanding your circle of acquaintances helps you improve, exposes you to new ideas, and prompts you to see things from a different point of view, which will help you generate new ideas of your own. It will help you to learn new working methods and pick up additional skills. And it will help you to become more innovative. Expanding your circle also expands your network, putting you into contact with more people and giving you potential access to their networks.

Let the Best Idea Win

Leaders in the middle of the organization who help to surface good ideas are creating what an organization needs most. They do that by producing synergy among their peers. And they will develop influence with their peers because when they are present, they make the whole team better.

To generate good ideas, 360-degree leaders listen to all ideas and never settle for just one. They also look in unusual places for ideas. Don't let the personality of someone with whom you work cause you to lose sight of the greater purpose, which is to add value to the team and advance the organization. If that means listening to the ideas of people with whom you have no chemistry, or worse, a difficult history, so be it. A 360-degree leader protects creative people and their ideas.

Don't Pretend You're Perfect

Since nobody is perfect, we need to quit pretending. People who are real, who are genuine concerning their weaknesses as well as their strengths, draw others to them. They engender trust. They are approachable. And they are a breath of fresh air in an environment where others are scrambling to reach the top by trying to look good. To "get real," admit your faults, ask for advice, worry less about what others think, be open to learning from others, and put away pride and pretense.

The Principles 360-Degree Leaders Practice to Lead Down

What makes 360-degree leaders unique—and so effective—is that they take the time and effort to earn influence with their followers just as they do with those over whom they have no authority.

As a 360-degree leader, when you lead down, you are doing more than just getting people to do what you want. You are finding out who they are, helping them to discover and reach their potential, showing the way by becoming a model they can follow, helping them become a part of something bigger than they could create on their own, and rewarding them for being contributors on the team.

Walk Slowly Through the Halls

One of the best ways to stay connected to your people and keep track of how they are doing is to approach the task informally as you move among them. To connect with people, travel at their speed. Express that you care and create a healthy balance of personal and professional interest. Professional interest shows that you have the desire to help them. That is something all good leaders share. Personal interest goes deeper—it shows your heart. When you take interest in your people as human beings, you need to be sure not to cross the line. There is a point at which interest becomes inappropriate.

See Everyone as a "Ten"

Three-hundred-sixty-degree leaders get more out of their people because they think more of their people. They respect and value them and, as a result, their people want to follow them. The positive, uplifting attitude that they bring to leadership creates a positive working environment where everyone on the team has a place and purpose, and where everyone shares in the win.

To shine in this area, see people as they can become. Let them borrow your belief in them. Catch them doing something right. Give them the benefit of the doubt. And understand that people usually rise to the leader's expectations.

Begin today to see and lead people as they can be, not as they are, and you will be amazed by how they respond to you. Not only will your relationship with them improve and their productivity increase, but you also will help them rise to their potential.

Develop Each Team Member as a Person

There is much more to good leadership than just getting the job done. Getting the job done makes you a success. Getting the job done through others makes you a leader. But developing people while helping them get the job done at the highest level makes you an exceptional leader.

In order to develop your staff, you need to keep growing yourself. Understand that development is a long-term process. Development is based on the needs of your people: You give them what they need in order to become better people. To do that well, you need to know people's dreams and desires.

Take responsibility for conforming your leadership style to what your people need, not expecting them to adapt to you. As a leader, your first responsibility is to help others define the reality of who they are. Sometimes that means having difficult conversations. The thing you need to remember is that people will work through difficult things if they believe you want to work with them.

Place People in Their Strength Zones

When employees are continually asked to perform in an area of weakness, they become demoralized, they are less productive, and they eventually burn out.

Successful people find their own strength zones. Successful leaders find the strength zones of the people they lead. When you place individuals in their strength zones, you change people's lives for the better, their jobs become rewarding and fulfilling, and you help both the organization and yourself. The ability to help people find the best place means discovering their true strengths, giving them the right job, identifying the skills that they'll need, and providing world-class training.

Model the Behavior You Desire

Leaders set the tone and the pace for all the people working for them. Therefore, leaders need to be what they want to see. Your behavior determines the culture. Your attitude determines the atmosphere. Your values determine the decisions. If your decisions are not consistent with your values, they are always short-lived. Your investment determines the return. Your character determines the trust.

Your work ethic determines the productivity. Your growth determines the potential.

Followers become like their leaders. They are influenced by their leaders' values. They adopt their working methods. They even emulate many of their quirks and habits. That's why we must always be aware of our own conduct before criticizing the people who work for us. If you don't like what your people are doing, first take a look at yourself.

Transfer the Vision

As a leader in the middle of the organization, you will be transferring what is primarily the vision of others. Leaders in the middle may not always be the inventors of the vision; they are almost always its interpreters.

To interpret the vision in a way that fires up people and sets them off in the right direction, include the following elements: clarity; connection of past, present, and future; purpose; goals; a challenge; stories that make the vision relational and warm; and passion. If there is no passion in the picture, then your vision isn't transferable.

Reward for Results

Whatever actions leaders reward will be repeated. That is why it is very important to reward results and to do it the right way. To reward results most effectively, give praise publicly and privately, back up praise with money, don't reward everyone the same, give perks beyond pay, promote when possible, and remember that you get what you pay for.

The Value of 360-Degree Leaders

Becoming a 360-degree leader isn't easy. It takes much work and it doesn't happen overnight. But it is worth every bit of the effort.

As you seek to grow as a leader, you will not always succeed. You will not always be rewarded the way you should be. Your leaders may not listen to you at times. Your peers may ignore you. Your followers won't follow. And the battle may feel like it's uphill all the way.

Don't let that discourage you. By becoming a better leader you add tremendous value to your organization. Everything rises and falls on leadership.

The following are five values that 360-degree leaders add to their organizations.

1. A leadership team is more effective than just one leader. Organizations need to develop leadership teams at every level. A group of leaders working together is always more effective than one leader working alone. And for teams to develop at every level, they need leaders at every level.

As a leader in the middle, if you develop a team, you will be making your organization better and helping it to fulfill its vision. You will be adding value no matter where you serve in the organization. As you do that, keep in mind that visionary leaders are willing to hire people better than themselves, wise leaders shape their people into a team, secure leaders focus on others and want them to do well, experienced leaders listen to their teams, and productive leaders understand that one is too small a number to achieve greatness.

2. Leaders are needed at every level of the organization. If a team starts out with a vision but without a leader, it is in trouble. Why? Because vision leaks. And without a leader, the vision will dissipate and the team will drift until it has no sense of direction. On the other hand, if a team starts out with a leader but without a vision, it will do fine because it will eventually have a vision. Leaders are always headed somewhere. They have vision, and that vision not only gives them direction but also gives their people direction.

Without a leader, decisions are delayed, agendas are multiplied, conflicts are extended, and morale is low. Without a leader, production is low and success is difficult.

3. Leading successfully at one level is a qualification for leading at the next level. Growing organizations are always looking for good people to step up to the next level and lead. To find out if a person is qualified to make the jump, they look at that person's track record in his or her current position. Leadership is a journey that starts where you are, not where you want to be. Great responsibilities come only after handling small ones well.

4. Good leaders in the middle make better leaders at the top. Good leaders maximize the performance of those on their team. They set direction. They inspire their people and help them work together. They get results.

Good leaders bring out the best not only in their followers but also in other leaders. Good leaders raise the bar when it comes to performance and teamwork, and this often challenges other leaders in the organization to improve.

Leaders in the middle of an organization are closer to the people in the trenches than are the leaders on top. As a result, they know more about what's going on. They understand the people who are doing the work and the issues they face. They also have greater influence at those lower levels than the top leaders do.

Today's workers are tomorrow's leaders in the middle of the organization. And today's leaders in the middle will be tomorrow's leaders at the top. While you function as a 360-degree leader in the middle of the organization, if you keep growing you will probably get your opportunity to become a top leader. But at the same time, you need to be looking at the people working for you and thinking about how you can prepare them to eventually take your place in the middle.

5. 360-degree leaders possess qualities every organization needs. The 360-degree leader possesses qualities that every organization wants to see in all of its employees, especially in its leaders. These include the following:

- Adaptability: quickly adjusting to change
- Discernment: understanding the real issues
- Perspective: seeing beyond your own vantage point
- Communication: linking to all levels of the organization
- Security: finding identity in self, not the position
- Servanthood: doing whatever it takes
- Resourcefulness: finding creative ways to make things happen
- Maturity: putting the team before yourself
- Endurance: remaining consistent in character and competence over the long haul
- Countability: being able to be counted on when it counts

HOW THE BEST LEADERS LEAD

by Brian Tracy

All successful leaders have role models, but what separates the best leaders is their ability to be a shining example to others. As author and business consultant Brian Tracy writes, "Leaders conduct themselves as though everyone is watching, even when no one is watching." Tracy is well aware that over the course of his long career, plenty of eyes have focused their gaze on him. Leadership is a topic to which the author has returned time after time. He views it as the single most critical factor in the success of any business. The position of leadership carries a burden of responsibility. Tracy's advice about being a role model is one of seven responsibilities he examines in his book *How the Best Leaders Lead: Proven Secrets to Getting the Most Out of Yourself and Others.*

As the subtitle indicates, the role of a leader is one that requires the constant refinement of the performance of a team, as well as of the leader himself. Tracy is one of a handful of authors who provide action items for any leader's to-do list rather than page after page of theory and rhetoric. In *How the Best Leaders Lead,* he balances the objectives between personal performance and the strengthening and conditioning of a workforce. It's a quest that begins with the individual. "The better you know and understand yourself," Tracy writes, "the better decisions you will make, the better results you will get." This applies in equal measure to a leader's personal and professional lives. An effective leader cannot attempt to have one personality in the office and another after hours. *How the Best Leaders Lead* helps individuals understand and maintain the balance necessary for effective management.

How the Best Leaders Lead is structured to help readers achieve results. It is full of itemized lists that cover topics from solving problems to communicating with power. Each section develops a particular skill set that leaders must master to achieve long-term success. As noted in this book's chapter on Tracy's book *Goals!,* these skill-building concepts are the result of Tracy's thousands of hours of study of leadership research. Tracy increases the potency of his recommended actions by including wisdom from authors such as Larry Bossidy, Henry Mintzberg, and Daniel Goleman, among others. Though his own works are frequently quoted by other authors, Tracy continues to feature a chorus of experts to lend strength to his own voice.

Part of what makes *How the Best Leaders Lead* an essential read for anyone pursuing success is the book's focus on introspection. At several points in the book, Tracy asks readers to take stock of themselves. This culminates in "The Leader's Questionnaire," a twelve-question examination that helps leaders define the goals of their business and frame a strategy to guide any company. Tracy writes that every leader should be able to answer the dozen questions without pause or debate. This level of confidence is what sets apart the best leaders, a category to which Tracy provides readers a more certain path.

HOW THE BEST LEADERS LEAD
Proven Secrets to Getting the Most Out of Yourself and Others
by Brian Tracy

CONTENTS

THE SUMMARY IN BRIEF

Leadership is the critical factor that determines the success of any business, department, or organization. The ability to select, manage, motivate, and guide employees to achieve results is the true measure of any leader's success.

In *How the Best Leaders Lead*, business expert and renowned author Brian Tracy reveals the strategies used by top executives and business owners everywhere to achieve astounding results in difficult markets against determined competition.

Tracy gives business leaders and managers at every level a series of practical, proven ideas and strategies that they can use immediately. He describes how you can plan for the future while managing the present, how to motivate people in turbulent times, how to communicate and get ideas across to others, and a variety of ways to build, manage, and motivate winning teams. He also tackles the issues involved in hiring and keeping the best people.

Great leaders determine their ideal leadership style for any situation, identify opportunities, and take concrete action. With this summary, anyone can learn how to become a better and more effective leader and get more done faster than they ever dreamed possible.

In addition, you will learn the following:

How you can put twelve military principles to use in your business
How to set clear goals and objectives for yourself and others
How to develop an exciting future vision for your business
How to set priorities and focus on key tasks
How to solve problems faster and make better decisions

THE COMPLETE SUMMARY

Introduction: The Race Is On

We are living in the most challenging times for business and economics that we have experienced in our lifetimes. Only the fit will survive. The race is on, and you are in it. If you are not committed to winning, to conquering against all odds, you will be brushed aside and passed over by people and companies more determined to win than you are.

The Seven Responsibilities of Leadership

There are seven basics that never change—the key responsibilities of leadership in any organization. On a scale of one to ten, your ability in each of these seven areas determines your value to yourself and your contribution. Here they are:

1. Set and achieve business goals. The number one reason for business and executive failure is the inability to achieve the sales, growth, and profitability goals for which the leader is responsible.

2. Innovate and market. As Peter Drucker said, the purpose of a business is to "create and keep a customer." Only through continuous innovation of products, services, processes, and promotional methods can companies create and keep customers.

3. Solve problems and make decisions. The only obstacles that stand between you and the business success you desire are problems, difficulties, hindrances, and barriers. Your ability to go over, under, or around these problems is central to your success.

4. Set priorities and focus on key tasks. Time is your scarcest resource. The way you allocate your time can be the critical determinant of everything you achieve—or fail to achieve.

5. Be a role model to others. Albert Schweitzer once wrote, "You must teach men at the school of example, for they will learn at no other." Leaders conduct themselves as though everyone is watching, even when no one is watching.

6. Persuade, inspire, and motivate others to follow you. Management consultant Tom Peters said that the best leaders don't create followers; they create leaders. You must motivate others to follow your vision, to support and achieve the goals and objectives that you have set, to buy into the mission of the organization as you see it.

7. Perform and get results. In the final analysis, your ability to get the results that are expected of you is the critical factor that determines your success.

The Heart of a Leader

Leadership is the single most important factor in the success or failure of a company or business. Your ability to step forward and lead your enterprise to success in competitive markets is both essential and irreplaceable.

The better you become as a leader, the better you will be in every area of your enterprise.

Leadership Requires Character

Leadership is more about who you are than what you do. Your ability to develop the qualities of effective leadership, the essence of what it takes to be a leader, is more important to your success as an executive than any other factor.

One of the great principles of personal development is "Whatever you dwell upon grows and expands in your experiences and personality."

You become more effective, day by day, when you think and act on the basis of the key qualities of effective leaders throughout the ages. You program these qualities into your personality and behavior by dwelling on them continually. You learn these qualities by practicing them in your daily activities as a person and as a leader in your organization.

The Seven Qualities of Leadership

There have been more than three thousand studies conducted over the years aimed at identifying the qualities of successful leaders. More than fifty qualities have been identified that are important to leadership. But there are seven qualities that seem to stand out as being more important than the others. The good news is that each of these qualities can be learned, and they must be learned by practice and repetition.

1. Vision This is the most important single quality of leadership. Leaders have vision. They can see into the future. They have a clear, exciting idea of where they are going and what they are trying to accomplish.

2. Courage This is the second quality that leaders have in common. Winston Churchill said, "Courage is rightly considered the foremost of the virtues, for upon it, all others depend." Courage means that you are willing to take risks in the achievement of your goals with no assurance of success.

3. Integrity This is the most respected and admired quality of superior people and leaders in every area of activity. The core of integrity is truthfulness. Integrity requires that you always tell the truth, to all people, in every situation. Truthfulness is the foundation of the trust that is necessary for the success of any business.

4. Humility Leaders have the security and self-confidence to recognize the value of others. The best leaders are those who are strong and decisive but also humble.

5. Foresight Leaders have the ability to look into the future and anticipate what might occur. Excellent leaders are good strategic thinkers. They have the ability to look ahead, to anticipate with some accuracy where the industry and the markets are going.

6. Focus The ability to focus personal and corporate energies and resources in the most important areas is essential to leadership. Leaders focus on results, on what must be achieved by themselves, by others, and by the company. Leaders focus on strengths—in themselves and in others.

7. Cooperation The ability to work well with others is essential for effective leadership. Your ability to get everyone working and pulling together is essential to your success.

FOUR WAYS TO CHANGE YOUR LIFE

*T*here are only four ways to change your life: First, you can do more of certain things. Second, you can do less of other things. Third, you can start doing something that you have not done before. Fourth, you can stop doing certain things altogether.

Leaders Know Themselves

The better you know and understand yourself, the better decisions you will make and the better results you will get.

What is the most important and valuable work that you do? The answer is *thinking*. The quality of your thinking determines the quality of your choices and decisions. The quality of your decisions, in turn, determines the quality of your actions. The quality of your actions determines the quality of your results, and the quality of your results determines almost everything that happens to you, especially in business.

Perhaps the most powerful stimulant of good thinking is pointed questions that force you to analyze and decide exactly what you want and what you are going to do to achieve it. Asking yourself serious questions—about your position, abilities, talents, performance, et cetera—will not only help you focus on your goals and aspirations; it will help you to develop greater clarity about who you really are inside and what is truly important to you.

The successful leader is, first and foremost, a successful person. The best leaders establish priorities and goals not only for their professional lives but also for their personal lives. They know, in both their professional and personal lives, what they want, who they are, who and what is important, where they are going and why, and what strengths and weaknesses will help or hinder them as they move forward. The best leaders are complete, balanced, self-aware, healthy individuals who live their professional and personal lives by the same rules.

Who Are You and What Do You Want?

Leaders know themselves. They know who they are and what they want. The more clarity with which you can answer the questions that you ask yourself, the more effective you will be as a leader. You will make better decisions, set clearer priorities, allocate people and money more diligently, and efficiently utilize your personal time and resources to accomplish more things that are more important. You will make fewer mistakes and get more things done with greater effectiveness.

By developing complete clarity about yourself and your situation, you will think and act more efficiently and accomplish greater results in everything you do.

Counterattack! The Business Lessons of Military Strategy

Great generals and military leaders have been studied throughout history to determine which qualities and abilities enabled them to prevail against fiercely determined and hostile enemy forces. Over the years, students of military history have identified twelve principles of military strategy that, when properly applied, lead to victory.

These principles of military strategy apply to business as well. Every one of them is essential to success in competitive markets. A weakness in a single key area can lead to business reversals or even bankruptcy.

1. The Principle of the Objective This refers to the importance of establishing clear objectives for every military action in advance and making them clear to each person who is expected to help to achieve them. Does everyone in your company know exactly which goals you are trying to achieve in your business?

2. The Principle of the Offensive This refers to switching over to the attack, to taking aggressive action against the enemy to achieve victory. Your company cannot win by playing it safe, retreating, or simply cutting costs.

3. The Principle of the Mass This refers to the ability of the commander to concentrate his or her forces at one point, the location of the enemy's greatest vulnerability.

4. The Principle of Maneuver This refers to the ability to move the attacking forces in such a way that they can outflank the enemy and attack where the enemy is most vulnerable.

5. The Principle of Intelligence This refers to the need to obtain excellent information concerning the actions and movements of the enemy. In business, the more you know and understand about your competitors and your marketplace, the more successful you will be.

6. The Principle of Concerted Action This refers to the ability of the general in command to ensure that all parts of his or her forces work together in harmony and cooperation in both offensive and defensive operations.

7. The Principle of Unity of Command This refers to the need for absolute clarity about who is in charge of every area of activity, from the commanding officer on down. Top companies have clear leadership at all levels.

8. The Principle of Simplicity This refers to the importance of clear, simple orders, commands, and battle plans that are easily understood by the people expected to carry them out.

9. The Principle of Security This refers to the importance of guarding against surprise attacks and unexpected reversals. In business, this principle requires that you look down the road and anticipate what could happen to hurt your business or threaten its survival.

10. The Principle of Surprise This refers to the importance of taking an action that is not anticipated by the enemy. In business, you must be looking for different ways to do business with different customers, in different markets, at different prices, using different distribution channels.

11. The Principle of Economy This refers to the importance of not expending any more soldiers and material to achieve a military objective than it is worth or than is necessary. In business, this means that you do everything at the lowest cost possible.

12. The Principle of Exploitation This refers to the importance of the winning army taking full advantage of a victory. In business, this means that you follow up and follow through when you achieve a market success or get a new customer.

Masterful Management

Henry Mintzberg wrote in *BusinessWeek* that too many leaders don't see themselves as managers. They believe that their job is "to do the right things," while others are responsible for "doing things right." That may look good in a consultant's PowerPoint presentation or an academic white paper, but the fact is that the best leaders are, first and foremost, managers. They make things happen. They get results. They organize people, allocate resources, implement strategies—whatever it takes to get things done.

In *Execution*, Larry Bossidy writes, "Only the leader can make execution happen, through his or her deep personal involvement in the substance and even the details of execution."

The Seven Roles of the Manager

In any enterprise there are seven key roles of the manager: planning, organizing, staffing, delegating, supervising, measuring, and reporting. Each of them is learned only through trial and error and continuous practice. But they are all *learnable*, and they must be learned for you to realize your full potential as a leader.

One of the most important management qualities is *flexibility*. The more mental tools and skills you have to get the most and the best out of your people, the more flexible and, therefore, the more effective you can be as a manager.

Each role is as important as any of the others. An executive can be excellent in many areas, but the areas where he or she is weak will hold him or her back from achieving everything that is possible.

The Seven Determinants of Business Success

There are seven key factors that are relevant to every business and organization: productivity, customer satisfaction, profitability, quality, innovation, organizational development, and people building. A failure or shortcoming in any one of these areas can lead to the collapse of the enterprise. Your job as a leader and a manager is to ensure that your company succeeds in each of these areas.

To fulfill your potential, you must become excellent at what you do. Choose your personal area of excellence. Your decision to excel in a particular area moves you into the top 10 percent in your field because most people never make that decision in their entire careers.

The key to moving from good to great in your field is to ask yourself the brutal question: "Why am I not already the best at what I do?" The answer is always the same. The reason you are not at the top of your field is because you have not decided to be there or you have not backed that decision up with the hard work that is necessary.

Hire and Keep the Best People

Your skill in hiring and keeping the best people will determine your success as a leader more than any other single factor.

In Jim Collins's best-selling book *Good to Great*, he writes that the key to building a great company is to "get the right people on the bus, get the wrong people off the bus, and then get the right people in the right seats on the bus."

The skill of hiring and keeping good people is not genetic. It is a skill that, like any other business skill, can be learned through practice.

Select the Right People

The selection process is the key to your success and the success of your company.

The rule is that if you select in haste, you will repent at leisure. As a manager, you are responsible for spending the time and effort required to make a good hire. As a leader, you have two responsibilities. One is to enable your managers to make the best decisions. Don't set deadlines for new hires unless you absolutely have to. Taking your time is one of the keys to successful recruitment.

Your second responsibility is to be involved in the hiring of employees at all levels in your organization. You may not do initial interviews for some employees, but no employees should be hired before you have seen and talked to them.

Improve Performance Professionally

Job descriptions and job requirements are changing so rapidly that you must continually redefine them for each employee. Here are five simple steps that you can use on a regular basis to improve the performance of every person who reports to you.

First, sit down and explain clearly what the employee is expected to do. Describe the results that you want from the job.

Second, set measurable standards of performance for the job you want done. Put numbers on everything. Put financial measures on every single output responsibility, if possible. One of the great rules in management is "What gets measured gets done."

Third, never assume that the employee completely understands what you are saying. When you have delegated an assignment, ask the employee to repeat it back to you in his or her own words.

Fourth, give regular performance feedback to tell people what they are doing well and what they can change or improve.

Fifth, inspect what you expect. When you delegate a job, you assign responsibility, but you are still accountable.

Building Winning Teams

All work is done by teams. Your ability to assemble and manage a high-performance team of individuals is one of the keys to your value and effectiveness as an executive at every stage of your career.

To help people become happy, productive members of the team, you must understand their motivations. People at work are most motivated by four factors.

The first is *challenging, interesting work*. Most people want to be busy and happy at work, doing things that keep them active and force them to stretch, to move out of their comfort zones, to continually learn and grow. People won't buy into the goals and objectives of a team if they are given only the most mundane tasks.

Second, people are highly motivated by working in *a high-trust environment*. This is created by keeping people in the know. Have regular weekly staff meetings where everyone gets a chance to talk about what they are doing in front of everyone else. This is one of the most powerful team-building exercises of all.

Third, people are motivated by being made *personally responsible for results*. Give people important, challenging work to do, and then support them while they do that work. The more responsibility a person takes on, the more he or she grows as a decision maker and leader and the more valuable he or she will be to your company.

Fourth, people are motivated by *opportunities for personal growth and promotion*. Many people will take or stay at a job that pays less than they can earn somewhere else if they feel that they are becoming better skilled and more competent as a result of the work they do.

Much to the surprise of most managers, money and working conditions are fifth and sixth on the list of what motivates people at work.

The Dynamics of Top Teams

Top teams have five characteristics in common: shared goals, shared values, shared plans, clear leadership, and continuous evaluation and appraisal.

Top teams and good leaders practice what is called *management by exception*. This means that once the task has been assigned, as long as it is on schedule and on budget, no reporting is necessary. The individual has to report back only if there is an exception to the agreed-upon plan and/or schedule. The better and more competent your people are, the more you can practice management by exception with them.

You can also practice *management by responsibility*. Make people completely responsible for the successful completion of a particular task. Then get out of their way and leave them alone. It is amazing what people will accomplish when they feel that they are personally responsible and that they have no excuses to fall back on.

Problem Solving and Decision Making

Your entire success as a person and leader is determined by your ability to solve problems effectively and well. Whatever title is written on your business card, your real job is problem solver. All day long, in every situation, you solve problems.

Leaders don't react to problems with anger or frustration; they look upon problems as the essential defining skill area of their work. As a leader, your job is to become extremely effective at solving any problem that is brought to you, large or small.

The Three Qualities of Genius

In becoming better at problem solving, you can develop within yourself these three qualities of genius:

1. The ability to concentrate single-mindedly on a single goal, a single problem, or a single question without growing tired or bored

2. Mental flexibility

3. Use of a systematic method to solve any problem

Systematic Problem-Solving Method

There is a systematic method of problem solving that is used by the most effective executives in almost every organization. The following ten-step process is incredibly effective in helping you overcome obstacles and achieve your goals:

Step 1: Define your problem or goal clearly in writing.

Step 2: Once you have defined your problem clearly, ask, "What else is the problem?"

Step 3: Restate the problem to make it easier to solve. If you settle for a quick definition of the problem, it could lead you down the wrong path.

Step 4: Determine all the possible causes of the problem. Ask the brutal questions. Get your ego out of the way.

Step 5: Determine all the possible solutions to this problem. Then force yourself to ask, "What else is the solution?"

Step 6: Once you have done a thorough and complete analysis of the problem and laid out all the possible causes and possible solutions, make a decision!

Step 7: Once you have made a decision, assign responsibility. Who exactly is going to carry out each part of the decision?

Step 8: Set a deadline. Set a schedule for reporting on progress.

Step 9: Implement the plan.

Step 10: Check and review later to see if the solution was successful.

Communicate with Power

Fully 85 percent of your success as a leader will be determined by your ability to communicate effectively with others. Everything you accomplish will be associated with other people in some way. And the people in your life will account for 85 percent of your happiness and your success.

The quality of your communication, therefore, determines the quality of your life and the quality of your relationships, of all kinds.

In your interactions with others, there are five goals that you want to accomplish:

1. You want people to like and respect you, which will reinforce and validate your self-image but also encourage others to want to hear you, not shut you out.

2. You want people to recognize that you are valuable and important, reinforcing your self-esteem but also giving others a reason to listen to you.

3. You want to be able to persuade people to accept your point of view, to sell your product, services, and ideas to others.

4. You want to get people to change their minds and to cooperate with you in achieving your goals.

5. Overall, you want to be more personally powerful and influential in all your relationships, personal and business.

These are the keys to success in leadership, life, and love.

Your Emotional Intelligence

In 1995, Daniel Goleman wrote the book *Emotional Intelligence*. He argued that EQ is more important than IQ.

He concluded that your ability to persuade others is the highest form of emotional intelligence and the true measure of how effective you are as a person.

People do things for their reasons, not yours. Motivation requires *motive*. To communicate and persuade effectively, you must find out what their motives really are.

The key is to get out of yourself and enter into the mind, heart, and situation of the other person. Focus on the needs and desires of the other person rather than your own.

Communicators are aware of the emotional element in effective communication—the importance of understanding the emotional motivations of the people with whom you're communicating. But any efforts to address emotional issues must be based in sincerity.

MAKE THEM FEEL IMPORTANT

The deepest need in human nature is to feel valuable and important. You trigger this feeling by doing everything possible to raise the person's self-esteem, to help him or her to like him- or herself even more.

You should imagine that every person in your company is wearing a sign around his or her neck, all day long, that says, "Make me feel important." In every interaction with every single person, you should respond to this basic human request. You should always be looking for ways to make people feel important and valuable as parts of your team.

THE LEADER'S QUESTIONNAIRE

*T*he best leaders are those who have a complete and intimate understanding of every facet of their business and industry. Leaders know everything about their own companies, their customers, their competition, and the business environment in which they operate.

A complete leader's questionnaire covers all the major strategic and management issues that leaders will need to address. Every leader should be able to answer each question with confidence, without hesitation. If you do not know the answers, or if you are unsure, it is important to find out as soon as possible. Without the answers to the questions, or with the wrong answers, you will make mistakes in marketing, sales, and business strategy that can be fatal to your business.

As Larry Bossidy writes, "Only a leader can ask the tough questions that everyone needs to answer, then manage the process of debating the information and making the right trade-offs. And only the leader who's intimately engaged in the business can know enough to have the comprehensive view and ask the tough, incisive questions."

Here are a few of the tough questions that you and the team you lead will need to answer:

1. What business are you really in? What does your company actually do for your customer to improve his or her life or work?
2. What is the mission of your company or firm? Your mission should be stated in terms of what you want to achieve, avoid, or preserve for your customers.
3. How do your customers talk about, think about, or describe your company to others? What words do they use?
4. Who is your perfect customer?
5. Describe your perfect customer psychographically. How does your perfect customer think and feel about buying what you sell?
6. What does your perfect customer consider of value? What benefits does your customer seek or expect in dealing with you?
7. What are your company's core competencies? What special skills or abilities does your company possess that enable you to fulfill the needs of your customer?
8. Who are your competitors? Who else sells the same product or service to your prospective customers?
9. Why do your customers buy from your competitors? What benefits do they receive from your competitors that they don't receive from you?
10. Which of your products or services give you your highest profits? Which of your products, services, markets, customers, or activities are the least profitable?

11. *What is your company's area of* specialization? *What is your area of differentiation or excellence?*
12. *What organizational changes should you make in your business, with regard to people, activities, work flow, and expenses, to improve both effectiveness and efficiency?*

Simplify Your Life

Everyone today has too much to do and too little time. You feel overwhelmed with your duties, tasks, and responsibilities. As a leader, those duties, tasks, and responsibilities are multiplied. The challenge is for you to simplify your life in such a way that you spend more time doing the things that are most important to you and less time doing those things that are not at all important. A great leader is someone who is effective, positive, in control, generally content, and even-keeled. If you are overwhelmed, you are probably none of these things. Simplifying your life will not only make you a happier person; it will significantly increase your success as a leader.

Here are six methods, techniques, and strategies that you can use to reorganize and restructure your life, simplify your activities, get more done, and enjoy more personal time and time with your family than ever before.

Determine your true values. Decide exactly what is most important to you. The most important question that you must ask, and answer, throughout your life is "What do I really want to do with my life?" Set peace of mind as your highest goal, and then organize your life around it.

Decide exactly what you want. Start deciding what you want by writing out a list of at least ten goals that you would like to accomplish in the next year. After you have written out this list, review the ten goals, and then ask: "What one goal, if I achieved it in the next twenty-four hours, would have the greatest positive impact on my life?"

Select your major definite purpose. Your most important goal becomes your major definite purpose. Then make a list of everything you can think of that you can do to achieve that goal. Organize the list by priority, by what is more important and what is less important. Then immediately begin the most important thing that you identified to achieve your most important goal.

Get your life in balance. The key to balance is to be sure that your exterior activities are congruent and in alignment with your interior values. A sense of happiness, peace, joy, and relief comes when you return to your values and make sure that everything you do is consistent with them.

Put your relationships first. Put the most important people in your life at the top of your list of priorities. Put everything else below them.

Take excellent care of your physical health. You can simplify your life by eating less, eating better, exercising regularly, getting thinner, getting regular medical and dental checkups, eating proper nutrients, and taking excellent care of yourself.

THE TRUTH ABOUT LEADERSHIP

by James M. Kouzes and Barry Z. Posner

Many of the best books that discuss how to achieve success as a leader are based on research conducted by the author. He or she may have surveyed a few dozen organizations and attempted to codify this data into a discernible strategy. However, there is one leadership book whose contents are based on three decades of research. This title has the distinction of bearing the fingerprints of more than one million leaders who responded to its authors' leadership assessment exercise. Over the course of their careers, authors James M. Kouzes and Barry Z. Posner found themselves answering the same questions about the secrets to leadership success. Combing through the data collected from their research, the pair began to formulate a set of leadership principles that could endure management trends and swings in the economy. The results of their search are ten fundamental leadership truths worthy of being chiseled into stone tablets. Kouzes and Posner reveal the timeless keys to great leadership in *The Truth About Leadership: The No-Fads, Heart-of-the-Matter Facts You Need to Know.*

One of the surprising revelations in *The Truth About Leadership* is the importance of each leader's role in an organization. Kouzes and Posner combat the image of the powerless middle manager by demonstrating the immense importance of a leader, regardless of whether he or she manages one worker or a thousand. "Leader role models are local," Kouzes and Posner write. This reveals an important concept for anyone looking to build upon his or her career success: It's important to achieve at every stop on a journey to the top. There are no stepping-stones that do not deserve a leader's total commitment.

Kouzes and Posner give readers an important eye-opener by reminding them that a leader's performance isn't being watched solely by those above him or her. The people entrusted to the leader's stewardship take their cues from the person to whom they report. *The Truth About Leadership* enforces a stalwart code of conduct and emphasizes credibility, values, and trust among its ten truths.

A successful leader recognizes that he or she has a responsibility to, as the authors term it, "model the way."

While strong personal characteristics form an individual leader's backbone, Kouzes and Posner suggest that the interaction a leader has with his or her team may be the most important skill to develop. They recognize in *The Truth About Leadership* that nothing extraordinary can occur without a well-nurtured connection between a leader and his or her people. Great accomplishments are the result of great collaborations. It's something Kouzes and Posner recognize from their own partnership, both as authors and as educators at the Leavey School of Business at Santa Clara University. Their work together has produced some of the most comprehensive examinations of the dynamics of leadership. What sets *The Truth About Leadership* apart is its ability to boil leadership down to its essence. Kouzes and Posner encourage readers to say yes to leadership. Their book makes it easy to comply.

THE TRUTH ABOUT LEADERSHIP
The No-Fads, Heart-of-the-Matter Facts You Need to Know
by James M. Kouzes and Barry Z. Posner

CONTENTS

THE SUMMARY IN BRIEF

In these turbulent times when the very foundations of organizations and societies are being shaken, leaders need to move beyond the pessimistic predictions, the trendy fads, and the simplistic solutions. They need to turn to what's real and what's proven in order to understand what the evidence tells us about how exemplary leaders get extraordinary things done. This is the imperative that best-selling, award-winning leadership experts James M. Kouzes and Barry Z. Posner have undertaken in their work.

Based on thirty years of research—and more than one million responses to Kouzes and Posner's leadership assessment—*The Truth About Leadership* explores the fundamental, enduring truths of leadership that hold constant regardless of context or circumstance. In ten time-tested truths, this summary reveals what all leaders must know, the questions they must be prepared to answer, and the real-world issues they will likely face.

The Truth About Leadership shows emerging and experienced leaders the heart of leadership and what they need to know to be effective. It also offers a dynamic new look at what it means to lead today. The lessons in *The Truth About Leadership* help leaders do their real and necessary work—bringing about the essential changes that will renew organizations and communities.

In addition, you will learn the following:

Ten fundamental truths about leadership
How sharing responsibility can help you become a more effective leader
Lessons that will sustain you in your personal and professional development
How a focus on values, commitment, and trust can help you become a
   successful leader

Introduction: What Everyone Wants to Know About Leadership

There are fundamental principles that inform and support the practices of leadership that were true thirty years ago, are true today, and will be true thirty years from now. They speak to what the newest and youngest leaders need to appreciate and understand, and they speak just as meaningfully to the oldest leaders, who are perhaps repurposing themselves as they transition from their lengthy careers to other pursuits in volunteer, community, or public sectors. They are truths that address what is real about leadership.

Here are ten fundamental truths about leadership and becoming an effective leader:

1. The first truth is that **You Make a Difference.** It is the most fundamental truth of all. Before you can lead, you have to believe that you can have a positive impact on others. You have to believe in yourself. That's where it all begins. Leadership begins when you believe you can make a difference.

2. The second truth is that **Credibility Is the Foundation of Leadership.** You have to believe in you, but others have to believe in you too. What does it take for others to believe in you? Short answer: credibility. If people don't believe in you, they won't willingly follow you.

3. The third truth is that **Values Drive Commitment.** People want to know what you stand for and believe in. They want to know what you value. And leaders need to know what others value if they are going to be able to forge alignments between personal values and organizational demands.

4. The fourth truth is that **Focusing on the Future Sets Leaders Apart.** The capacity to imagine and articulate exciting future possibilities is a defining competence of leaders. You have to take the long-term perspective. Gain insight from reviewing your past and develop outsight by looking around.

5. The fifth truth is that **You Can't Do It Alone.** Leadership is a team sport, and you need to engage others in the cause. What strengthens and sustains the relationship between leader and constituent is that leaders are obsessed with what is best for others, not what is best for themselves.

6. The sixth truth is that **Trust Rules.** Trust is the social glue that holds individuals and groups together. And the level of trust others have in you will determine the amount of influence you have. You have to earn your constituents' trust before they'll be willing to trust you. That means you have to give trust before you can get trust.

7. The seventh truth is that **Challenge Is the Crucible for Greatness.** Exemplary leaders—the kind of leaders people want to follow—are always associated with changing the status quo. Great achievements don't happen when you keep things the same. Change invariably involves challenge, and challenge tests you. It introduces you to yourself.

8. The eighth truth is that **You Either Lead by Example or You Don't Lead at All.** Leaders have to keep their promises and become role models for the values and actions they espouse. You have to go first as a leader. You can't ask others to do something you aren't willing to do yourself.

9. The ninth truth is that **The Best Leaders Are the Best Learners.** Leaders are constant-improvement fanatics, and learning is the master skill of leadership. Learning, however, takes time and attention, practice and feedback, along with good coaching. It also takes willingness on your part to ask for support.

10. The tenth truth is that **Leadership Is an Affair of the Heart.** Leaders make others feel important and are gracious in showing their appreciation. Love is the motivation that energizes leaders to give so much for others. You just won't work hard enough to become great if you aren't doing what you love.

These are enduring truths about leadership. You can gain mastery over the art and science of leadership by understanding them and attending to them in your workplace and everyday life.

Truth 1: You Make a Difference

Everything you will ever do as a leader is based on one audacious assumption. It's the assumption that *you matter.*

Before you can lead others, you have to lead yourself and believe that you can have a positive impact on others. You have to believe that what you do counts for something.

The Truth Is That You Make a Difference. It is not a question of "Will I make a difference?" Rather, it's "What difference will I make?"

You Are the Most Important Leader

Leader role models are local. You find them close to where you live and work.

You also definitely find leader role models "close to home" in your organization. The media, and many leadership gurus, focus a lot of attention on people at the top of the organization—founders, CEOs, generals, presidents, and the like. They make it seem as if these top dogs are the only ones responsible for everything that's great, and everything that's lousy, about organizations. It's a subtle thing, but it perpetuates the trickle-down theory of leadership: All things start at the top and trickle down to the bottom. But when you actually look at the data, you see a very different picture.

The leader who has the most impact on your day-to-day behavior is, in fact, not the CEO, the COO, the CFO, or any other C—unless, of course, you report directly to that person. The leader who has the most influence over your desire to stay or leave, your commitment to the organization's vision and values, your ethical decisions and actions, your treatment of customers, your ability to do your job well, and the direction of your career, to name but a few outcomes, is your most immediate manager.

This means that if you're a manager, to your direct reports *you* are the most important leader in the organization.

THE FIVE PRACTICES OF EXEMPLARY LEADERSHIP

1. *Model the way.*
2. *Inspire a shared vision.*
3. *Challenge the process.*
4. *Enable others to act.*
5. *Encourage the heart.*

Truth 2: Credibility Is the Foundation of Leadership

Leadership begins with you and your belief in yourself. Leadership continues only if other people also believe in you.

The Truth Is That Credibility Is the Foundation of Leadership. What does it take to be the kind of person, the kind of leader, others want to follow and will follow enthusiastically and voluntarily?

It turns out that the believability of the leader determines whether people will willingly give more of their time, talent, energy, experience, intelligence, creativity, and support. Only credible leaders earn commitment, and only commitment builds and regenerates great organizations and communities.

Constituents Have Clear Expectations of Their Leaders

Leadership is a relationship between those who aspire to lead and those who choose to follow. You can't have one without the other. Leadership strategies, tactics, skills, and practices are empty without an understanding of the fundamental dynamics of this relationship.

In every relationship people have expectations of each other. Sometimes these expectations are clearly voiced, and other times they're never discussed, but nonetheless, expectations are present in every human relationship. In surveys of tens of thousands of people around the world asking them to select the qualities that they most want in a leader, the results reveal there are a few essential "character tests" someone (you) must pass before others are willing to grant the designation of "leader."

Before anyone is going to willingly follow you—or any other leader—he or she wants to know that you are *honest, forward looking, inspiring, and competent.* Before they are going to voluntarily heed your advice, take your direction, accept your guidance, trust your judgment, agree to your recommendations, buy your products, support your ideas, and implement your strategies, people expect that you will measure up to these criteria. Credibility ties it all together.

In the investigation of admired leadership qualities, the data reveal that more than anything people want to follow leaders who are credible. Credibility is the foundation of leadership.

Truth 3: Values Drive Commitment

Imagine you're sitting in a meeting with a group of your colleagues. The door to the conference room opens, and in walks someone you've never met before who says, "Hi, I'm your new leader." What questions immediately come to mind that you want to ask this person?

People have lots of questions they would want to ask, but by far the most frequently asked is "Who are you?"

People want to know your values and beliefs, what you really care about, and what keeps you awake at night. They want to know who most influenced you, the events that shaped your attitudes, and the experiences that prepared you for the job. They want to know what drives you, what makes you happy, and what ticks you off. They want to know what you're like as a person and why you want to be their leader. They want to understand your personal story. They want to know why they ought to be following you.

Before you can effectively lead others, you have to understand who you are, where you come from, and the values that guide you.

The Truth Is That Values Drive Commitment. You cannot fully commit to something that isn't important to you. No one can. You can't fully commit to something that doesn't fit with who you are and how you see yourself. In order to devote the time, to expend the energy, and to make the sacrifices necessary, you have to know exactly what makes it worth doing in the first place.

Your ultimate success in business and in life depends on how well you know yourself, what you value, and why you value it. The better you know who you are and what you believe in, the better you are at making sense of the often incomprehensible and conflicting demands you receive daily. You need internal guidance to navigate the turbulent waters in this stormy world. A clear set of personal values and beliefs is the critical controller in that guidance system.

Listen to Your Inner Self

If you are ever to become a leader whom others willingly follow, you must be known as someone who stands by his or her principles.

Values represent the core of who you are. They influence every aspect of your life: your moral judgments, the people you trust, the appeals you respond to, the way you invest your time and your money.

Clarity of values gives you the confidence to take the right turns, to make the tough decisions, to act with determination, and to take charge of your life.

Truth 4: Focusing on the Future Sets Leaders Apart

Angela Gu was in her first year as assistant controller, overseeing the accounts-payable function in finance for Wal-Mart China. While Wal-Mart had opened eleven stores in six cities across China, it had plans to triple the store count and enter into more new cities over the following three years. At that time the finance department was set up by city, and Angela could see that if the accounts-payable function grew at the same rate as the company expanded it would grow from about two hundred people to more than eight hundred people within a few years. She imagined the challenges and problems this would create for her area, "including the people management, procedural control, and compliance and costs related to personnel, travel, training and telecommunications."

Anticipating the future challenges the company would face, Angela proposed an alternative to the CFO—a centralization initiative—and received approval to move ahead. The program involved all divisions in the home office and local cities, including human resources, merchandising, and operations, in addition to finance. The effort paid off almost immediately in terms of productivity, improved control, and standardization and established a platform for future efficiency-driven programs. Within a year the average number of accounts-payable associates serving one store was reduced by 40 percent, and within three years the actual head count in accounts payable had been reduced by nearly 50 percent, despite the almost fourfold expansion of new stores. Angela explains:

> The initiative was quite new, with no other precedent to refer to, but the vision of a national accounts payable center excited me. You can always choose to follow whatever you have been doing—which demands from you no extra thinking or efforts—or you can focus on accomplishing something different that would do good for the enterprise.

Being forward-looking paid dividends for Angela and for Wal-Mart. This kind of anticipatory thinking can do the same for you.

The Truth Is That Focusing on the Future Sets Leaders Apart. Your constituents expect you to know where you're going and to have a sense of direction. You have to be forward-looking; it's the quality that most differentiates leaders from individual contributors. Getting yourself and others focused on the exciting possibilities that the future holds is your special role on the team.

Spend More Time in the Future

Developing the capacity to envision the future requires you to spend more time in the future—meaning more time reflecting on the future, more time reading about the future, and more time talking to others about the future. It's not an easy assignment, but it is an absolutely necessary one. It also requires you to reflect on your past to discover the themes that really engage and excite you. And it means thinking about the kind of legacy you want to leave and the contributions you want to make.

None of this can be done by a pessimist. You must remain optimistic and hopeful about what is yet to come. A positive difference can only be made by a positive leader.

Truth 5: You Can't Do It Alone

Leadership is not about the leader per se. It is not about you alone. It's about the relationship between leaders and their constituents. It's about the connection you and your teammates have with one another. It's about how you behave and feel toward one another. It's about the emotional bond that exists between you and them. Exemplary leaders know that they must attend to the needs and focus on the capabilities of their constituents if they are going to get extraordinary things done.

Ask Great Questions

Rather than thinking that you have all the answers, you need to be able to ask great questions. Great questions send people on pioneering journeys in their minds. They're a lot more likely to discover novel ideas when you set them free to explore on their own. The answers are out there, and they will be found among your constituents as long as people feel safe in offering them.

Asking questions is just one way that you can communicate that you believe in other people's abilities. Giving them choices, providing them with discretion over how things are done, and fostering accountability are other ways. People want to feel in charge of their own lives. They want to be in control. They want to determine their own destinies. They want to know that their input matters, that their ideas are good ones, that their answers are correct, and that their decisions will be supported. It's your job as a leader to increase people's sense of self-determination, self-confidence, and personal effectiveness.

Interact with Others

High-quality relationships don't happen spontaneously. They require leadership. It's your job to interact with others in ways that promote connection, collaboration, confidence, and competence. When you do, you'll see learning, innovation, and performance soar.

The Truth Is That You Can't Do It Alone. Leaders alone don't make anything great. Leadership is a shared responsibility. You need others and they need you. You're all in this together. To build and sustain that sense of oneness, exemplary leaders are sensitive to the needs of others. They ask questions. They listen. They provide support. They develop skills. They ask for help. They align people in a common cause. They make people feel like anything is possible. They connect people to their need to be in charge of their own lives. They enable others to be even better than they already are.

Truth 6: Trust Rules

A PricewaterhouseCoopers study of corporate innovation among the *Financial Times* 100 showed that the number one differentiating factor between the top innovators and the bottom innovators was trust. That means that if people don't trust you, your organization is likely to underperform and be slow to innovate.

If you are going to build cohesive teams, then you must also create a structure for trust in your organization. Without it you can't lead.

The Truth Is That Trust Rules. Trust rules your personal credibility. Trust rules your ability to get things done. Trust rules your team's cohesiveness. Trust rules your organization's innovativeness and performance. Trust rules your brand image. Trust rules just about everything you do.

Increase Your Trust, Increase Your Influence

Researchers have found that the level of trust that constituents have in their leaders determines the amount of influence they will willingly accept. In an experiment on the impact of trust on group problem solving, leaders in a high-trust condition had greater influence on group members and were more willing to accept influence attempts by group members than were leaders in a low-trust condition. This same study also found that high trust led to greater acceptance of group member interdependence, more cooperation, and enhanced information flow among all group members.

Studies involving soldiers in combat in Iraq found that the more the soldiers trusted their platoon leaders, the more willing they were to accept their leaders' influence concerning their motivation to become better group members, strive for excellence, and improve as people. Even in a traditional command-and-control environment, trust comes first and following comes second, not the other way around.

Trust motivates people to go beyond mere compliance with authority. It motivates them to reach for the best in themselves, their teams, and their organizations.

Truth 7: Challenge Is the Crucible for Greatness

When people think of the business leaders they admire, they think about people who have turned around failing companies, started entrepreneurial ventures, developed breakthrough products and services, or transformed industries. Challenge was the context in which these leaders operated, and change was the theme of all their campaigns.

You don't have to study historical leaders to learn this lesson. You can just look at everyday leaders such as yourself and those down the hall or across the street. For example, here is what Katherine Winkel, marketing communications coordinator at Monsanto, had to say about a discussion in a seminar about peers' personal-best leadership experiences:

The similarity that most stuck out in my mind at the time, and indeed remains with me, was that in each story the person described having to overcome uncertainty and fear in order to achieve his or her best. Whatever the case, staring down uncertainty and ultimately overcoming this hurdle was a major theme.

Typically, you would think people would describe uncertainty and fear as negative or even demotivating factors in leadership, but here it seems they are almost prerequisites for success! It has taught me that uncertainty is a necessity that drives us to do our very best.

The personal-best leadership cases, as Katherine observed, were about triumphs over adversity, about departures from the past, about doing things that had never been done before, about going to places not yet discovered. They were all about challenge and change.

The Truth Is That Challenge Is the Crucible for Greatness. The study of leadership is the study of how men and women guide people through uncertainty, hardship, disruption, transformation, transition, recovery, new beginnings, and other significant challenges. It's also the study of how men and women, in times of constancy and complacency, actively seek to disturb the status quo, awaken new possibilities, and pursue opportunities.

As the late John Gardner, adviser to four U.S. presidents and founder of Common Cause, was fond of saying: "What we have before us are some breathtaking opportunities disguised as insoluble problems." Sometimes leaders have to shake things up. Other times they just have to grab hold of the adversity that surrounds them. Whether challenge comes from the outside or the inside, leaders make things happen. Leadership and challenge are simply inseparable.

Truth 8: You Either Lead by Example or You Don't Lead at All

Jazz virtuoso Dizzy Gillespie once said, "That trumpet is lying in the case every day, waiting for me." In the same sense, leadership is waiting for you every day. It's waiting for you to take action. It's waiting for you to show others that you mean what you say. It's waiting for you to demonstrate that you know how to get people moving. In the final analysis, leadership is about playing that instrument called "you." But when you perform, you have to make sure that you play in tune. Your audience won't applaud dissonant notes.

That was certainly the insight that Casey Mork, manager of a new product team, shared about one of his supervisors, someone Casey felt wasn't clear about his values, never "had a true voice," and said one thing and did another. "As could be predicted," explained Casey, "with the lack of a model at the top, our group failed in internal cohesion, customer experience and business results." Casey learned what every aspiring leader must realize: You've got to walk the talk, not just talk the talk.

Leaders are responsible for modeling behavior based on the values they communicate. The leader must then live by them, in plain view of those he or she expects to follow the values. A leader must go beyond just talking about organizational values—such as "customers are always different"—he or she must actually demonstrate how to apply those values.

Casey understood that leading is not about telling others what to value and what to do. You have to model the way you want others to feel, think, and act. You have to show others that you are going to do exactly what you are asking them to do.

The Truth Is That You Either Lead by Example or You Don't Lead at All. Enduring leadership truth number two is *"Credibility Is the Foundation of Leadership."* Your actions had better be consistent with your words. In the final analysis, people believe what you do over what you say. As journalist and author Alan Deutschman writes in his book *Walk the Talk*, "Leaders have only two tools at their disposal: what they say and how they act. What they say might be interesting, but how they act is always crucial."

Truth 9: The Best Leaders Are the Best Learners

The potential to lead exists in you. If you apply your head, your heart, and your courage, you can learn to lead.

Leadership is not preordained. It is not a gene, and it is not a trait. There is no hard evidence to support the assertion that leadership is imprinted in the DNA of only some individuals and that the rest of us missed out and are doomed to be clueless.

The Truth Is That the Best Leaders Are the Best Learners. Leadership can be learned. It is an observable pattern of practices and behaviors and a definable set of skills and abilities. Skills can be learned, and when we track the progress of people who participate in leadership-development programs, we observe that they improve over time. They learn to be better leaders as long as they engage in activities that help them learn how.

No matter how good you are, you can always get better.

Learning Is the Master Skill

Studies show that leadership can be learned in a variety of ways. It can be learned through active experimentation, observation of others, study in the classroom or reading books, or by simply reflecting on one's own and others' experiences.

Certain styles contribute to more effectiveness in some practices, but there is no one best style for learning everything there is to know. The style is not the thing.

What is more important is the extent to which individuals engage in whatever style works for them.

Passion for Learning

You have to have a passion for learning in order to become the best leader you can be. You have to be open to new experiences and open to honestly examining how you and others perform, especially under conditions of uncertainty. You have to be willing to quickly learn from your failures as well as your successes and to find ways to try out new behaviors without hesitation. You won't always do things perfectly, but you will get the chance to grow.

Another dynamic that gives rise to the need for aspiring leaders to be first-rate learners is the astounding pace of change in the world. Not only do you have to be able to learn, but you also have to learn how to learn, constantly absorbing and teaching yourself new ways of doing old things and new ways of doing new things.

Truth 10: Leadership Is an Affair of the Heart

Leaders shouldn't turn a blind eye to reality or hide it from their teams. You must be honest with your constituents about the state of the organization's or the nation's health. Then you have a choice.

You can tell people they're doomed, criticize the ideas they present, contradict them at every turn, and offer little or no support as they struggle to survive. Or you can give them hope. You can tell people that if they apply themselves—and if they're willing to struggle and suffer—they will overcome one day. You can tell them you have confidence in their abilities, help them to broaden their perspectives, build on their ideas, support them as they look for solutions, and recognize their contributions. It's not hard to recognize the right option to choose.

Positive energy is especially important in volatile times. When the news is worrisome, and often downright scary, it's pretty easy for folks to become negative. And people become negative even faster when they see it in their leaders, whether the leaders show it overtly in speeches or just mope around a bit. Negative leadership breeds negative emotions. And these negative emotions are far more damaging to an organization's and an individual's health than doing nothing at all. In uncertain and challenging times, it's your obligation as a leader to accentuate the positive. If you don't, you're either keeping things the same or making them worse.

The Truth Is That Leadership Is an Affair of the Heart. Leaders put their hearts in their businesses and their businesses in their hearts. They love what they're doing and they stay in love with leading, with the people who do the work, with what their organizations produce, and with those who honor them by using their products and services. They show they care by paying attention to people, sharing success stories, and making people feel important and special. Exemplary leaders are positive and upbeat, generating the emotional energy that enables others to flourish.

HOW TO SHOW YOU ARE TRUSTWORTHY

*R*esearch has shown that a few key behaviors contribute to whether or not others perceive you as trustworthy. Here are four rules to keep in mind:

Behave predictably and consistently.

Communicate clearly.

Treat promises seriously.

Be forthright and candid.

Epilogue: Leaders Say Yes

Everything you do as a leader begins with one word: "yes." Until you say yes, nothing great can happen.

Reminders About the Truths

You can make a difference. Leadership begins when you believe in yourself and believe that you can make a positive difference in the world.

Others have to believe in you too, and gaining followers can be tough. Followers come when you work hard to earn their faith and confidence.

You have to be clear about what's important to you whether you're going to devote yourself fully to something. Values drive commitment.

Leaders focus on the future, whether it's the future of a group, an organization, a nation, or the planet. Big dreams that resonate with others inspire and energize.

While the leader may initially provide the spark of an idea, it takes a group of people—sometimes small and sometimes large—to make something extraordinary happen. And when beginning something brand new, the truth that trust rules is especially relevant. There isn't much else to go on. You just have to show that you trust others. Your trust in them will bring greater trust in you.

All leaders are severely tested, and there will always be detractors—those who will tell you that it's impossible, that it can't be done, that you're not capable, and that your dream is foolish. Despite the obstacles and despite the naysayers, you just have to go out there and do it. You have to make mistakes, bounce back, and persist. You have to go first as a leader. You have to be the example that others can follow.

Leadership is not about wishful thinking. It's about determined doing. There are no shortages of problems to solve. Leadership is not about telling others that they ought to solve these problems. It's about seeing a problem and accepting personal responsibility for doing something about it. And it's about holding yourself accountable for the actions you take.

Leaders aren't bystanders. They are active participants who work tirelessly to mobilize others to want to struggle for shared aspirations. Leaders believe that they have an obligation to do something to bring about change and that, with the active engagement of others, they can move things forward.

You Have to Say Yes to Leadership

You have to say yes to begin things. You have to say yes to your beliefs, you have to say yes to big dreams, you have to say yes to difficult challenges, you have to say yes to collaboration, you have to say yes to trust, you have to say yes to learning, you have to say yes to setting the example, and you have to say yes to your heart.

Are you ready to say yes to leadership? When you are ready to say yes, doors will open to entirely new adventures in your life. When you are ready to say yes, people will join you on the quest. When you say yes, you will discover your own truth about leadership.

THE ART OF THE START

by Guy Kawasaki

I f someone were to tally the mentions of various organizations in any business book on the subject of success, there is one name that would sit atop the list: Apple. The computing colossus began life as so many companies do, particularly in the technology industry: as a start-up born of the creativity and drive of budding entrepreneurs. Building a company from the ground up into a powerful organization is one of the pinnacles of success in business. It requires a certain set of skills that emphasize vision, action, and the ability to improvise. Who better to help a person strengthen his or her entrepreneurial spirit than someone who worked at Apple during its initial climb to greatness?

As one of Apple's original "evangelists," Guy Kawasaki helped Apple push the Macintosh to the forefront of the world of home computing. Upon his departure from Apple, Kawasaki turned his attention to venture capital, becoming the CEO and founder of Garage Technology Ventures. He also became a prolific business author. His eight books deal with subjects that range from product creation to handling one's competition. With each book, Kawasaki's full-throttle writing style and attention to detail ensnare another audience of devoted followers. For entrepreneurs, Kawasaki's book *The Art of the Start: The Time-Tested, Battle-Hardened Guide for Anyone Starting Anything*, is a must-read title.

Kawasaki's mind operates at the pace of the machines he once promoted with Apple. He is one of the most prolific bloggers in the technology sphere. As a result, any piece authored by Kawasaki is crammed with information. *The Art of the Start* is no exception. Kawasaki schools readers on every stage of the business-development process. He doesn't waste a word on philosophy, preferring instead to charge headlong into action plans. Step-by-step instructions give readers a definitive method for each skill discussed in the book. While *The Art of the Start* lacks the humor that crops up in Kawasaki's later work, it is still one of the most enjoyable reads for anyone wishing to start a company. His passion for the first stage of a company's development jumps off the page.

Kawasaki views the term "entrepreneur" as a mind-set possessed by those who want to rewrite the future. He does not sugarcoat the fact that the journey to the future is fraught with peril. However, the individual who will pursue his or her vision until it is achieved will likely view the trip as one filled with joy. Kawasaki dove head-long into writing *The Art of the Start* and hasn't looked back. Readers who are able to keep up with his frenetic pace will be rewarded with a palette whose colors can paint any future they can envision.

THE ART OF THE START
The Time-Tested, Battle-Hardened Guide for Anyone Starting Anything
by Guy Kawasaki

CONTENTS

THE SUMMARY IN BRIEF

"Entrepreneur" is not a job title: It's the state of mind of people who want to alter the future. Doing, not learning to do, is the essence of entrepreneurship. Guy Kawasaki writes that his goal is to help you use your knowledge, love, and determination to create something great without getting bogged down in theory and unnecessary details. In *The Art of the Start*, he presumes that your goal is to change the world, not study it.

At Apple in the 1980s, Kawasaki was a powerful leader who turned ordinary consumers into evangelists. As founder and CEO of Garage Technology Ventures, he has field-tested his ideas with dozens of newly hatched companies.

In *The Art of the Start*, Kawasaki takes you through every phase of creating a business, from the very basics of raising money and designing a business model through the many stages that will eventually lead your company to doing the right thing and giving back to society.

In addition, you will learn the following:

What the entrepreneur's key tasks are. Every start-up must make meaning, make mantra, get going, define its business model, and weave a "MAT" of critical milestones, assumptions, and tasks.

How a new company can articulate what it is all about. Pitching, positioning, and writing a business plan are the ways in which a start-up defines itself and communicates its message to others.

How you can "activate" your business. Bootstrapping (operating on little cash), recruiting, and raising capital will all give you the human and financial resources you need.

How you can "proliferate" your business. Creating win-win partnerships, building a brand, and "rainmaking" (generating large amounts of business) all expand your start-up beyond its original horizons.

What the entrepreneur's obligation is to repay society. In exchange for the right to exist and do business, each of us is required to give back to society and to be a *mensch*—a generous, honest, socially responsible, fully moral person.

THE COMPLETE SUMMARY

Causation: The Art of Starting

To alter the future, you as an entrepreneur must do the following:

1. Make meaning. Create something that makes the world a better place.

2. Make mantra. This is a powerful, emotional statement of what the company is all about.

3. Get going. Get your product or service to market, even though it's not perfect.

4. Define your business model. Do the following:

Target your customer specifically.

Keep it simple. Describe your business model in ten words or fewer with little or no business jargon.

Copy somebody. Relate your business model to one that's already successful and understood.

5. Weave a "MAT"—milestones, assumptions, and tasks. Compile these three lists:

- Milestones you must meet (e.g., complete design specifications, raise capital)
- Assumptions about your business (e.g., market size, gross margins)
- Tasks necessary to design, manufacture, sell, ship, and support your product or service

Make business cards and letterhead (twelve-point font, minimum) immediately. You also need a Web site and a domain name.

Articulation: The Art of Positioning

Positioning is a clear statement of why the founders started the organization, why customers should patronize it, and why good people should work at it. Good positioning is . . .

Customer-centric. It's all about what you do for your customers.
Empowering. It shows your employees they're making the world better.
Practical. It's easily understood and believed by customers, vendors, employees, journalists, and partners. It uses plain English, not industry jargon. And it is founded on the core competencies of your organization.

Positioning Your Startup

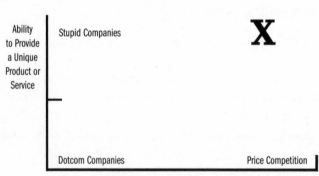

Value to Customer of the Product or Service

Clearly differentiate yourself from the competition. Instead of near-universal descriptors likes "high quality" or "easy to use," offer concrete proof points that convey your unique qualities.

Pick a company name that will make your positioning easier. Use a first initial that's early in the alphabet, and avoid words that begin with X or Z.

The availability of a domain name should be a factor in naming the organization. You need a domain name that people can easily remember and use.

Everyone in the company, including your directors and advisers, should understand the positioning. Put it into a short document and discuss it in an all-hands meeting.

Articulation: The Art of Pitching

In the first minute of your pitch, don't lead off with a heartfelt autobiographical tale. Explain what your company does. Then your audience can listen to everything else with a more focused perspective. If they remember that alone, your pitch will be better than 90 percent of the competition.

You want to communicate enough to get to the next step. If it's funding, then you want a meeting with more partners in the firm. If it's a sale, then you want a test installation or a small purchase. If it's a partnership, then you want a meeting with more people in the organization.

Your audience doesn't necessarily understand the importance of what you're saying, so every time you make a statement, consider following it with an answer to the question "So what?" Know your audience. A great pitch starts with the research you do before the meeting. Visit the organization's Web site, use Google searches, read reports, and talk to your industry contacts. Ask the person who invited you: "What are the most important things you'd like to learn about us? What attracted you to our idea? Are there any special issues or questions I should be prepared for?"

Keep the pitch down to ten slides and twenty minutes to allow for discussion. The CEO should do 80 percent of the talking. The rest of the team (no more than two others) can present the one or two slides pertaining to their expertise.

Realistic Segmentation

Describe only your "total addressable market"—not the totality of every nickel that's spent on something related to your product or service. You'll show that you truly understand the market—and that you're realistic about the segments that you can address.

Strive for a balance: Provide enough detail to prove that you can deliver—and enough aerial view to prove you have a vision. Don't even mention liquidity unless you have at least five potential acquirers that the investor is unlikely to know about—this shows you truly know your industry. Saying the industry leader will buy you out will only scare investors away.

After the pitch, take notes on the audience's responses. At the end of the meeting, summarize what you heard to make sure you got it right. Then go back and write the presentation from scratch. Let this version reflect what you've learned to date.

Continue to develop your pitch. When you're familiar and comfortable with it, you'll give it most effectively. For most people, real fluency takes about twenty-five repetitions. If your pitch is short and provides a compelling story of how you solve a real problem, it'll be better than 99 percent of the rest.

Articulation: The Art of Writing a Business Plan

A business plan isn't terribly useful to a start-up because so much of it is based on assumptions. The plan document is actually one of the least important factors in raising money. If an investor is leaning positive, the plan only reinforces his or her thinking. If the investor is negatively inclined, the plan will probably not change his or her mind.

Still, many investors do expect a plan. And in the later, due-diligence days, the investor will ask for a plan because it has to be "in the file." The main reason for writing a plan is to force the founding team members to work together and consider any issues they had overlooked or glossed over in their initial euphoria.

Uncover Holes in the Team

Writing a plan uncovers holes in the team. If you see that no one can implement key elements of the plan, you need someone else on board. A good business plan is a detailed pitch. If you get the pitch right, you'll get the plan right.

Write a pitch that follows these ten slides: title slide; problem; solution; business model; underlying magic; marketing and sales; competition; management team; financial projections and key metrics; and current status, accomplishments to date, time line, and use of funds. Practice on mentors, colleagues, and relatives. Get the team in a room and discuss what you've learned. Fix the pitch, then write the plan.

Use the slides for your pitch as the framework for your plan. Instead of a title slide, write an executive summary—a clear, concise (about four-paragraph) description of the problem you solve, how you solve it, your business model, and the underlying magic of your product or service. It's the most important part of your business plan because it determines whether people read the rest of it.

Business Plan Writing Tips

Use these tips when writing your plan:

Keep it under twenty pages.
Pick one person to write it, to give it a single voice.

Keep your financial projections down to two pages. The most important projection is your cash flow statement for the first five years. Generally, investors want five years of projections—or however long it takes to get to "significant" revenues—to help them understand the scale of your business and determine how much capital you require.

Include key metrics, e.g., number of customers.

Include assumptions that drive your projections.

To make your plan stand out from others, have a credible referral source bring it to the attention of the reader.

Also, provide a list of customers the reader can call to find out how much they need your product or service—or, even better, how much they're already using it.

Activation: The Art of Bootstrapping

Bootstrapping is about surviving the critical, capital-deprived early days—about thinking big and starting small. It means managing for cash flow, not growth or market share.

Here are the preconditions for successful bootstrapping:

People already know, or it becomes immediately obvious, that they need your product or service.

A megatrend is breaking down barriers for you. A prime example is the Internet.

You can piggyback on a product or service that already has a large, installed base.

Here's what else you must do to bootstrap successfully:

Do a "bottom-up" forecast, starting with such real-world variables as the number of phone calls that each salesperson can make per day, until you develop a realistic forecast.

Get to market immediately (exceptions: a biotech or medical device company). You get immediate cash flow and real-world feedback.

Of course, if there are quality problems, your image could suffer, which is why there is such tension involved in deciding between shipping your product and perfecting it.

Bootstrapping Tips

To bootstrap successfully, you must also do the following:

Hire affordable talent—inexperienced young people full of raw ability and energy. They'll try anything!

Know what you're really good at. "Off the shelf" is good if you can save money on products and services that have become commoditized.

Sell directly. A distribution system isolates you from your customer and requires a large sales volume.

Position yourself against the market leader. This works only if (a) the leader actually is, and remains, worth positioning against (think Enron); (b) the leader doesn't get its act together and erode your advantage; or (c) your product or service really is superior.

Stay in touch with reality. Ask the important questions about who we are, what we need, and what we are doing. Realism is so important that you need someone on your team whose role and temperament keep you in touch. This person should have at least ten years of operating experience (as opposed to being a consultant or analyst), including firing or laying off someone. The role may shift from one person to another. The important thing is that the right person be available to give you a reality check when you need it.

Outsource. Overstaffing causes many problems, so outsource as many functions as you can—but only payroll and other back-office work that others can do as well as you.

Build a board. Include outsiders. Good guidance is always valuable.

Sweat the big stuff—developing your product or service, selling it, and collecting the money. Whenever possible, do the small stuff (office space, furniture, computers, et cetera) cheaply.

Execute. The real enemy of bootstrapping is failing to execute. Some recommendations:

Set and communicate goals.

Measure progress and report results—at first, every thirty days.

Establish a single point of accountability. If it takes more than ten seconds to figure out who is responsible for a goal, something is wrong. Besides, someone who is being measured and held accountable is highly motivated.

Reward the achievers.

Follow through until an issue is either done or irrelevant.

Establish a culture of execution. The CEO must set the right example—answering inquiries, solving problems, and promoting people who deliver results, thus sending an unmistakable message: In this organization, execution counts.

Activation: The Art of Recruiting

Good recruiting starts at the top: A CEO must hire a management team that is better than he or she is. And the team must hire employees who are better than they are. Both CEO and team must have the humility to admit that some people can perform a function better than they can. And they need the self-confidence to recruit these people.

To avoid hiring the wrong people, use the following techniques:

Don't confuse correlation and causation. A candidate may have worked at a successful organization without actually contributing to its success. Analyze his or her actual performance and results.

Dramatize your expectations. Make it clear that working in a start-up is different. You might scare off a few desirable candidates, but it is worth it to avoid ending up with people who cannot function in a start-up atmosphere.

Learn to read references. U.S. laws prohibit providing job references that could damage a candidate's ability to get a job, so whenever you don't get a superlative reference, consider it a negative one.

Look to your current employees to bring in good staff.

Good hires should not only be better than a CEO and management team; they should also be different from them. Hire people with diverse and complementary skills.

Your candidates must also be infected with enthusiasm for what you do. Take a chance with a reasonably qualified candidate who already believes in what you're doing.

What if the candidate has been with a failed organization? Failure is usually a better teacher than success. But avoid the person who has a consistent history of working for failures. You want smart people—not necessarily "degreed" people.

Double-Edged Sword

Industry experience is a double-edged sword. Understanding the industry lingo and possessing preexisting relationships are helpful. But a candidate who is stuck in his or her way of thinking can be a problem.

The same goes for functional experience: Sometimes it will carry over to a new industry; sometimes it won't.

You should often ignore a functional weakness. When head count is low and there is no room for redundancy, you need tremendously talented people. High achievers tend to have major weaknesses. People without major weaknesses tend to be mediocre.

Ask a candidate who his or her important decision makers are—children, parents, friends—and then answer the candidate's concerns too.

Don't prepare an offer until the end of the hiring process. It is not a negotiating tool to get the candidate to say yes, but simply a way to confirm a verbal agreement.

Sometimes the candidate's education and background aren't quite right, but your intuition says "grab him"—or the candidate is perfect on paper (education, work experience, et cetera), but your intuition tells you to pass. Unfortunately, your intuition is often wrong.

Balancing Intuition

To balance any undue influence from your intuition, do the following:

Prepare a structure for the interview beforehand. Decide on exactly the attitude, knowledge, personality, and experience that are necessary for the position.

Ask about specific job decisions that the candidate has made.

Stick to the script. Minimize spontaneous follow-up questions; resist making up new questions in real time.

Don't overdo the open-ended, touchy-feely questions. Instead of "Why do you want to work for this organization?" ask, "What were your biggest accomplishments and failures?"

Take copious notes so you can accurately remember what each candidate said.

Check references early to decide whether the candidate is even acceptable—not as a confirmation of a choice you have already made.

Despite your best efforts, the new hire might not perform to your expectations. If you don't terminate people who aren't working out, you increase the probability of having to lay off people who are.

Establish an initial review period, with incremental milestones and concrete performance objectives. Agree that after ninety days, there will be a joint review, at which both sides will discuss what's going right, what's going wrong, and how to improve performance. (Some issues will be your fault!)

THE MALL QUESTION

*O*ne last question you should ask yourself about job candidates: Is this the kind of person you would actually walk up to at the mall? If not—or if you would avoid him or her—don't make the hire. Life is too short to work with people you don't naturally like—especially in a young, small organization.

Activation: The Art of Raising Capital

To meet the people who can lend you money, you need an introduction by a credible third party—preferably a source that your potential investors respect, such as a current investor. When you pick a lawyer, an accountant, and a PR counselor, look for connections as well as competence. Ask them to introduce you to sources of capital.

Other entrepreneurs are another source. A call or e-mail from an entrepreneur to his or her investors saying, "This is a hot company—you should talk to them," is powerful. If you are starting a nonprofit, look at the organizations that your target foundations have funded.

If you don't know such people, get out there and get connected.

Show Forward Momentum

You also have to show evidence of forward momentum. The factor that counts most is sales—evidence that people are willing to put money in your pocket.

Momentum can take other forms: for a church, attendance at services; for a museum, the number of visitors.

Investors are not attracted to a company that hasn't cleaned up its act. You should have no issues in intellectual property (e.g., lawsuits), capital structure (e.g., ownership of most of the organization by a few founders), management team (e.g., married or related cofounders), stock offerings (e.g., common stock sold to friends and relatives at high valuations), or regulatory or tax compliance.

If any of the above has not been or cannot be cleaned up immediately, tell the investors—early.

If you worked for a failed organization, accept as much blame as is justified without blaming anyone else. What's important is not that you failed—it's that you learned from your failures and are eager to try again.

Some Competition Is Good

Never tell potential investors that you have no competition. A moderate level of competition is good because it validates the market. And the fact that you're aware of your competition shows you've done your homework. If you're accurate about the things that you can do and the competition can't, you will build credibility.

Your competition might simply be the status quo. Pick something, because saying you have no competition is a nonstarter.

After all this, an investor might show interest—then stall. He or she might still be watching you: Did you try to establish contact after the pitch? Did you answer questions that came up in the pitch? Did you provide supplemental information that supports your case? Have you closed the big customers or met milestones early? Have other high-quality investors written you a check?

From Persistent to Pest

If you have tangible accomplishments and significant improvements, continue to make contact (but only if you have something to report—otherwise, you've gone from "persistent" to "pest").

Raising money is a long, hard process—and that's if it goes well. Venture capitalists don't know any more than you do about your sector. Also, getting a top-tier investor does not guarantee that you will succeed. These firms make many bets, and they assume that most won't pan out. Plus, the moment that you take a dollar of outside money, you lose control. You are obligated to all shareholders, even those with a minority position.

Lower your expectations. Outside investors can open doors, help you kick-start sales and partnerships, help you find future investors, and prevent you from making mistakes that they've seen before. But that's about it.

Proliferation: The Art of Partnering

You enter into partnerships to drive your financial performance. Define the deliverables and objectives in such "spreadsheet" terms as additional revenues or new markets. If you base a partnership on spreadsheet numbers and define deliverables and objectives, you have tripled the probability of its success.

Successful partnerships start with a true win-win agreement that leverages the strengths and needs of both partners.

Many partnerships are formed between two organizations of vastly different sizes, so it is tempting to cut win-lose deals.

But such deals won't last. Oppression is not a sustainable system. Also, if you want the middle and lower ranks to support the partnership, both sides have to see the union as a win. Beware of win-lose partnerships, no matter how attractive the terms.

Internal Champions

To keep the partnership going, both organizations need an internal champion—not the CEO but a single point person who truly believes in the relationship. The success of the partnership should be his or her only goal. The internal champion should be empowered to cut across internal departments, priorities, and turfs.

Don't send a draft of the partnership agreement to get the discussion rolling. Instead, get together face to face. Discuss the deal points and write down the ones you agree on. Follow up with a short e-mail outlining the partnership "framework." Then reach closure on all details by e-mails, phone calls, and follow-up meetings. Finally, draft your legal document.

Then find a lawyer who genuinely wants to do deals, not prevent them.

Always include an exit clause. People are more likely to take chances and be innovative if the partnership is not set in stone.

Schmoozing

It is much easier to build partnerships with people who already know you. The process of building connections is called "schmoozing," "networking," or "discovering what you can do for someone else."

Attend trade shows, conventions, seminars, and conferences.

When you are talking to people, ask good questions, then shut up. Good schmoozers don't dominate conversations. They start them off with interesting questions—and then listen.

Within twenty-four hours of meeting someone, follow up with an e-mail or phone call.

Make it easy to get in touch. Carry business cards with your e-mail address and phone number. Promptly respond to e-mails and voice mails.

Unveil your passions. If you can talk only about your business, you're boring. But if you are knowledgeable about six subjects, you can connect to almost anyone in the world. (If you have no passions, then at least read voraciously to learn a little about many things.)

Do favors. Help people—especially people who seemingly can't do anything for you. And do it without expectation of return. Somehow, you will be repaid.

Proliferation: The Art of Branding

Brand building starts with adoption. To encourage adoption, you must do the following:

Reduce product complexity and flatten the learning curve. A customer should be able to get basic functionality right out of the box.

Make the manual a marketing opportunity. The better the manual, the more enjoyable the customer's experience and the better your word-of-mouth branding. Include a thorough index.

Test your product on someone over forty-five. The feedback of teenagers is irrelevant—they can figure out anything. Create a user interface that an ordinary adult can handle.

Keep the price and conversion costs low.

Proselytize

If you have done all this, then you are well positioned to "proselytize"—to ask satisfied customers for help in spreading the word and building a community around your product or service.

Brand building also means attracting publicity and press coverage. If your customers generate buzz, the press will write about you. But you should also make friends before you need them. Help reporters from publications you've never heard of. Later on, they'll remember you.

Decide whether your story is appropriate for a particular publication. Identify and work with the reporter in your field. Pitch that reporter only if your story really is useful for his or her readers.

Be a foul-weather friend. Whether or not things are going well, always return phone calls and maintain good relations with the press.

Always tell the truth. If you've been honest when times are bad, they will believe you when times are good.

Your employees can also help you build your brand. Make sure that everyone has at his or her disposal several snappy one-liners that enable him or her to proselytize for the organization.

Do you need a PR firm or a PR department? They can force you to create a solid branding message, open the door for you with members of the press via preexisting relationships, schedule meetings and interviews, provide postinterview feedback, and help you improve your presentation skills. They cannot take second-rate products and services and generate countless articles about them or make the company always look good.

Proliferation: The Art of Rainmaking

Rainmaking means generating large quantities of business. Two conditions make rainmaking difficult. First, you don't know who will actually buy your product and what it will be used for. Thus, one challenge is to get your first version into the marketplace to find out where it blossoms.

Also, few customers want to take a chance on a new offering from a small, undercapitalized organization. The second challenge is to overcome this resistance.

Take the Money!

If you see your offering being used in unintended ways, don't try to reposition it so that the intended customers use it as intended. Take the money! But also learn where and why you are succeeding, then adjust your business to reflect this information.

To sell effectively, you must establish credibility and develop personal contacts, which begin with effective lead generation. The most effective technique is to conduct small-scale seminars to introduce the product (not to advertise, telemarket, make glossy brochures, or exhibit at trade shows).

The next-best methods are, in order, giving speeches, getting published, networking, and participating in industry organizations.

To generate business, you must also find the true decision makers by asking their secretaries, administrative aides, and receptionists. Here is how you can work with gatekeepers to get access:

Understand them. Their job is to enable the executive to do his or her job—partly by guarding his or her time (which many people, like you, might waste).

Don't try to buy them. Have a credible introduction and a rock-solid proposition; then treat every gatekeeper with respect and civility. After you've gained access (whether it worked out well or not), follow up with an e-mail, handwritten note, or gift.

Empathize. This person is not making much money—certainly a pittance compared to the executive. And he or she could probably run the place better. So don't assume the gatekeeper has to put up with you.

Never complain. Even if the person is wrong, your complaint will circle back, and you can kiss your access good-bye. Forever.

Dream Accounts

Rainmakers typically want to land the big, prestigious customer who provides tons of money, plus credibility. The problem is that these accounts are already successful and established. They're the least likely to embrace your innovative product or service.

So if your dream account doesn't "get it," find customers who are at least willing to consider you. They're typically not using anything. You are enabling them to do something they can't do—as opposed to having to displace an entrenched competitor.

Let Them Talk

Let your sales prospects talk. If a prospect is willing to buy, he or she will often tell you what it will take to close the deal. Create a comfortable environment. Ask permission to ask questions, listen to the answers, and take notes. Explain how your product or service fills the prospect's needs.

Begin by mentioning all your benefits—and let prospects react. They will typically tell you which ones are appealing.

If nothing resonates, ask what would. Then focus on the answer, because you've just gotten valuable information on "how to sell to me."

If the customer says, "You don't have your act together," either you really don't or you have stepped on someone's toes. Review your pitch and interpersonal skills to determine which it is. If you offended someone, figure out how to make amends.

"You're incomprehensible" means "Redo your pitch from scratch, cut out the jargon, and practice." The burden of proof is on you. If you need customers who are "smart enough to understand why they need our product," you'll starve.

"You're asking us to change, and we don't want to" means you are in the right market but talking to the wrong customers. Find customers with a problem that you can solve.

"You're a solution looking for a problem" means you should keep mutating your value proposition until it really appeals to a customer. If you can't create real value, you might really be a solution looking for a problem.

"We've decided to standardize on another product (or service)" means that you are probably trying to sell to the wrong person—if your product or service is truly, demonstrably better. Avoid the gatekeeper and try to get access to the real customer.

Support your selling by letting customers test-drive your product or service. They react very well to being trusted to make their decision after some actual hands-on experience.

Also, offer a smooth adoption curve—ask to deploy the product or service in small pieces of the business, in a limited and low-risk manner. Satisfaction could trigger further adoption.

Encourage everyone in the company to make it rain by doing the following:

- Set goals for specific accounts.
- Track leading indicators.
- Recognize and reward true achievements. Don't allow people to submit intentionally low forecasts. Intentions are easy; rainmaking is hard.

Obligation: The Art of Being a Mensch

Your goal should be to achieve menschhood. "Mensch" is the Yiddish term for a person who is ethical, decent, and admirable. It is the highest form of praise one can receive from the people whose opinions matter.

Every person and organization exists in the larger context of society. Don't do things that benefit you and your organization to the detriment of the rest of society. Also, if you want to build a truly great, lasting organization, you must set the highest moral and ethical standards for employees. A mensch provides a good role model for this.

Being a mensch means helping people who cannot help you.

A mensch does what is right—not necessarily the easy thing, the expedient thing, the money-saving thing, or the thing he or she can get away with.

Finally, a mensch pays society back. There are many "currencies" other than money: giving time, expertise, and emotional support. A mensch joyfully pays back—for goodness already received—and pays forward with no expectation of return.

SUCCESS BUILT TO LAST

by Jerry Porras, Stewart Emery, and Mark Thompson

Despite the financial and material rewards that many people attach to the definition of success, the majority of people who fit the label's description would be glad to do what they do without earning a dime. Achieving a goal or reaching a certain plateau can afford one the tag of "overnight success," which in itself is a misnomer. Authors Jerry Porras, Stewart Emery, and Mark Thompson demonstrate to readers that success should be measured not by temporary gains but by the lasting pursuit of fulfillment. Their book, *Success Built to Last*, is an aggregate of success stories. It presents the results of hundreds of interviews with individuals whose devotion to their pursuits proves that success is less about money and more about love.

The individuals who populate *Success Built to Last* are dubbed "Builders" by the authors. This group, regardless of the respective industries in which they operate, demonstrates the principles the authors describe as the backbone of a successful life. Each one possesses an all-encompassing love of his or her pursuit. The authors point out that the pursuit of success is so daunting and arduous that love is the only emotion that can sustain a person who treads this treacherous path. In lessons that incorporate the wisdom of the poet Maya Angelou, Nobel Peace Prize recipient Archbishop Desmond Tutu, and others, *Success Built to Last* guides readers through the challenges that prevent a person from joining the ranks of the Builders.

Builders succeed because of their ability to conquer their own minds. Porras, Emery, and Thompson point out that many of the people who inspired the book do not fit the profile of a brash, dragon-slaying hero. In many cases, Builders are reserved, tentative, and introverted. What sparks them to life is the interaction with the single idea or objective for which they have unlimited passion. Readers learn that this level of joy propels the Builder past any personal foibles and causes him or her to acquire laserlike focus. This focus is essential when it comes to responding to the inevitable failures that dot the line of a successful life. Builders turn these events from catastrophe to opportunity and never allow a bad moment to escape examination after the fact.

Success Built to Last doesn't limit itself to theory. The authors create a plan to help readers turn their passions into action. This begins with the pursuit of what they term Big Hairy Audacious Goals (BHAGs). Using the example of the United States's attempt to put a man on the moon by the end of the 1960s, Porras, Emery, and Thompson reveal that a BHAG gives a passionate person a target but not a step-by-step method to reach it. The achievements higher than any other are those that, at the outset, many deemed impossible. Builders devote their lives to proving the naysayers wrong, but as the authors indicate, this devotion is sourced from the heart. By following their examples, readers can find their passion points and let the chase begin.

SUCCESS BUILT TO LAST
Creating a Life That Matters
by Jerry Porras, Stewart Emery, and Mark Thompson

CONTENTS

THE SUMMARY IN BRIEF

Imagine discovering what successful people have in common, distilling it into a set of simple practices, and using them to transform your company, your career, and your life.

Authored by three thought leaders in organizational development and self-improvement—including *Built to Last* coauthor Jerry Porras, *Success Built to Last* challenges conventional wisdom at every step.

It draws on face-to-face, unscripted conversations with hundreds of remarkable human beings from around the world, including billionaires, CEOs, presidents of nations, Nobel laureates, and celebrities. Meet unsung heroes who've achieved lasting impact without obvious power or charisma. Famous or not, almost all started out ordinary.

Above all, discover how successful people stay successful and how you can too. In addition, you will learn the following:

Why leadership is pointless without an understanding of what success means

Why it's so hard to do what matters and what you can do about it

What you have in common with people who have impacted the world in which we live

How these enduringly successful people harvested their victories and failures and found the courage to follow their passions

Why it's dangerous not to do what you love

Why you don't have to be charismatic to be successful

How to overcome adversity

THE COMPLETE SUMMARY

From Great to Lasting—Redefining Success

When you feel pressure to pursue the elusive outcome of traditional success, it's often driven by the burden of making a living, pleasing others, or achieving status. Ironically, it appears that success often will fade, vanish, or become the dungeon of your soul unless it is not your primary objective.

Builders—enduringly successful people—tell us that when success just means wealth, fame, and power, it doesn't last and it isn't satisfying. Builders insist that success may never come unless you have a compelling personal commitment to something you care about and would be willing to do with or without wealth, fame, power, or public acceptance as an outcome.

Builders mostly toil with every ounce of their energy and persistence, with heart and soul, for their whole lives. They become lovers of an idea they are passionate about—for years and years—creating something that continually seduces them into obsessing over every detail, losing track of the passage of time. In a real sense, it's something that they'd be willing to do for free, for its own sake. They do it because it matters to them.

For Builders, the real definition of success is a life and work that brings personal fulfillment and lasting relationships and makes a difference in the world in which we live.

Part I: Meaning—How Successful People Stay Successful

It's dangerous not to do what you love. The harsh truth is that if you don't love what you're doing, you'll lose to someone who does.

All You Have Is Personal Capital

You may have noticed that we now live in a global economy where job security is a contradiction in terms. All you have is your personal capital, and we're not talking about your money. It's your talents, skills, relationships, and enthusiasm. Making success last takes a level of tenacity and passion only love can sustain. Making a life is as important as making a living. Builders do both.

"The job of leadership today is not just to make money, it's to make meaning," said John Seely Brown, who presided over research for two decades at Xerox PARC. "Talented people are looking for organizations that offer not only money, but . . . spiritual goals that energize . . . [and] resonate with the personal values of the people who work there, the kind of mission that offers people a chance to do work that makes a difference."

Be warned: The relentless irritation of not loving what you do makes you a pain to be around and has been clinically proven to chip away at your health. "We spend our health building our wealth," said author and financial adviser Robert T. Kiyosaki, paraphrasing the old proverb. "Then we desperately spend our wealth to hang onto our remaining health."

Rational Optimism or Irrational Exuberance

No one can tell you what risks you should take. Instead, you must choose a path that you love, for better or for worse, because only then will you have the good-hearted stubbornness to stretch for your full potential and survive the inevitable slings and arrows that await you on your journey.

You've got to love what you're doing or you can be sure there will be someone else who will. Falling in love with all the rational and irrational exuberance that is involved is the only way you have a prayer of creating success that lasts.

Portfolio of Passions

Although one passion usually dominates Builders' lives and defines their successes in the eyes of the world, it's a mistake to believe there is just one passion that must be pursued at the expense of all others.

Builders may look like racehorses sprinting with blinders on, but most live large and complicated lives filled with many different personal and professional passions. The myth that there is only one thing to do with your life is not an idea that we could get many to endorse.

It's Not About Balance Ironically, at the same time society insists that you do one thing with your life, cultural norms pressure you to have a "balanced" life split into neat little slices. The problem here is thinking there's a right answer—the notion that balance can be defined by a time-allocation pie chart representing work, family, community, and if you're lucky, you in there somewhere too.

If you define balance in the sense that it requires equal proportions of life partitioned into four or five politically correct parts, then CEOs and presidents don't have balance, nor do most Nobel laureates. The Dalai Lama doesn't either, nor does Nelson Mandela or Bono. Martin Luther King Jr. and Mother Teresa did not have balance. Enduringly successful people, many of whom live a life that's a gift to the world, don't raise balance as a major issue—not because they have it masterfully handled, but because they are busy doing what matters to them.

It's a struggle for everyone at some point. If you're feeling a twinge of guilt about balance, there is a probability that you don't want more balance, exactly, but need more of something that you can't admit you want. The balance you're seeking is a meaningful portfolio, not a balanced one. The reason that balance is so painful and elusive is that it's not what you really want. What you hunger for is a place for all of your passions—not balance as culturally defined.

MAYA ANGELOU'S PORTFOLIO

*M*aya Angelou became the first best-selling African American author (I Know Why the Caged Bird Sings), one of the most popular living poets of our time, an Emmy Award–winning actress and producer, a university professor, a mentor to Oprah Winfrey, a civil rights activist and Martin Luther King Jr.'s protégée, and the first African American woman admitted to the Directors Guild of America. If there is a secret to her success, it is that she has found many ways to feed her soul. "You can't simply sit on the sidelines and bemoan one's outcast state; it's not enough," she told Mark Thompson. "This experience, this life, is our one time to be ourselves."

Integrity to Meaning

Endeavors are not things from which these remarkable people can ever fully retreat or retire. That's why they stay successful for so long. To ask them why they're still "working" is to dismiss their passions as trivial pursuits.

That mistake is often made in interviews; it seems like an innocent question but only tends to indicate that the interviewer doesn't get it. Builders' passions create meaning in their lives that is nothing short of a lifelong obsession from which they seek no escape.

People become fascinated by the lifestyles of the rich and famous, perhaps longing for the adulation, glamour, and imagined self-satisfaction in those lives. It may be tempting to believe you can find success by studying their stories and assuming that whatever they did is a road map you can follow. But that's a dead end. That's not what billionaires or the best CEOs do. That's not what heroes like Mother Teresa or Mahatma Gandhi did. That's not what the world's enduringly successful people do.

If there is one thing they all do consistently—one value they all share in common—it is integrity about what matters to them and makes a difference in their lives and work.

Whenever they are faced with a decision, they look to find meaning in that opportunity that is very personal to them. They do not waste their time if it doesn't matter.

One Value That Builders Have in Common Although Builders keep their lives and careers on track by placing high value on personal meaning, individual interpretation and expression of "what matters" varies enormously.

As it turns out, all of the stories of enduringly successful people have some improbable quality to them. What helps successful people stay successful is their stubbornness about sticking with their own journey based on their own values, not a magic path followed precisely by everyone else.

The lesson here is that you can't—or shouldn't—hijack someone else's value system. To do so would be a violation of integrity about what matters in your life. There is no more personal decision than what meaning means to you. Only you can make that choice.

OVERCOMING FAILURE

Jimmy Carter grew up in relative isolation outside Plains, Georgia, a community of five hundred people. No one in his family had ever finished high school before, and this fellow goes to college to study nuclear physics, jumps into politics, and ends up the thirty-ninth president of the United States.

He would have to reinvent his definition of success, however, after his first term. "When I left the White House, I was in despair," Carter said. "I think everybody has to be prepared in life for failures or disappointments or frustrated dreams or even embarrassments. . . . You have to accommodate changing times but cling to unchanging principles. If you do have an extreme change in your life that is unpleasant, what are the principles that don't change, on which you can build a new life, an expanded life, a better life, a more adventurous life?"

Part II: Thought Styles—Extreme Makeovers Start in Your Head

The Silent Scream

Happy endings come from listening to that little voice inside your head—some call it a whisper—about what matters to you. It is a voice that echoes through every cell in your body, straining to be heard like a silent scream. It's a nagging, often irritating "need" craving a response.

The tragedy for most people is that there is a gaggle of other voices trying to drown out the whisper. Whether it's the ranting of your own self-doubt or the concerns of loved ones and business partners, there are many forces vested in seeing you not change. These forces would be more comfortable if risky notions—like following your passion—were locked silent in the basement of your soul.

Builders plow ahead despite self-doubt, delusional bosses, desperate spouses, and outlaw in-laws who have high control needs. And of course there are always those incoming hostiles—media messages proclaiming that without consuming the right stuff, you cannot be successful or happy.

You Don't Have to Be Charismatic to Be Successful

Due to hardship, genes, or both, many of the Builders we interviewed lacked the kind of confidence you might expect in a leader. Many were tentative, even nervous, introverts. But when they talk about what really matters to them, it's like watching shy, mild-mannered Clark Kent step into a phone booth and, a moment later, leap out a superhero. Despite the way social worker Norma

Hotaling felt about herself at any given moment, her cause had the charisma she needed to keep her going through hard times, to help her magnetize and motivate a strong support community and unlock barriers such as low self-esteem and limited knowledge in an area.

"It came down to this," Hotaling insisted. "I will do this and make a difference or I'll commit suicide. It's just that simple and just that hard." What could the rest of us accomplish with a fraction of that clarity?

The Cause Has Charisma Many Builders will tell you that breaking away from the boundaries set in their own minds—despite the realties of their tortured past—was one of the most difficult, necessary, and rewarding achievements.

"You must release yourself from the repression of your mind," noted Roberta Jamieson, who became chief of the Six Nations of the Grand River and CEO of the National Aboriginal Achievement Foundation in Toronto. "You are no longer a prisoner. You are not that person. You are a part of a long and great history. You are entitled to make decisions. You have gifts to share that belong to your people. It is your responsibility to share your talents with others. Throw off the shackles that keep you down—stop tearing at yourself and others because you don't feel good about yourself."

Your personality is not what determines enduring success. It's what you do with your personality that counts. We found that the personalities of Builders come in all sizes. Some are painfully shy and others seem aggressively in your face. The essential difference with Builders is that they've found something to do that matters to them and are therefore so passionately engaged that they rise above the personality baggage that would otherwise hold them down. Whatever they are doing has such meaning to them that the cause itself provides charisma and they plug into it as if it were an electrical current.

Enduringly successful people—whether they're shrinking violets or swashbuckling entrepreneurs—serve the cause, and it also serves them. It recruits them, and they are lifted up by its power.

Builders cling to a personal commitment that's so compelling to them— something so important to them that they would actually do it for free—that they must do it despite popularity, not because of it.

Trust Your Passion Life takes "passion, determination and skill," says Condoleezza Rice, former U.S. secretary of state. You can't skip any of those three and expect to enjoy success built to last.

One of the best ways to unleash the charisma that Builders feel for a cause, calling, career, or other major objective is to see whether or not they're really willing to immerse themselves in it. Opportunity comes from expertise, not just luck, talent, and passion. If you find it impossibly tedious to become an expert about what you think matters to you, then you're not chasing a dream;

you're just daydreaming. You can't claim the buried treasure if you aren't willing to dig for it.

That is not to say that it's easy or that you won't suffer frequently. But if you find you can't or won't persist in learning more about it, then it's going to be very tough to hang on when the inevitable obstacles get thrown in your way. This isn't earth-shattering news. Being the best at what you do is essential.

The Tripping Point—Always Make New Mistakes

There is rarely a person who doesn't have a pile of embarrassments or stunning defeats in his or her portfolio. Most highly accomplished people describe themselves as so proficient at making mistakes that, if you didn't know better, you might think they were losers. If there is just one thing that all enduringly successful people have in common, it is that they are all really great at failures.

Life is short, but some days are really long. Many Builders face lifelong adversity, phobias, or flaws that they never overcome—but they find a way to manage. They refuse to let their goals and dreams be held ransom by their feelings in that awful moment when everything has gone wrong.

When Positive Thinking Doesn't Work It's not that enduringly successful people keep a "positive attitude" regardless of the situation. Most Builders have a hard time choosing an attitude when they first hit a setback. It hurts. What makes Builders different has to do with having a "ThoughtStyle" that moves them from negative emotion to constructive action quickly. Builders go to work dealing with a setback directly instead of struggling to put a smile on their face. They don't pretend to be happy when things go wrong, and they refuse to completely surrender to the current disappointment. It's not that they feel good; they just harvest what they can from the setback and keep taking action.

"It's natural to feel like hell when things turn out badly," laughed Desmond Tutu, the Nobel Peace Prize–winning archbishop. He leaned forward, almost whispering. "But don't let that stop you. Emotions are a storm that sweeps through your life." This defeat you've had matters less than what you ultimately want to create.

Builders don't try to "fix" that they feel bad; they believe that learning from the experience and getting on with their goal is the "fix." They feel the pain but cherish what they're building more than the misery of the moment—they believe that their dream deserves to be created and that they have an essential role in it, no matter how awful they feel today.

Builders shift their focus back to what they want to ultimately achieve—that thing they are committed to building. Instead of struggling to choose their attitude, they shift their focus to what works, and when they do that, their attitude improves. In a culture that seems bent on perfection, entitlement, and instant gratification, it is often forgotten that most overnight successes require decades of failure to achieve their dreams.

Persistence and Perfectionism—the Dark Side Two of the tripping points that make the adventure particularly difficult are what Builders describe as an overly self-critical tendency toward perfectionism and persistence for its own sake. Of course, both attributes are necessary and noble aspirations of high achievers.

It's true that you can't get much of anything done without perseverance. Stories of persistence making the vital difference are legendary, and the pursuit of perfection is something to which many high performers aspire.

While an obsession with perfection is typically listed in the leadership and success literature as your worst enemy and persistence as your greatest asset, both are an addiction. People persist at all sorts of bad habits—like believing they must be perfect. The answer is neither perfection nor persistence but choosing what to persist at.

You've Paid the Tuition, Collect Your Paycheck Every Builder says setbacks are to be searched for lessons. At a minimum, the lesson may be not to do the same thing again, or at least to do it differently. Perhaps what becomes clear is how committed you are to doing what you're doing, allowing you to see different options that you wouldn't have recognized otherwise.

Builders don't use a weakness or a setback as a reason to distrust themselves. They don't marginalize themselves or the problem. If you fail to dissect the problem to see what is working and what isn't—if you keep throwing away the experience—you may be doomed to repeat it. Builders put the content to work for them.

The question is not whether they won or lost this round but what they will do with the feedback. Innovation is failure sped up.

Wounds to Wisdom

Builders don't deny their flaws, nor do they allow them to paralyze action. They might feel embarrassed or overwhelmed by them at times, but they still don't marginalize themselves or the problem. They don't even "overcome" their "disability." They manage it, include it, cope with it, and don't let it stop them. In many cases, they embrace so-called disabilities as the building blocks of greatness.

It's a difficult and nonintuitive step to think of the adversity that you are facing as an opportunity to find a way to make the challenge or flaw itself somehow useful. There is a much bigger prize awaiting you. The perceived disadvantage may hold the seeds of your genius.

By embracing their pain, Builders gain something more powerful than just the ability to learn from mistakes or harness the value of persistence. It's even more than just empathy. The special knowledge and skill you can gain from painful personal experience seems to transcend even empathy.

Some Builders who were once thought to have lost the genetic lottery and suffered learning disabilities have instead found that they won a prize: discovery of a special talent and a novel way to break out of the pack.

Letting Go of What Doesn't Work   At its highest and best level, perhaps that horrible thing in your life—that failure or disability or source of outrage—is the genius. Gandhi could not have found his voice without pain. CEOs Charles Schwab, John Chambers, and Richard Branson could not have built their companies without their dyslexia. By their nature, Builders are obsessed with creating or building something—and they're on a never-ending quest for something of value they can use. When it comes to their flaws, nothing goes to waste.

One of the things that Builders do discard quickly is blame. When you talk with them, what is clearly missing is the natural human tendency to dwell on blaming other people and things for their problems. Builders may explode, grieve, and privately blame everything and everyone, but most appear to drop it quickly. Instead, they look at what they can change and deal with that directly without prolonged whining. Wallowing in blame of yourself or others doesn't actually deal with the problem or allow progress toward the goal.

Builders don't try to rewrite history or to wipe the slate clean. They don't pretend it didn't happen. They simply decide to dismiss the case and move on. Obsessing about grudges keeps them alive; letting them go forces them to die as you get back to business.

" 'Dismiss' is a very strong word," said Reverend Deborah Johnson. "When something is dismissed, it's over. When it's dismissed, you don't keep going back to it." That's what successful people do. They don't necessarily call it "forgiveness." But they do abandon blame as a way of life.

Part III: Action Styles—Turning Passion into Action

Earning Your Luck

The overwhelming majority of Builders claim that their success has been a serendipitous journey, and the luck they enjoyed was usually earned, often at great cost. They have done that by focusing on doing work that is meaningful to them and going deep to discover relevant clues along the way. They have set big goals and engaged completely in the work at hand.

As a consequence, Builders are better prepared to turn things that, on the surface, may seem bad or useless into opportunities. What may appear to be brilliance, heroism, or passive good luck is actually a saga of passion, depth, and skill. Because they love what they do, Builders invest the time to acquire detailed knowledge about things that matter. It is focus and knowledge more than brains and brawn that allow them to observe the subtleties of their path and then take advantage of serendipitous events. Builders describe their path as adventures filled with bad breaks and unplanned good fortune. Only a prepared mind and open heart prevail.

Big Hairy Audacious Goals

Are Builders saying goals and plans are pointless? No, they are often essential. In fact, Builders use planning and goals—often big goals—to put themselves into a serendipitous position. Big Hairy Audacious Goals (BHAGs) don't just exist in parallel to your ideology; they are a manifestation of it. They are an extension of who you are and what matters to you.

A BHAG engages people—it reaches out and grabs them in the gut. It is tangible, energizing, highly focused. People get it right away—it takes little or no explanation. It has a clear finish line, so the organization can know when it has achieved the goal; people like to shoot for finish lines. BHAGs involve a consistent pattern of making bold, risky investments in audacious projects—to stimulate forward progress while still preserving core values and ideology.

BHAGs give you something tangible to be authentic about. Much has been said about the need for leaders to be authentic, but Builders will tell you to be careful about what that means. Your BHAG must be real, but the world doesn't want to know everything you're thinking. Your behavior has to match your words. And your words should take the form of personal stories rather than clever quotes from heroes you've never met.

For Builders who stay true to what they know and what matters to them, things actually have a tendency to turn out better than they imagined. This is one of the more subtle, but critical, powers of BHAGs. They instantly capture your heart and head. They deliver clear direction. Don't confuse direction with a road map, however. Builders have the former but not the latter. Take the race to the moon, for example. What is often forgotten is that when the BHAG of "a man on the moon and back before the end of the decade" was conceived, America had no clue how to actually accomplish this.

Bold Risks Measured in Small Steps

Most people don't do well with ambiguity. Builders do. Ambiguity is the enemy of audacity and innovation. It strikes fear in our hearts and doubt in our heads. When was the last time you were able to sell an idea to your boss, your partner, or your team without an exact battle plan for getting it done? Did they not want a detailed process for getting there and certainty about the outcome?

It's human nature to crave certainty and repudiate ideas that don't have guarantees. And yet very few things do. Great ideas and great careers don't have perfect plans before launch dates.

Responsible Chutzpah

Builders exercise an odd mixture of accountability and audacity. It's tough to find the right word for this leadership quality. The Yiddish dictionary gets close: We're talking about a responsible form of chutzpah—the nonconformist, gutsy audacity to create something despite all odds, for better or for worse.

The difference here is that long-term Builders are accountable—they are people who deliver for themselves and the outside world at the same time. Accountability means "to stand and be counted," as a part, a cause, an agent, or a source of an event or set of circumstances. "Audacious accountability" means you consider your life from the point of view that how it goes and what happens is up to you. You may or may not be to blame for what happens to you, but either way you are responsible for doing something about it. Builders don't claim to feel in total control, but they do have the audacity to embrace the idea that they alone are building this life for a reason, rather than life being something that happens to them while they're making other plans.

Very few Builders even give their work an intimidating label like "mission," "calling," "cause," or "higher purpose." Such a pedestal can develop as an unnecessary torment. Indeed, Builders describe their objectives as essential— that they must be done, that they deserved to happen.

Measuring What Matters and Keeping Score

Without feedback, you cannot adapt or improve. Measurement provides that feedback. And every time you get more information about how to do better, you are making a deposit in your personal capital account.

Measuring things helps you take account of progress on your long hike toward your goal, but it won't tell you if you're headed in the right direction. It's important to start with the end in mind, but it could be a dead end if you're in too much of a hurry to set a goal (for yourself or for the sake of others) without checking in and finding a meaningful passion in life.

The goal-setting process is both powerful and dangerous because it can make you effective at achieving an objective without any assurance that it's the right mountain for you to climb. Goals, by their nature, don't necessarily require focusing on inspiration as much as they do focusing on perspiration and the sheer pragmatic effort of getting things done.

It's important to curb the rational impulse to set goals too soon on your journey. Goals become a barrier to success and satisfaction when they're not really yours. This is what we call the Secret Life of Goals—when the milestones take on a life of their own. Goals can dictate success for its own sake or by someone else's definition, not necessarily success that matters to you and the stakeholders you care about.

Naked Conversations—Harvesting Contention

It might not sound intuitive, but the best thing you can do about contention is throw fuel on the flames. One of the oddly inspiring "ActionStyles" of enduringly successful people is that they actually seek out contention. We're talking here about gloves-off, brutally frank dialogue. It's what some pundits call naked conversations.

Many entrepreneurs light up when you raise the topic. It's something they look forward to, and many say their teams see contentious meetings as a "perk" of working for them. These naked conversations are not intended to be personally abusive. The focus is on issues, not people. What Builders ignite is actually a sort of controlled burn. The purpose is to encourage contention in a very precise way to draw out the best, most passionate, and most creative ideas from their team.

Struggle with the Issue and Not Each Other Builders don't fend off contention; they manage it as a source of inspiration. If you can foster a safe place to air the issues, you constructively unleash power that would otherwise become toxic—festering and infecting things later. In addition, creative contention can help your team avoid its own delusions of grandeur and dangerous self-agreement.

Many companies hold "workout" sessions where it's required to get all the issues out on the table. When people really commit themselves to frank discussion, these meetings can be an effective way to create an appropriate, politically correct environment to do what's usually politically incorrect at work.

These meetings can be used to shift the focus from personality conflicts to the actual problems that need to be solved by providing a safer, more honest dialogue without as much whining and name-calling. They provide a place to share the facts behind your worst fears and greatest hopes, rather than allowing them to continue to collide by accident.

The sooner you can do this, the better. Encouraging contention in the early stages of an initiative helps you discover where the problems are and fix them while they are small. Without a forum or time and place to attack and resolve the issues, relatively small problems can become counterproductive obsessions.

Creating Alignment—The Environment Always Wins

Builders have this odd notion that many of the people they meet are potential members of their communities or teams—as recruits, customers, vendors, volunteers, friends, you name it.

If you want success that lasts, then you're better off if you think about your relationships as being built to last with people whose roles change—sometimes they work for you, sometimes you work for them, sometimes they leave your organization and become your customers or vendors or regulators or competitors.

But if you consider them on your virtual "team," the only thing that changes is their role. You still have the relationship.

The thing that matters is meaning. It drives everything. Builders focus their attention on the things that matter to them, and they know a lot about that stuff. They are experts on what matters to them—their portfolio of passions. They talk responsibly in the domains of their expertise; otherwise they say, "I don't know." Seconds later, they tell you what they do know about their passion or goal.

Builders are fanatical about framing what they say in terms of their goals and values. Their answers to most questions they are asked end with a segue back to the goal or mission with which they are passionately engaged.

Intuitively they are always pushing and shoving the three circles—Meaning, Thought, and Action—into alignment. Everything that has meaning gets organized in a ThoughtStyle which then is turned into words and deeds—and ActionStyles—that support what matters to them. They use every opportunity to reaffirm goals and meaning.

The only thing that provides lasting success is the day-by-day practice and struggle to move the three circles toward alignment in your life and work. It's an adventure that you are better off embracing with all of your heart and soul, because it is a challenge that never ends.

GREAT WORK, GREAT CAREER

by Stephen R. Covey and Jennifer Colosimo

The ability to deliver consistent performance is a challenge for anyone who achieves a level of success. In subjective disciplines such as film, popular music, and literature, the demands can be doubly torturous. A musician who writes and records a successful album may struggle with his or her next project. The executives in the music industry clamor for a follow-up that will move as many units as its predecessor. Meanwhile fans and critics alike sit in judgment over whether the previous success was a peak from which down is the only direction. This is inevitably why artists say that pleasing oneself is the true measure of success. It's a sentiment that applies to business as well.

Stephen R. Covey, PhD, is intimately familiar with the pressures that accompany a runaway success. In 1989, Covey released his book *The 7 Habits of Highly Effective People: Powerful Lessons in Personal Change*. The self-help title became a colossus. It sold more than fifteen million copies and was released in thirty-eight different languages. The seismic shift caused by Covey's book would have allowed him to tread the public-speaking circuit for the remainder of his career, never needing to explore beyond his best seller's ideas. Instead, Covey continued to write and publish books that help individuals achieve success. In *Great Work, Great Career: How to Create Your Ultimate Job and Make an Extraordinary Contribution*, Covey teams with executive coach and change-management consultant Jennifer Colosimo to motivate readers to construct a meaningful career of sustained success.

Part of the reason Covey refused to rest after the success of *The 7 Habits* forms one of the central themes of *Great Work, Great Career*. Long-term success, according to the authors, has little to do with acclaim or financial rewards. A great career is one that focuses on making vital contributions and solving the problems that halt the progress of human advancement. Studies that examine job satisfaction often indicate that lack of personal engagement leads to lower levels of satisfaction. The great career that Covey and Colosimo push readers to create is one in which the individual follows his or her passion and finds fulfillment from within. The authors have little interest in the external rewards and verbal praise that cloud a person's pursuit of his or her ideals.

Great Work, Great Career calls upon people to quiet the outside world and listen to their conscience as a guiding voice. With practical steps wrapped in spiritual overtones, the book serves as a reminder that fulfillment is circular in nature. The success that comes from a great career is meant to be shared. The authors encourage readers to think less about getting a job and more about becoming a volunteer. The key is to build a career that provides self-satisfaction while inspiring the passion to make a difference. It is a book fit for the current era of economic uncertainty. In an era when the traditional career path has eroded into an unrecognizable desert, Covey and Colosimo encourage readers to shake the dust from their shoes and take to the skies.

GREAT WORK, GREAT CAREER
How to Create Your Ultimate Job and Make an Extraordinary Contribution
by Stephen R. Covey and Jennifer Colosimo

CONTENTS
1. Great Work, Great Career
2. What Will Be Your Contribution?
3. Discover Your Cause
4. Contribute Your Best
5. How Will You Make Your Contribution?
6. Build Your Own Village

THE SUMMARY IN BRIEF

Anybody can have a great career. Your line of work doesn't matter. It's all in how you define "great career." If you define it as something that brings you a lot of money and power, then you might or might not achieve that "Alexander the Great" level of greatness. Of course, a livable wage is important, but isn't there more to a great career than just a paycheck?

There are two key hallmarks of a great career. A person with a great career makes a distinctive contribution and generates a strong feeling of loyalty and trust in others. Anyone, regardless of title, position, or profession, can do these things.

Great Work, Great Career is about today and tomorrow. It's about getting a great job now and enjoying a great career for life. When we say a person has had a great career, what do we mean? Would you describe your current career as "great"? When you get to the end of your productive life, will you be looking back on a great career? And how will you know?

Authors Stephen R. Covey and Jennifer Colosimo grapple with these provocative questions. They have been associated in their work for many years as avid students of what it takes to build a great life and career. They provide tools and insights that will help you find answers for yourself, whether you're looking for a job or want to make the job you have more meaningful.

In addition, you will learn the following:

How you can bring a unique combination of talent, passion, and conscience to the world of work

Why it is important to find and define the cause that matters most to you

How to understand your strengths and leverage them to make the contribution only you can make

How to create your own community of people who can help you in your great career—and how you can help them in turn

Why it is important to write out your personal contribution statement

THE COMPLETE SUMMARY

Great Work, Great Career

Fiona Wood was a young English athlete who wanted a career in medicine. She followed the usual track through medical school, married, and, while raising six children, completed a specialty in plastic surgery. After moving to Australia, she went to work in Perth at a clinic for the treatment of burn victims.

The agony and scarring suffered by her patients moved her to wonder if there could be better ways to treat them. She knew that the longer a burn takes to heal, the worse the scarring. If only she could speed up the healing process from weeks to days, much of the pain and disfigurement might be avoided. Her experiments led her to invent "spray-on skin," a method of applying new skin cells over burns. According to Dr. Wood, the technique starts healing in days instead of the weeks needed for conventional skin grafts to work.

Then, on the night of October 12, 2002, her small hospital was flooded with victims of a terrorist bombing in Bali, many of them horrifically burned. Wood and her small team worked without rest for days and managed to save twenty-five of their twenty-eight burn patients. Spray-on skin was part of the treatment. This accomplishment brought worldwide acclaim to Wood, and for the next four years she was voted in national polls "Australia's most trusted person."

It's About the Contribution

Wood clearly shows us what it means to have a great career. It's not the acclaim or the fame; it's the contribution. A great career is all about solving great problems, meeting great challenges, and making great contributions.

Speaking of their life's work, the French use the word "métier," which originally meant "ministry" or "service." It's a good word. It contains echoes of giving of self, ministering to the needs of others, and finding the satisfaction that comes from providing a real and meaningful service. A great career rises not from a need for outside affirmation but from within you, from your own curiosity, from your own unique mix of talents and passion. It also rises from your conscience—from the whispers deep inside that point you to what you should do.

Obviously, a person like Fiona Wood could not make her contribution without gaining the skill to do so. But her conscience is just as key to the making of her great career as her competence. A great career requires both of these dimensions—the desire and skill to contribute and a character worthy of the trust and loyalty of others.

The Shift to the Knowledge Economy

We are now living in a time when great forces are converging to produce a new world. The landscape of the economy is undergoing a seismic shift, and with it the landscape of opportunity for each one of us.

The new Knowledge Age is full of turmoil and uncertainty. One daunting consequence of the shift from the Industrial Age to the Knowledge Age is the disappearance of job security. The lifetime job with a pension at retirement is about finished and probably not returning.

Still, there is a positive side to this risky but exciting new time: You can secure a great future for yourself by becoming an indispensable solution to important problems. Instead of pointing with alarm at these developments, we should welcome this complicated new world with passion for the opportunities it presents. There's no shortage of problems, just a shortage of answers.

Begin (or Begin Again) Your Great Career

The word "career" comes from the French word "carrière," which originally meant "going around in a circle," like a car on a circular racetrack. "Carrière" can also mean "quarry," a place where people go to break rocks all day. Unfortunately, too many of us experience our careers in this way. We feel like we're going around in circles, getting nowhere. Or we feel like we're hacking away uselessly like prisoners in a rock quarry.

If you feel this way about your career, it's time to rethink everything. You are no longer bound by the old mind-set that you're just a cog in a machine, a gear in some great bureaucratic wheel that goes around in meaningless circles.

The Knowledge Age entices us to ask questions, to challenge old assumptions, to look at the old intractable problems of the world and bring to them our unique answers. It challenges us to look at human need, poverty, misunderstanding, pain, ignorance, and fear and say to the world, as Wood states, "It doesn't have to be that way."

Charles Dickens: A Case Study

At a point early in his career, the young author Charles Dickens was discouraged. He had a wife and four children to support, with another child on the way, and was essentially out of a job. Plagued by self-doubt and mounting financial pressures, he found it hard to write and spent long, sleepless nights walking the streets of London.

As he talked by night with struggling street people, observing firsthand the social strains of child labor, poverty, and hopelessness, an idea formed in his mind. These sights fueled his passion to help the poor, and he began to see beyond his own problems. How could he make a difference? What did he have within himself to contribute to making a better world?

On October 14, 1843, Dickens sat down to write with a renewed zeal. He combined this newfound passion with his genius as a writer to create a small book that he hoped would change the world, as well as his own fortunes. Six weeks later, he published *A Christmas Carol*, an immortal story that at once became wildly popular and transformed public opinion. Some observers connect the beginning of Britain's social reform movement with the publication of the book. For Dickens, it was also the beginning of a prosperous writing career. His novels made him rich, which enabled him to get involved in educating and reintegrating the poor into society through his Urania Cottage charity.

What was it that recharged Dickens and refocused his great career? He found that unique combination of natural talent, passion for a cause, and the call of his conscience to fill a great need in the world. What was true for Dickens is true for anyone.

It all comes down to finding work that (1) taps your talent, (2) fuels your passions, and (3) satisfies your conscience. But it's not just about you. It's also about answering a significant need.

What Will Be Your Contribution?

At the core, there is one simple, overarching reason why so many people remain unsatisfied in their careers. It stems from an incomplete paradigm of who they are, their fundamental view of themselves.

Your value as a human being is not outside yourself—it comes from inside. Deep down, you must know that you are a being of virtually infinite potential and, unlike a machine, you have the power to choose what you will be.

Too many of us base our self-worth on externals, on being compared to other people. So many people equate their self-worth—or the worth of what they achieve—with money. If thirty years of data are to be believed, salary is actually not as motivating to people as making a contribution in which they themselves believe. Salary is an expectation, not an incentive.

Some people have been socialized to constantly compare themselves to others, to the point that the locus of their identity moves from themselves to other people's opinions of them—to how well they stack up. They lose their identity. This is true "identity theft." They become incapable of making a unique contribution because they have devalued and lost what is uniquely worthwhile about themselves.

In the Industrial Age, people simply asked, "What's my job description?" Now, according to Peter Drucker, "Knowledge Age workers must learn to ask, 'What should my contribution be?' This is a new question in human history. Traditionally, the task was a given. Until very recently, it was taken for granted that most people were subordinates who did as they were told. The advent of the knowledge worker is changing this, and fast."

Working in the Knowledge Age with the old paradigm of the Industrial Age leads nowhere. Passively carrying out a job description in the turbulent realties of this new world can quickly leave you irrelevant, stranded on the sidelines. Why? Because your job description is obsolete the moment it's written. If you are not constantly changing to adapt to the challenges your organization faces, you'll be left behind.

If you have an Industrial Age paradigm, you see yourself as a tool used by others. On the other hand, if you have a Knowledge Age paradigm, you see yourself as a solution provider who brings a singular set of tools to solving significant problems. The difference between the Industrial Age paradigm and the Knowledge Age paradigm is fundamental. It's the difference between a passive person with no initiative and an active person who takes responsibility for the future.

Adopting a Knowledge Age paradigm means that you bring your individual portfolio of strengths to relevant, meaningful problems and challenges. You are not a job description with legs. You are a knowledgeable, skilled, proactive, thinking, and creative human being with unlimited potential; and you can leverage that portfolio of strengths to make your own unique contribution.

Identify Your Portfolio of Strengths

A key step is to identify a portfolio of strengths you can leverage. These strengths can be divided into three categories: your talents, your passion, and your conscience.

Why these categories? Because they sum up what you are—not just what you do. You are more than just a bundle of capabilities; that would make you a machine. You are more than just your passion and instincts: That would make you merely an animal. A key distinction is your conscience—the part of you that whispers what you *should* do with your life, what your *responsibility* is. Your talents, passion, and conscience together add up to a whole person.

Talents What unique knowledge, talents, or skills do you have that can help you make a contribution? The category of talent is all about the tools you carry with you. In the Industrial Age, the company owned the tools and the means of production; the talents of individual workers were pretty much irrelevant. That's not so anymore.

In the Knowledge Age, as Drucker says, we each literally own "the means of production. . . . Those means are in our heads and at our fingertips. . . . Intelligence has become the new form of property. Focused intelligence, the ability to acquire and apply knowledge and know-how, is the source of wealth."

Passion Enjoying your career is just as important as using your talents, and that brings us to the category of passion. What job-related opportunities are you passionate about? Never downplay your own passion. Your passion is what fulfills you. It's a fire that comes from within, not from without.

Think about times when you were so passionate about a project, you couldn't think about anything else. Did you need to be supervised? Of course not.

Of course, your passion and talents don't necessarily connect. But often you will find your talents through your passion.

Conscience Once you've defined your passion, you need to examine your conscience. The category of conscience surprises some people. Why should you listen to your conscience as you build your great career? Because your conscience, your moral compass, will whisper to you and tell you what contribution you should make. So answer this question very thoughtfully: What is your real responsibility to your organization, your customers, and your coworkers? Your conscience tells you what your responsibility is.

DISCOVERING YOUR PASSION

Often you will find your talents through your passion. Back in the 1940s, a young American, Julia Child, found herself living in Paris because of her husband's job. There she discovered a passion for French cuisine and a talent she never knew she had. On her arrival in France, she had lunch in a little restaurant in Rouen. That first meal of oysters and sole meunière was a revelation to her, like nothing she had ever experienced before.

It was "absolute perfection. It was the most exciting meal of my life." She became fascinated by truffles and pâtés and cheeses and wines—"wrestling with the subject of butter in sauces"—everything stirred her interest.

Pursuing her passion, Child applied to the finest school for chefs in Paris, Le Cordon Bleu. "By now I knew that French food was it for me. I couldn't get over how absolutely delicious it was. My friends considered me some kind of nut. . . . They did not understand how I could possibly enjoy doing all the shopping and cooking and serving. Well, I did!"

Discover Your Cause

The twenty-first-century economy is giving everyone a wild ride. It seems that turbulent times are here to stay. The seismic shift to a knowledge economy has so disoriented many people that they have a hard time getting their footing. Some see only disaster. They see only millions of jobs gone up in smoke, whole industries laid waste, and an economic landscape barren and scarce.

To others, the landscape has never been greener. The volatile, burned-over economy of the new century provides opportunities no one ever dreamed of in industries that didn't even exist a few years ago. What seems to some a disaster holds the seeds of renewal for others.

Regardless of the economic climate, so much depends on the paradigm or mentality that governs your thinking and actions. If you have a scarcity paradigm, you see only burned ground around you—sparse opportunities, limited possibilities. On the other hand, if you have an abundance paradigm, you see prospects springing up everywhere.

We've never had such opportunity as we do today. Turbulent times offer the chance, the opening, the break people have been looking for. If you're let go from your job, you're free to change everything.

Just look at Steve Demeter of San Francisco, who used to work on ATMs for a big bank. When he got interested in programming applications for the iPhone, he created Trism, a game he sold on the Internet for five dollars per download, and made a quarter-million-dollar profit in two months.

Most of us probably won't be starting our own businesses launching iPhone games. But plenty of existing businesses still need your energy and talent. Yes, hundreds or thousands of others may be competing for those jobs. And the job you already have might be in danger. You can lament this situation or you can act.

Here are two mind-sets you'll need. First, become a volunteer, not an employee. Second, become a solution, not a problem.

Become a Volunteer, Not an Employee

Stop thinking about "getting a job" and start "volunteering for a cause." A job is something you do for money. A cause is something you work at because you believe in it. People used to talk about their vocations, not their careers. The term "vocation" literally means "calling"—a cause you are driven to serve based on a deep commitment and a conviction that it's worthwhile.

So change your mind-set. Think of yourself not as an employee but as a volunteer. Where an employee has a job description, a volunteer has a cause. A job description is external, and the employee reactively accepts it. A cause is internal, and you proactively volunteer for it. The motivation for a job comes from outside you, while the motivation for a cause comes from within you.

One difference between a great career and a mediocre career is finding a cause you can volunteer to serve. We're not talking about earthshaking causes like solving world hunger or curing cancer. We're talking about any worthwhile cause, regardless of your profession. Until you see your work as a cause, you won't find the passion for it that marks a great career.

Become a Solution, Not a Problem

Become a solution for your employer. Adopt a solution mind-set. Especially in tough times, your employer or prospective employer doesn't lack problems to solve and challenges to meet. So stop thinking that opportunities are lacking— they're not. The "we're not hiring" message so many companies put out is simply not true. They are hiring, and they will hire you if you are the best solution to a problem they must solve.

So how do you become a solution instead of a problem? The most important thing you can do is to truly become a knowledge worker. This means you must gain profound knowledge about the needs you feel called on to serve. Obviously, to gain that kind of knowledge you must really research the company you want to work for—or, if you're trying to save your job, the company you already work for. It's not an exaggeration to say that getting the job you want is 90 percent research.

To begin, you must clearly define the need or problem you are driven to solve. Here's the key question: What is the job that needs to be done—the job only you can do? Please don't define this job only in terms of an inward-looking job description. The job that needs to be done is the one your customers need from you—whether those customers are external or internal to your organization.

Obviously, if you can offer a solution to some critical problem, you've suddenly become very valuable to your employer. The classic way to define a business problem is to identify the gap between current reality and some desired outcome. If you can put meaningful numbers to the outcome, your solution becomes more meaningful.

What is the size of the problem? What is the measurable impact in terms of money, quality of product or service, or customer relationships? Can you express the gap in terms of "X to Y"?

What is the timing of the problem? Does it occur every day? month? hour? How long would it take to solve? By when could you show progress? Express the timing in terms of "from X to Y by when."

In the Knowledge Age, curiosity and research ability are paramount if you're going to get the job you want.

Have a Solution Conversation

After you've invested the time to understand the challenges a company faces, present yourself as a solution to its problems, not as just another job seeker. Do not go just for a job interview. Go instead for a Solution Conversation.

Describe the need they have and how you can help them meet it. Show a better understanding of their significant issue than the people they already employ. Explain the opportunity you bring to them to meet that need. Show them what life would be like with you and without you. Suggest a trial period—even at your own expense if you have to—until they're convinced that you really are an answer they've desperately needed.

In such an interview, they will learn a few things about you. They will learn that you are a leader. You take initiative to make good things happen. You don't wait to be told what needs to be done; you already know.

One caution: Remember that interviewers hire people they feel are trustworthy. Don't exaggerate anything for effect; don't pad your résumé. Stay focused on the company's needs and what you can realistically bring to those needs. Know your facts, but frequently check the facts against the interviewer's perception. For example, "Am I on track?" "Is that how you see it?" Use a helpful voice, not a self-important voice. If you approach the Solution Conversation with EQ, you will get the attention of decision makers. You will blow them away with the depth of your preparation and discipline.

Another caution: Don't come across as a threat. You might look presumptuous to people if you march into their offices, publicly air their problems in front of them, and position yourself as the solution they've always needed. There's a right way to do this and a wrong way. There's a helpful tone of voice and an arrogant tone of voice, and you need to know the difference.

Contribute Your Best

If you know your strengths and have discovered your cause, you're just about ready to write your Contribution Statement. This statement will provide the direction for everything you do in your current job, or even for your entire professional life.

Before you write your Contribution Statement, let's deal with a common and understandable feeling you might have: You might not think you have much to contribute. It could be you've tried to get job after job and have been turned down. Maybe you don't feel valued at work or believe you're too young or too old or too unimportant to contribute anything. You may feel alienated, frustrated, or obstructed on your career path.

Frankly, many of these feelings come from your view of yourself, not from the views of others. If you have a Job Seeker paradigm, you see yourself as a prepackaged product that you're trying to push on a buyer. Your résumé is your product brochure. On the other hand, if you have a Contributor paradigm, you see yourself as a solution to a genuine problem, concern, or opportunity. You have a proposal that will make a difference. Your main challenge is to change your paradigm of yourself from helpless job seeker to powerful contributor.

Write Your Contribution Statement

Your Contribution Statement is similar to a life mission statement, except that a Contribution Statement defines the high purpose you want to serve and what you intend to achieve in your career or in your current role.

This statement is your "personal value proposition," a summary of your strengths and your commitment to a cause that transcends any particular job. You can also write a Contribution Statement for your current role at work. Spend the time to give this statement your best thinking and quality research. It will pay you back a hundredfold.

Follow these six steps to write your Contribution Statement:

1. Write a tribute to an influential person. Think about the most effective, influential people you have ever known personally. Choose one of them and write a tribute to that person. It could be a teacher, a coworker, a friend, or a leader you have worked for. What contribution did that person make to your life? Writing this tribute to another person will help you crystallize in your own mind the kind of contribution you might make in your role.

2. Write down the tributes you would like to receive from other key people in your work. These people could include your boss, your fellow team members, and/or your customers.

3. Review your strengths. What unique knowledge, talents, or skills do you have that can help you make a contribution? What job-related opportunities are you passionate about? What is your real responsibility to your organization, your customers, and your coworkers?

4. Review your cause. What company or industry are you interested in (or already employed in)? What key problem(s) does it face? What is the size of the problem in costs, quality, or relationships? What is the timing of this problem? What solution will you propose?

5. Draft your Contribution Statement. Taking all of this input into consideration, draft your Contribution Statement. Write freely. Take your time. You can always go back and rethink, refine, and reshape your statement.

6. Share your Contribution Statement. If you're applying for a job, consider sharing your statement with the interviewers. Make it the centerpiece of your Solution Conversation. If you want to upgrade or transform your job, share your statement with your supervisor. Make an appointment to discuss it in depth. Listen to your supervisor's input. Make a plan together to enable you to make your contribution.

How Will You Make Your Contribution?

Now that you've written your Contribution Statement, your task is to make it happen. You have to give up being helpless—at the mercy of the economy or your boss or your weak education (or too much education) or your thin résumé or your youth or your age or your gender or your race or your face or your special case. In other words, you have to give up being a victim.

The job market can be a daunting place—hiring freezes, downsizing, restructuring of whole industries, reductions in workforce—it all means fewer traditional, secure, well-paying jobs. It also means a lot more competition for many of the best jobs.

At the same time, employers face a host of new challenges in this turbulent era while still grappling with the old problems. To familiar issues like improving sales, product development, and marketing they add global competition, social responsibility, and online commerce. Ironically, while employers offload employees, they have to hire more and more part-timers, consultants, and contractors. They must still get the work done.

That's where you come in. No company wants to hire just for the sake of hiring, but they all want to solve problems. They need your contribution like a thirsty man in the desert needs water, but they must first recognize that you *have* water to offer.

There are certain hard moments that, if we are strong, will make all the difference in our lives. Hard moments are conflicts between doing what leads to success and just giving up.

Work in Your Circle of Influence

Now, what if nobody answers your phone calls or e-mails or carefully considered proposals? What if your employers aren't ready to see you in a new or expanded role? What if you're really not in a position to become much of a solution to the problems they care about? What if the obstacles to your success look overwhelming? If so, you need to work on your Circle of Influence, not your Circle of Concern.

Imagine a circle that contains all the barriers to your career success. This is your Circle of Concern. Now imagine another, smaller circle inside the Circle of Concern. It contains all the people, knowledge, tools, and capital you have to work with. This is your Circle of Influence. It might be very small for now, but if you invest your energies in growing that Circle of Influence instead of wasting your energies worrying about your Circle of Concern, your power to build your career will grow.

Elisabeth Kübler-Ross: A Case Study

A marvelous example of a person who started small within her Circle of Influence is Dr. Elisabeth Kübler-Ross, a Swiss psychiatrist who, in the 1950s, began her career as a lowly intern in a very large hospital. Doing exhausting rounds, as all new doctors do, she was disturbed by the way the hospital staff treated terminally ill patients. The dying were lied to about their condition, ignored, and often left to die alone. So she began to break out of the routine and just sit with patients in the last stage of life, listening to their stories as they poured out their hearts to her. And she noticed that they would feel better, more at peace, after these visits.

Gradually, Dr. Kübler-Ross became more and more knowledgeable about how to treat the spirit of these patients who could no longer be treated for their physical ailments. Other doctors asked her to help their patients. Hospital administrators became interested in her work, which was entirely outside her job description. Eventually, a publisher approached her, and in 1969 she wrote *On Death and Dying*, a landmark book that transformed how the medical profession deals with patients at the end of life.

By working within her own small Circle of Influence, an intern of no particular importance with no institutional authority expanded that circle to influence the whole world. When she started her career, she had few resources within her Circle of Influence—only her basic medical education and her own talents, passion, and conscience. But she sensed a vast need and began to leverage her few resources to fill it.

Build Your Own Village

There's another key principle to live by if you want a great job and a great career: "building your own village." That means creating and maintaining authentic relationships with key people and mutually supporting each other. They help you in building your great career, and you in turn contribute to their success. Your career success depends not only on yourself but also on the people around you. In the workplace you never achieve anything worthwhile alone.

One of the most common bits of advice for the job seeker is to "network." In some respects, networking is a relic of the Industrial Age. Too often, networking comes down to having a lot of contacts—a big list of names you will never know what to do with or a drawer full of business cards from people you can't even place anymore. Industrial Age thinking sees people as tools. People are tempted to see one another as "means to an end." They seek out others only when they need something from them.

By contrast, in the Knowledge Age, people are important in themselves. Authentic relationships with coworkers, customers, and suppliers are becoming essential. So network from a Knowledge Age mind-set rather than an Industrial Age mind-set. The best networkers are building a village of people who value one another for more than just what they can do for one another.

Contribute to the Village

We tend to assume that some jobs, like those of a teacher or social worker, are more about service than others. Some professions are even categorized as "service jobs," but this is a misleading paradigm. People with great careers always have a service paradigm. If you believe that what you do truly makes the lives of others better, if you satisfy a real business need or delight a child or inspire the mind, then you are serving others in your work.

One of the great paradoxes of life is that the self-serving careerist never has a great career. That's because such a person's vision never extends beyond the next rung on the corporate ladder. Someday, someone will sum up your career. Will you be just another link in a giant, impersonal network? Or will you be remembered as one who served and contributed and gave your best to the "village"?

How do you build your village?

1. Identify the members of your village. There are two kinds of people: those you serve and support and those who serve and support you.

2. Create an Emotional Bank Account. You know what a financial bank account is. You make deposits into it and build up a reserve from which you can make withdrawals when you need to. An Emotional Bank Account is a metaphor that describes the amount of trust and confidence in a relationship. When you plan your time, deliberately schedule activities to build your relationships with the members of your village.

3. Carve out space for yourself on the Internet so people know to turn to you for expertise in your field. You should start a career blog. On your blog, you can publish your career Contribution Statement, which will draw followers who value your contribution. Showcase your generic résumé. Regularly post your ideas, discoveries, readings, and accomplishments related to your contribution. Invite people who share your passion to add their own content. And stick with it—the richness and longevity of your blog can make a huge difference in building a great career.

4. Practice synergy. The village you build might ultimately be your greatest career achievement. It might even become the source of great new advances in understanding your field. It's a natural principle that you cannot achieve anything truly worthwhile alone—at least not in the world of work.

The energy you invest in *regularly* and *frequently* building your village will pay dividends not only in advancing your career but also in personal satisfaction. You will get into the habit of service, which is the foundation of a great career. With a synergy mind-set, you will learn from the best people in your life. And when you need them, they'll be there for you because you have been there for them.

INDEX